IMAGES
of America

BOATS AND BOATING ON CRANBERRY LAKE

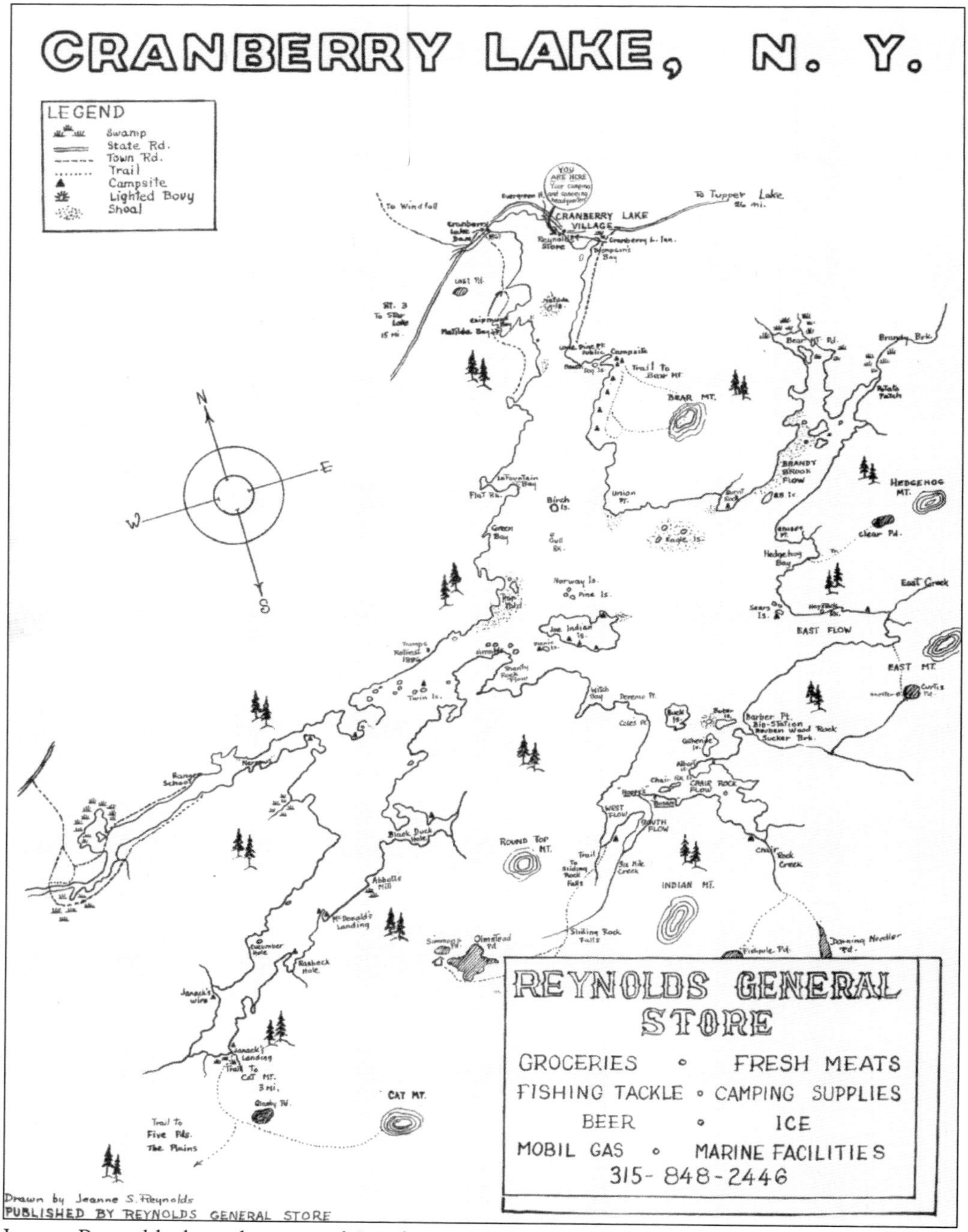

Jeanne Reynolds drew this map of Cranberry Lake in 1967.

On the cover: Both as pleasure steamer and workboat, the *Helen* was a popular ride. Many photographs have taken on iconic status and are part of the lore of Cranberry Lake. Here on a bright, calm day, passengers pose on the upper deck and prow for this 1906 postcard. On one copy of this card, the sender wistfully asks, "Can you find us here?" (Courtesy of Peter VandeWater.)

IMAGES
of America

BOATS AND BOATING ON CRANBERRY LAKE

Allen P. Splete
for the Cranberry Lake Boat Club

ARCADIA
PUBLISHING

ISBN 978-0-7385-6520-0

Published by Arcadia Publishing
Charleston SC, Chicago IL, Portsmouth NH, San Francisco CA

Printed in the United States of America

Library of Congress Control Number: 2009920002

For all general information contact Arcadia Publishing at:
Telephone 843-853-2070
Fax 843-853-0044
E-mail sales@arcadiapublishing.com
For customer service and orders:
Toll-Free 1-888-313-2665

Visit us on the Internet at www.arcadiapublishing.com

To my wife, Marilyn, as her writing and editing skills made this book possible

Contents

ACKNOWLEDGMENTS

Ernest Giraud, Clint Farnsworth, Jay Edel, and Hal Brown reviewed many boat pictures with me. Their knowledge of boats on the lake was very helpful to one who never professed to be a boat expert.

Jeanne Reynolds, William Gleason, and Susan Smeby helped me check facts about boats and the people involved with them. Susan, Jeanne, and Peter VandeWater shared pictures and postcards from their scrapbooks.

Mary Ann Remelé, Robert Thurston, Eugene Carver, Rod Leavell, John and Mary MacAleese, Barbara Slater, Ernest Giraud, Mark Friden, Penny Giraud, Lucia VerSteeg, Susan Heffner, Lyle Boss, Charles Lewis, and Leiper Read shared special memories beyond the call of duty. Suzanne Liberty helped compile information from the Cranberry Lake Boat Club Survey in 2008.

Thanks to all the unnamed others who provided important information for the book. Special thanks go to Dan Miller of the Antique Boat Museum in Clayton; Laura Foster of the Frederic Remington Art Museum in Ogdensburg; Hallie Bond and Angela Snye of the Adirondack Museum in Blue Mountain Lake; Flora Nyland, college archivist for the F. Franklin Moon Library at the State University of New York Environmental Science and Forestry (SUNY ESF), Syracuse; Larry Rathman, maintenance supervisor at the Cranberry Lake Biological Station (SUNY ESF), Cranberry Lake; Rebekah Collinsworth of Arcadia Publishing; and Roby's Photo Shop, Damascus, Maryland.

My wife, Marilyn, was a full partner in this undertaking. David Johnstone provided editorial assistance. Heidi Splete Johnstone and Michael Splete provided technical support.

Atwood Manley and Paul Jamieson, Adirondack historians, helped pique my curiosity about Cranberry Lake. Little did they know it would lead to this work. It seems fitting to let Paul have the final word. "Year-round Adirondackers generally leave book-writing to outsiders and summer residents. There is too much to do in the woods."

FOREWORD

In the summer of 1909, a group of interested residents formed the Cranberry Lake Motor Boat Club, and Cranberry Lake has had a boat club ever since. Hence this book has been written to commemorate 100 years of happy boating on lovely Cranberry Lake. As a year-round resident of Cranberry Lake for 60 years, I have witnessed the comings and goings of many a boat, both privately owned pleasure craft and commercial boats. In the pages that follow, we hope you will find pleasure in this pictured history of the numerous vessels of all sizes and descriptions that have plied the wide waters of Cranberry Lake, as well as a short history of the folks who have owned them. Enjoy!

—Jeanne Reynolds, Town of Clifton historian

It was not long after arriving in Wanakena as a weekend camper that I began to learn of the rich and fascinating history of the area. Along with other interested neighbors, we founded the Wanakena Historical Association in 1998. We all enjoyed learning more about the hows and whys of Cranberry Lake, Star Lake, and Wanakena. Now, much to my surprise, I have become involved with the centennial celebration of the Cranberry Lake Boat Club by collecting pictures and information for this book. This experience allowed me to gain added insight regarding the wonderful history of boats used on Cranberry Lake and the Oswegatchie River. One quickly realized that the boats associated with Wanakena, whether for pleasure or work, from the beginning years to the present time, were as intertwined as the Oswegatchie River and Cranberry Lake. Reviewing the pictures and information in this book will provide many memories for those who have lived all their lives in the area. I believe this book also gives visitors and new residents a wonderful view of the past. I know everyone reading this book will enjoy it and that it will add to their knowledge of the boating history of Cranberry Lake.

—William Gleason, Town of Wanakena historian, president Wanakena Historical Association

INTRODUCTION

The Cranberry Lake Motor Boat Club was founded in 1909 and is believed to be the longest continually operating boat club in the western Adirondacks. This book is part of the 2009 centennial celebration. In July 2007, the centennial committee of the boat club asked club members and friends to search their attics, basements, and garages for anything old that related to boats on the lake in general and the boat club in particular. By the summer of 2008, old postcards, family photographs, local histories, trophies, and even a boat propeller were appearing. This book is the culmination of that effort.

The Oswegatchie River flows from the Adirondack Mountains past Wanakena. It widens into Cranberry Lake, pushing back into a number of creeks and flows. The South Bay region is called the head of the lake. Where the river narrows again at Cranberry Lake village is called the foot of the lake.

Cranberry Lake has a longer and richer history than can be recounted here. This book focuses on specific events that occurred in and around the lake that are part of the story of its boats, the people who paddled, rowed, sailed, and piloted them, and those who made their living with boats.

In 1854, the New York State legislature laid the groundwork for creating a reservoir at Cranberry Lake by declaring the Oswegatchie River a public highway and asserting its right to regulate the passage of logs and improve the river. In 1867, the first dam was built at the foot of the lake, forever changing the shape of the lake and leaving a stand of dead and decaying trees and stumps along the shoreline. In 1873, Verplanck Colvin surveyed the Cranberry Lake region for New York State. It was one of the last regions identified in the Adirondacks. By 1900, the sights and sounds of a thriving lumbering industry were part of the Cranberry Lake scene. The wood-burning *Howlett* carried cargo; the *Ironclad* towed log booms that stretched across the lake. There were many others.

Beginning in the late 1800s, local guides who knew the woods and water would take hunters and fishermen to camps around the lake in Rushton canoes, Adirondack guide boats, and motorboats.

Along with the sportsmen came the tourists. Many were prominent names. Frederic Remington, artist, illustrator, and sculptor, was a frequent visitor to Cranberry Lake between 1889 and 1900. He visited with Canton friends at Tramps Retreat and Witch Bay. Occasionally an illustration or an Adirondack tale would make its way into print. "A Good Day's Hunting in the Adirondacks" and "Spring Trout Fishing in the Adirondacks" appeared in *Harper's Weekly* in 1890 and 1892, respectively. J. Henry Rushton of Canton, builder of the famous Rushton canoes and guide boats, spent time on the lake to renew his health and paddle about. Reuben Wood, whose name is familiar to fly fishermen who still use the fly he invented, first came in 1878. He used to clamber up on a large boulder at the mouth of Sucker Brook and tell fishing stories to friends who gathered around. A memorial inscription on the boulder reads, "In memory of Reuben Wood, a genial gentleman and great fisherman who was fond of these solitudes." Marc Chagall, the acclaimed Russian-born artist who lived in France, spent the summer of 1944 at Cranberry Lake and did a painting named *Cranberry Lake* at that time. Ralph Brown, credited as the inventor of the inboard/outboard motor and a national figure in the early days of aviation, had a cabin at Wanakena.

Over the years, the Cranberry Lake Boat Club has accommodated and encouraged the coexistence of those seeking peace with those looking for the excitement of a fast ride. Paddlers and kayakers roam the lake alone or in groups. People on water skis and Jet Skis and in Zodiacs zoom along. Fishermen put trolling motors on their boats and idle along the shoreline. Toddlers, grandparents, and all ages between enjoy the pace of an afternoon on a pontoon boat. The classic inboard and outboard motorboats parade next to the new ones. Sailboats seek the breeziest spots.

Boats and Boating on Cranberry Lake traces the evolution of boating on Cranberry Lake. It spans the years from the late 1800s to 2008. Chapters describe and illustrate the mundane and the extraordinary in the saga of paddlers, sailors, workboats, pleasure boats, regattas, races, and docks. Each chapter covers the topic beginning with early examples and ending with newer ones.

The following unsigned and undated statement surfaced in the files of Clifton town historian Jeanne Reynolds:

> One of the first requirements of camp ownership is a boat of some sort. Since we are some distance from any source of supplies, a motor boat [*sic*] is a great convenience, but a canoe is all that's really necessary. Someone, somewhere has observed that sensitiveness to noise is the first sign of intelligence. Nevertheless outboard motors are increasing in numbers and noise to an alarming degree. Kids love them, the fisherman of the itinerant type find them a great convenience. It is noticeable also that every outboard fan is a potential in-board [*sic*] engine owner. On many lakes near urban centers kicker-boats have already been banned. Perhaps someday, some manufacturer will take the hint and build outboard motors with mufflers attached. As they are today, they are a boon to thousands but a curse to many who remember the mystic beauty of an Adirondack silence undisturbed by anything louder than the cry of a loon.

One

PADDLERS AND SAILORS

In the beginning, New York's backwoods country around Cranberry Lake was hard to get to. Once one arrived there, one felt a long way from the outside world. One could stay awhile for the fishing, to hunt, or perhaps just for the solitude and quiet. To get around, one would walk or use a boat: the canoe, the guide boat, then the rowboat, skiff, and sailboat. There were strong backs and sturdy hands on paddles, oars, and tillers.

Some boats in this chapter are in museums. Some are still in use on the lake. Owners willingly pulled them out of boathouses and garages for photographs or dug though old family albums to find photographs taken years ago.

Fishermen and hunters used the services of local guides to provide transportation, advice, a campfire-cooked supper, and shelter. Some of the best known were Bill Mott, who died when his boat smashed into Gull Rock on a foggy night in 1934; William MacAleese Sr., who ran the Evergreen Hotel after 1918 and always had a dependable inboard boat to guide parties of fishermen and hunters; William MacAleese Jr., who ran the Evergreen Hotel, told stories, and guided deer hunters, just like his father; Fred Howland, who bought the *Wanakena* and *Helen* from Frank Wilder's Cranberry Lake Transportation Company and guided sportsmen for many years; Rudy Hayes, who was quite a guide in his younger days but later ran a boat storage and repair shop on the lake; Wilfred Morrison, a well-known guide from Wanakena, who was best known for winning a game violation trial in 1933; Spencer Howland, a guide who was known as the best boatman on the lake in the 1950s; Al Snyder, who worked for the College of Forestry summer camp as caretaker and master mechanic and knew every inch of the lake; and Frank Starkey, a terrific woodsman and excellent guide.

Today boaters rely on state-of-the-art maps and global-positioning devices. There are still canoes, guide boats, rowboats, and sailboats on the lake, joined by the popular kayaks. It is still quiet; one can still hear the loons.

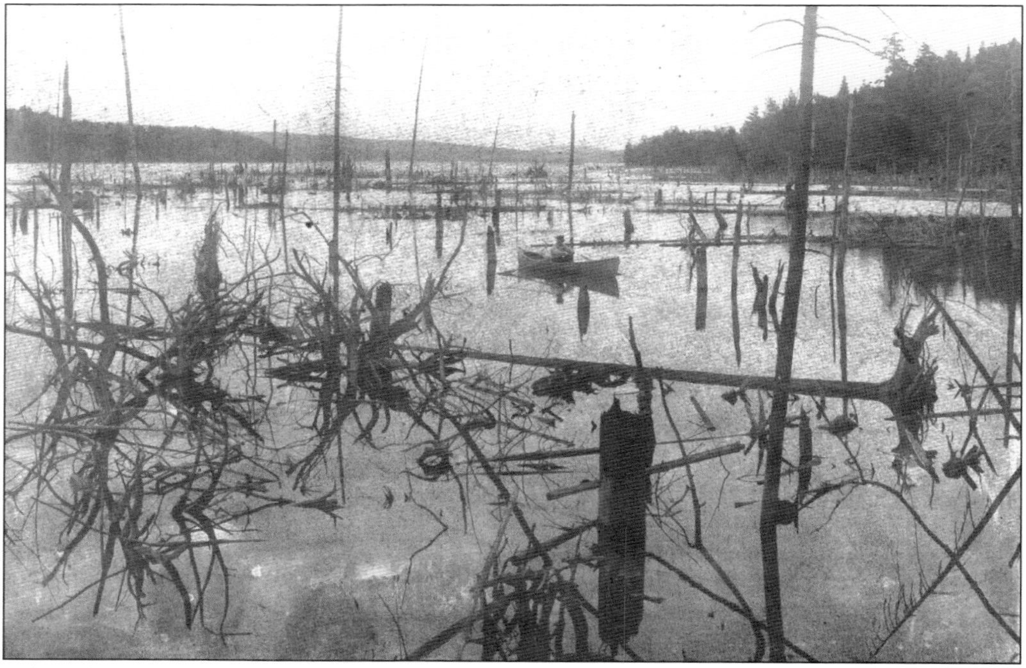

When the first dam was built at the foot of Cranberry Lake in 1867, no attempt was made to clear the flooded land. This left stands of dead and decaying stumps and a soft, bottomless mud floor. A guide boat paddler, possibly John Janack, who later manned a fire tower on nearby Cat Mountain, is wending his way into Dead Creek Flow in the 1880s or 1890s. (Courtesy of the Wanakena Historical Association.)

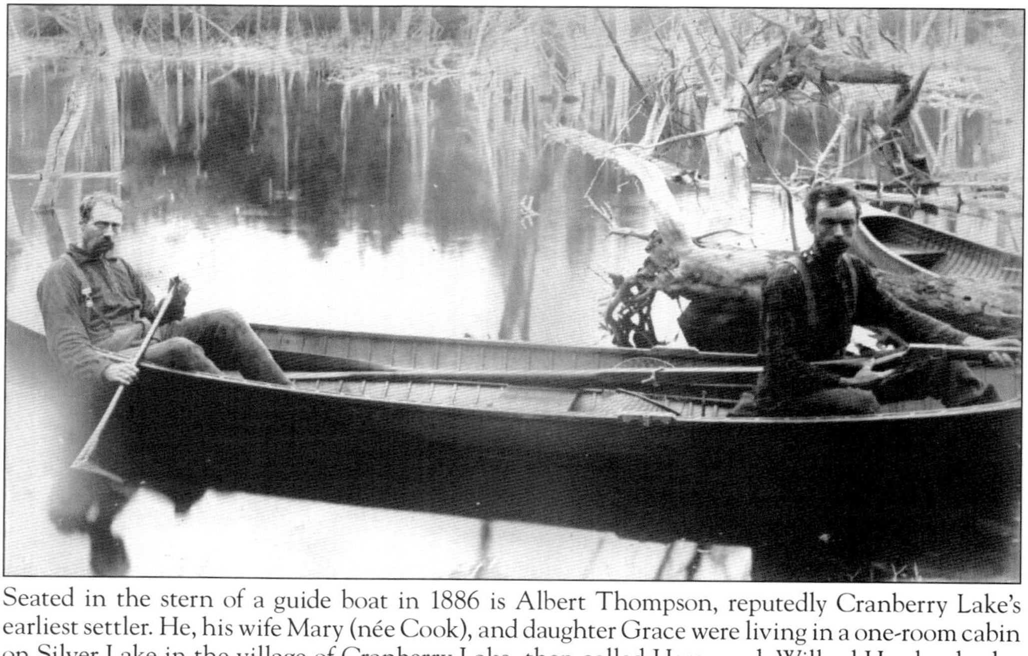

Seated in the stern of a guide boat in 1886 is Albert Thompson, reputedly Cranberry Lake's earliest settler. He, his wife Mary (née Cook), and daughter Grace were living in a one-room cabin on Silver Lake in the village of Cranberry Lake, then called Harewood. Willard Howland, who built a log house at Chair Rock in 1905, is in the bow of the boat. (Courtesy of Randy Hayes.)

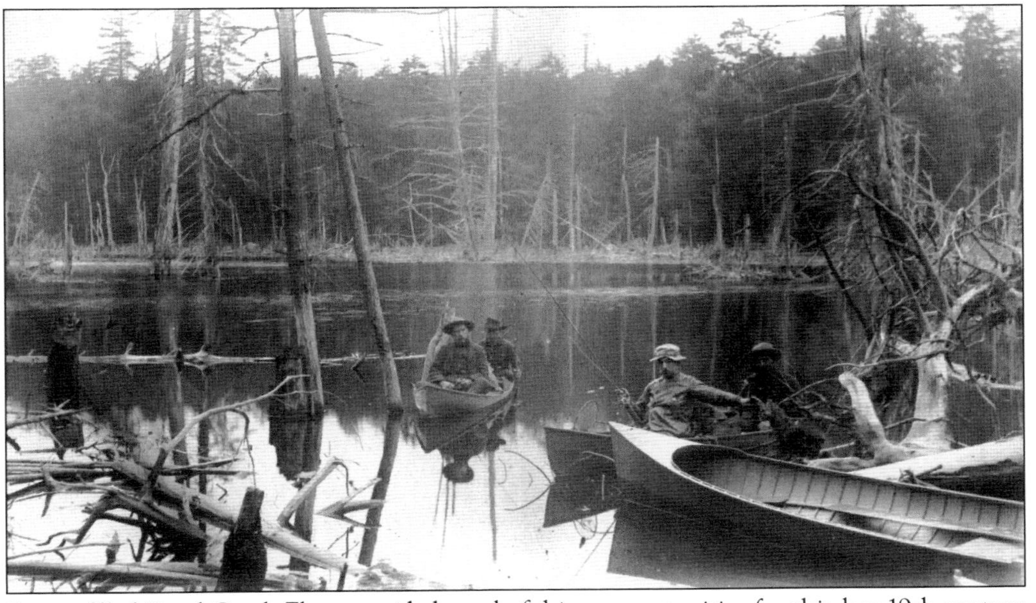

Stump-filled Dead Creek Flow provided ample fishing opportunities for this late-19th-century group of unidentified anglers in guide boats. The Adirondack guide boat is a descendant of the Colonial military bateau. It is light, steady, dry, and strong, with fine lines and greater carrying capacity than a birch bark canoe. It suited the needs of both settlers and professional guides. (Courtesy of Randy Hayes.)

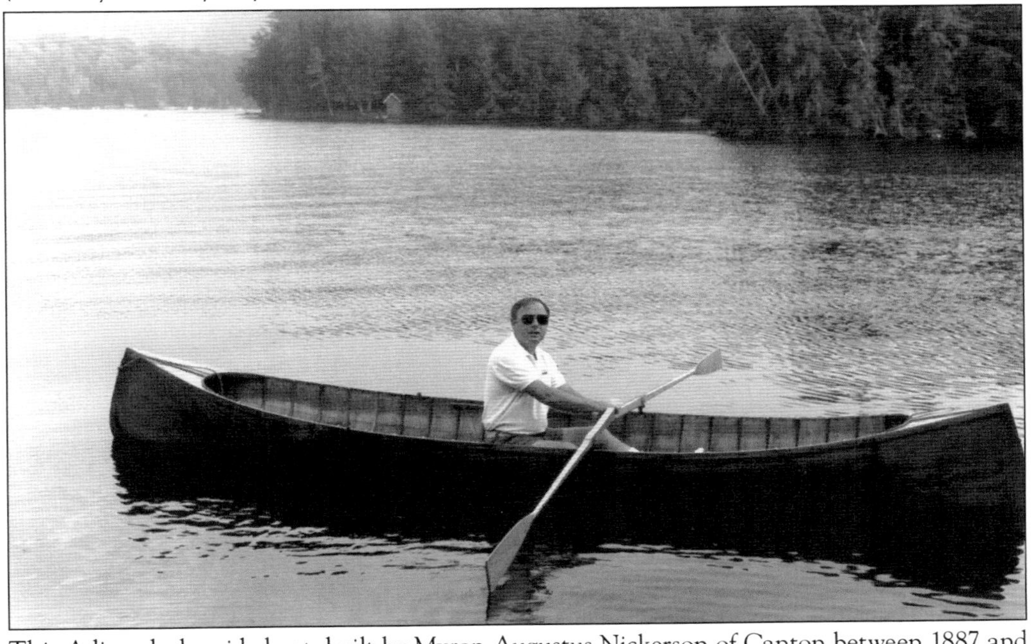

This Adirondack guide boat, built by Myron Augustus Nickerson of Canton between 1887 and 1907, was launched and rowed by Allan Newell and Everett Smith at the No-Octane Regatta in 2007. A well-known builder of guide boats and similar small craft, Nickerson learned the trade from J. Henry Rushton at his boat shop in Canton. The boat was last used on Cranberry Lake. Here it is being rowed by Jay Edel. (Courtesy of the Antique Boat Museum.)

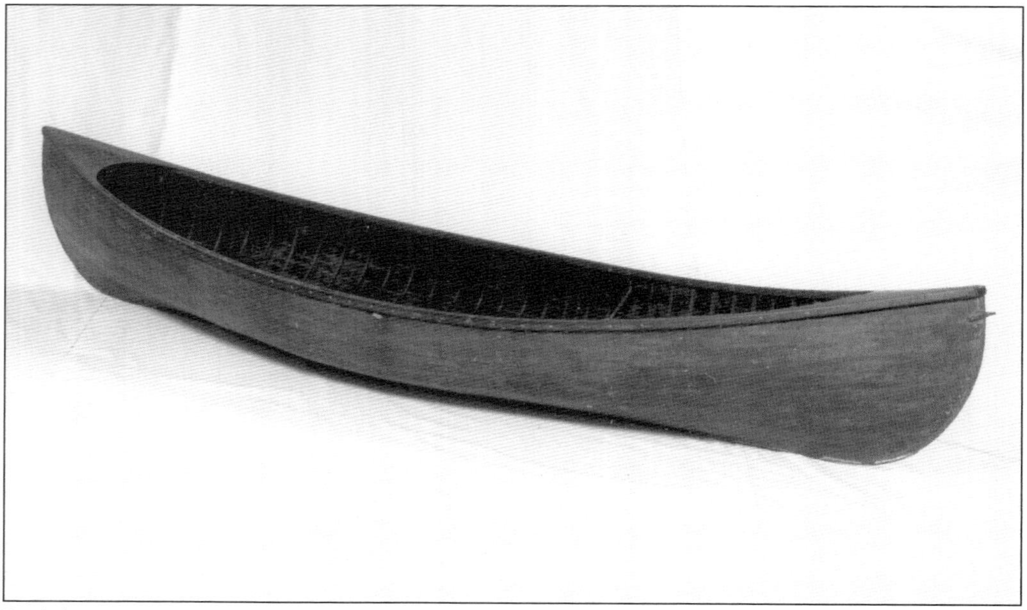

Built between 1880 and 1890, this double-ended, wooden, strip-built canoe has rear and center wooden seats with brackets attached to keep the boat from springing. It was built by Harry Green of Hermon, a "fine mechanic" and carpenter who worked out of his barn. He was a contemporary of J. Henry Rushton, known for building canoes, but used strip planking, which Rushton never did. (Courtesy of the Adirondack Museum.)

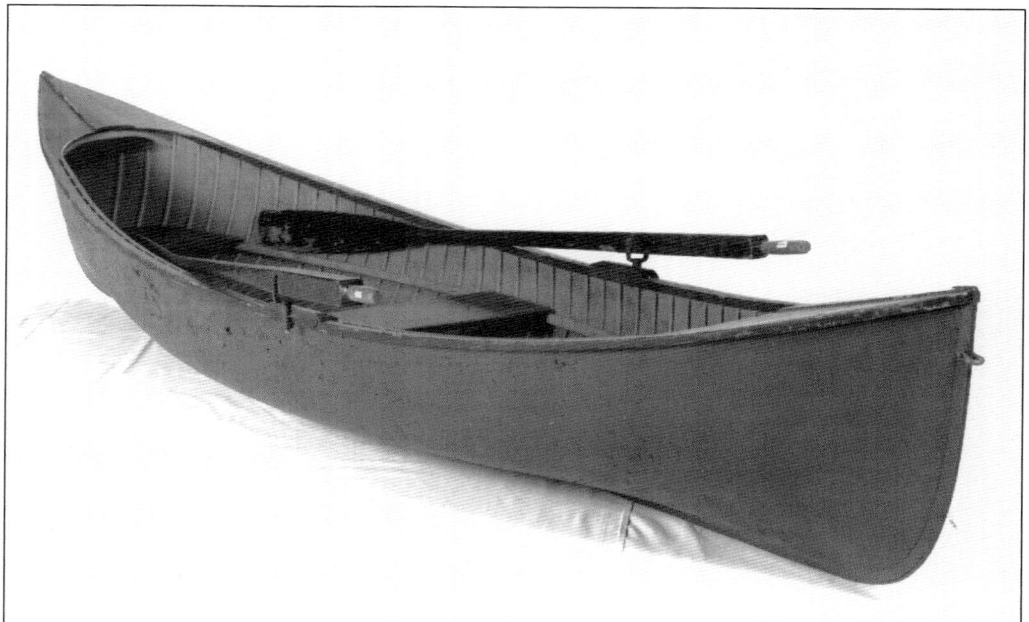

Green built many boats for the Cranberry Lake region. This one, a double-ended wooden canoe built around 1890, weighs 98 pounds and is 14 feet long. It belonged to Bill Rasbeck (1840–1917), a popular Cranberry Lake guide well liked by artist and outdoorsman Frederic Remington. (Courtesy of the Adirondack Museum.)

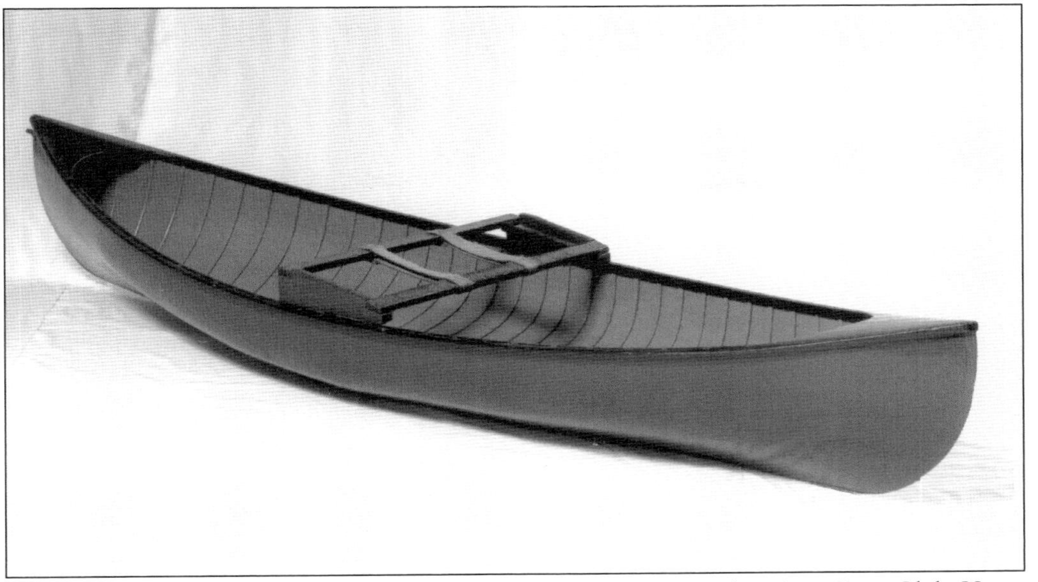

Judge Irving G. Vann was the first commodore of the Cranberry Lake Motor Boat Club. Harry Green of Hermon built this "carry boat" in 1895 for him to use at his summer residence on Buck Island. It has a carrying yoke and was used as an alternative to the guide boat for portable water transportation in the Adirondacks. (Courtesy of the Adirondack Museum.)

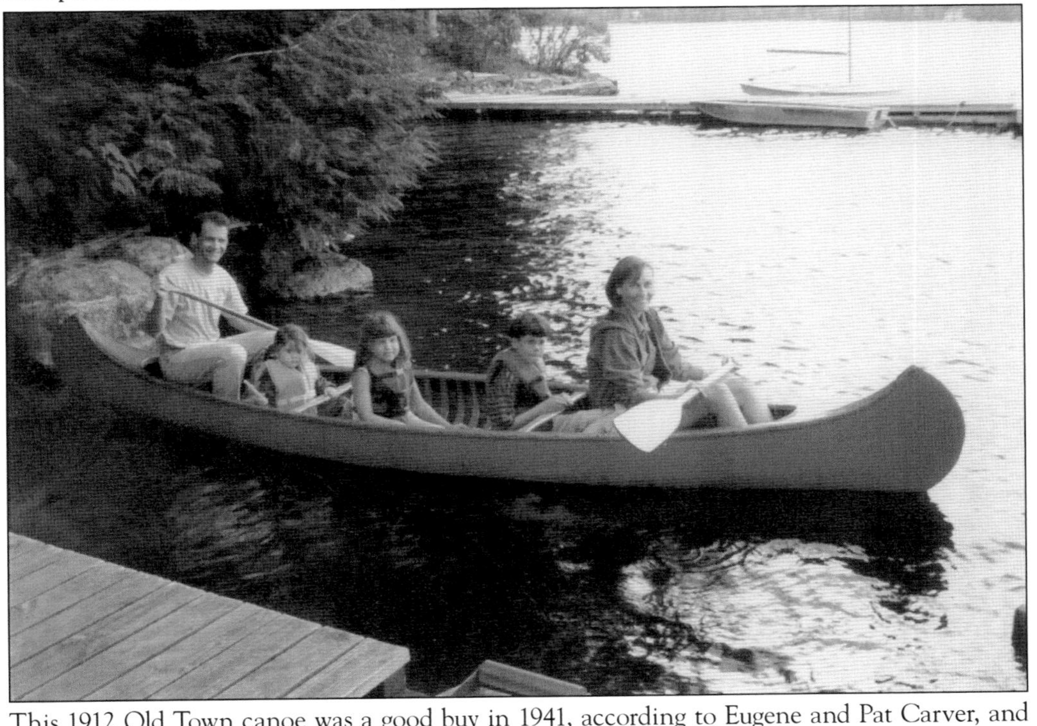

This 1912 Old Town canoe was a good buy in 1941, according to Eugene and Pat Carver, and is still enjoyed by family members today. About to leave the dock in Matilda Bay are, from left to right, Mark Gittleman in the stern, children Sarah Gittleman, Elena Gittleman, and Adam Gittleman, and Joan Gittleman in the bow. (Courtesy of Eugene Carver.)

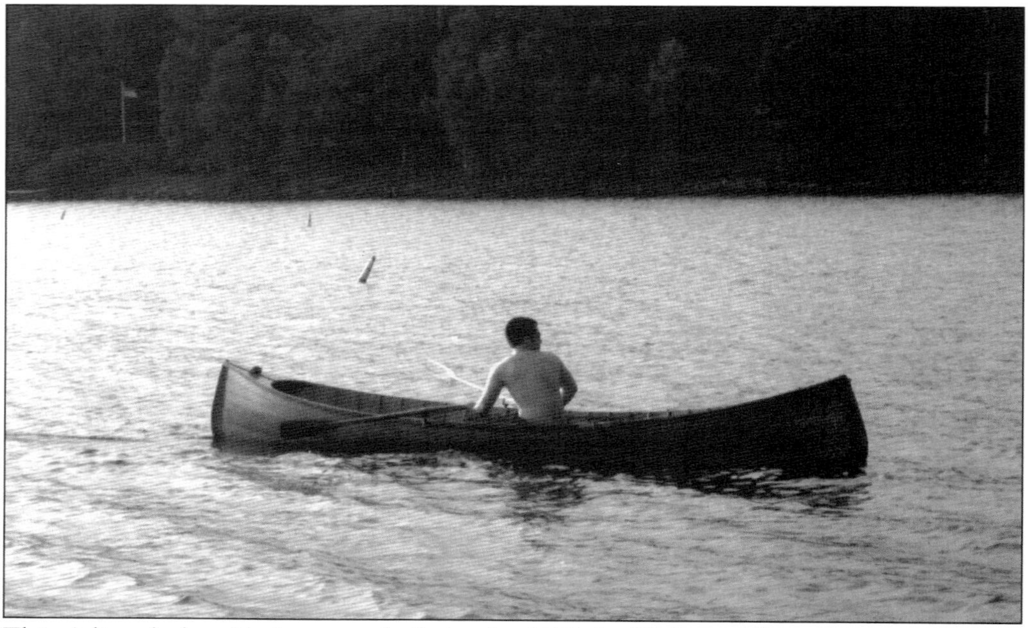

This Adirondack guide boat was built in the 1880s by William Allen Martin, one of the earliest- and best-known of the Saranac Lake guide boat builders. His extremely light boats were known locally as "Martin's Eggshells." It is strip built of alternating colors of wood and has flagpole mountings on both the bow and stern decks. Matthew Covell is at the oars in this 2004 photograph. (Courtesy of Bruce Covell.)

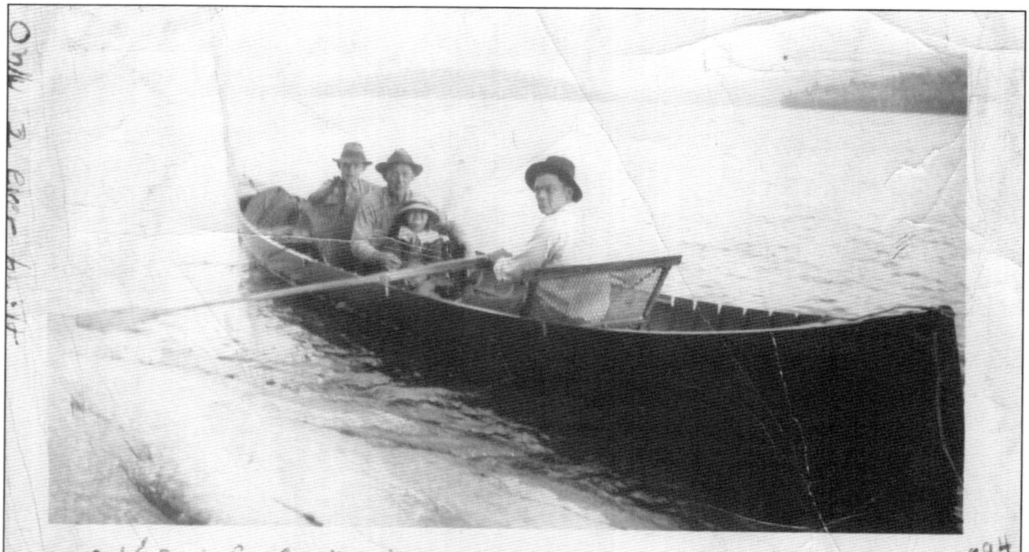

At 21 feet, this guide boat is believed to be the longest guide boat found in the Adirondacks and one of only two ever made. It was built by Bill McCaffrey of Bloomingdale in 1894. Pictured in the original boat in 1938 are, from left to right, George Leslie Robinson, George Eli Robinson, Barbara Slater, and Gilson M. Slater (rowing). The stern was later cut off to accommodate a motor. (Courtesy of Barbara Slater.)

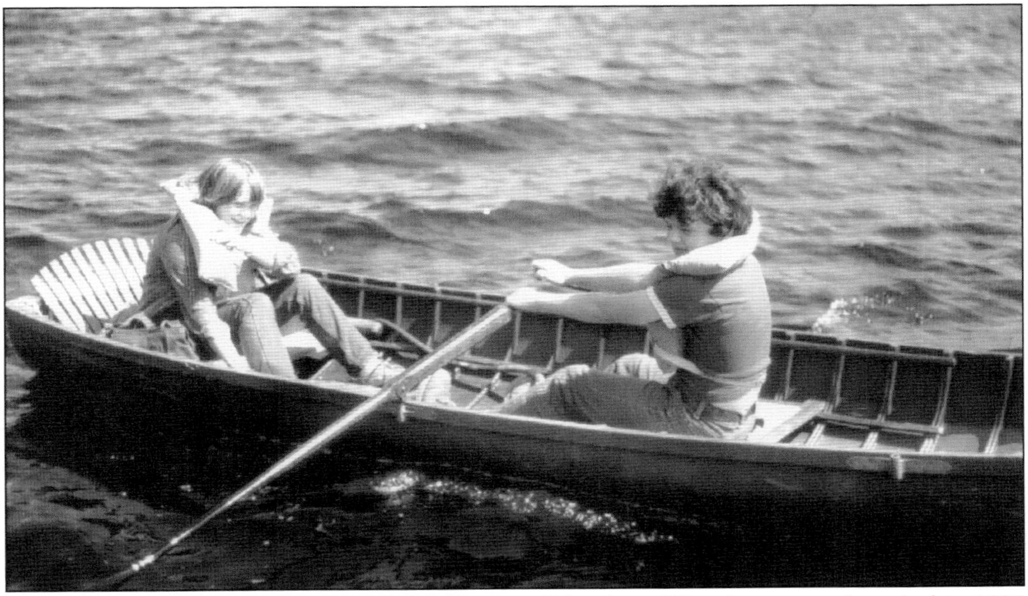

Lucian (Lou) Plumley, director of the Ranger School in Wanakena, purchased this 1894 McCaffrey guide boat from Gilson Slater in the 1940s. The stern end of the guide boat had been cut off to make an 18-foot boat, which, at that length, could avoid payment of a motorboat registration fee. Plumley then constructed and caned new seats for his grandson Andy Giraud, who is shown rowing the boat with his sister, Amy, in the 1970s (above) and solo with the motor in the 1980s (below). The boat is still on Cranberry Lake and is currently in storage for restoration. (Courtesy of Ernest Giraud.)

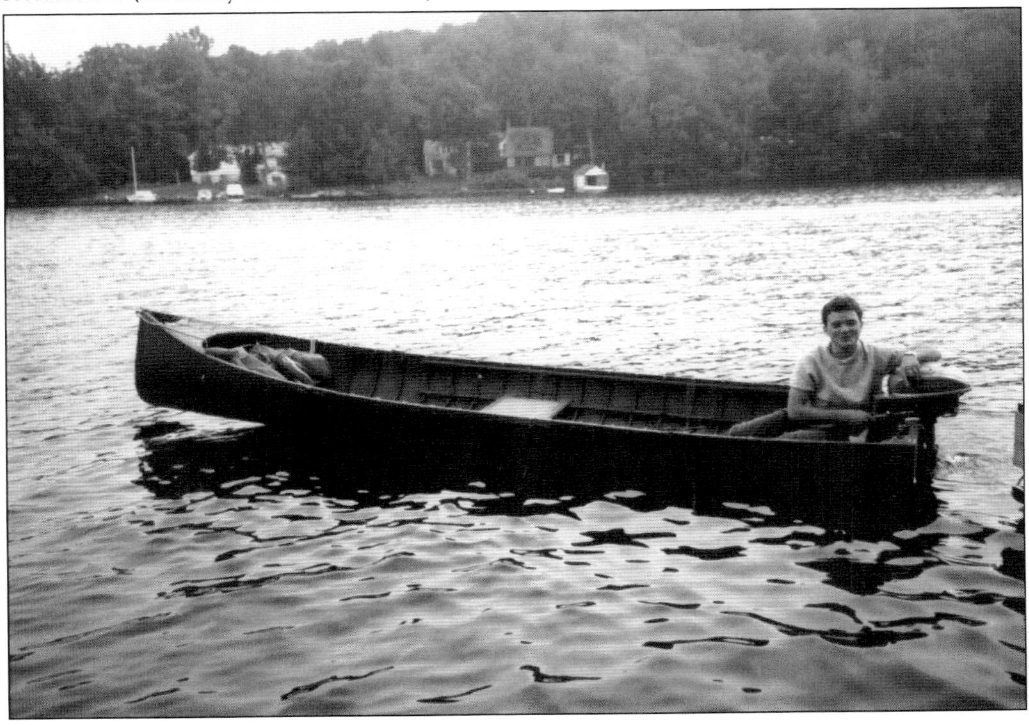

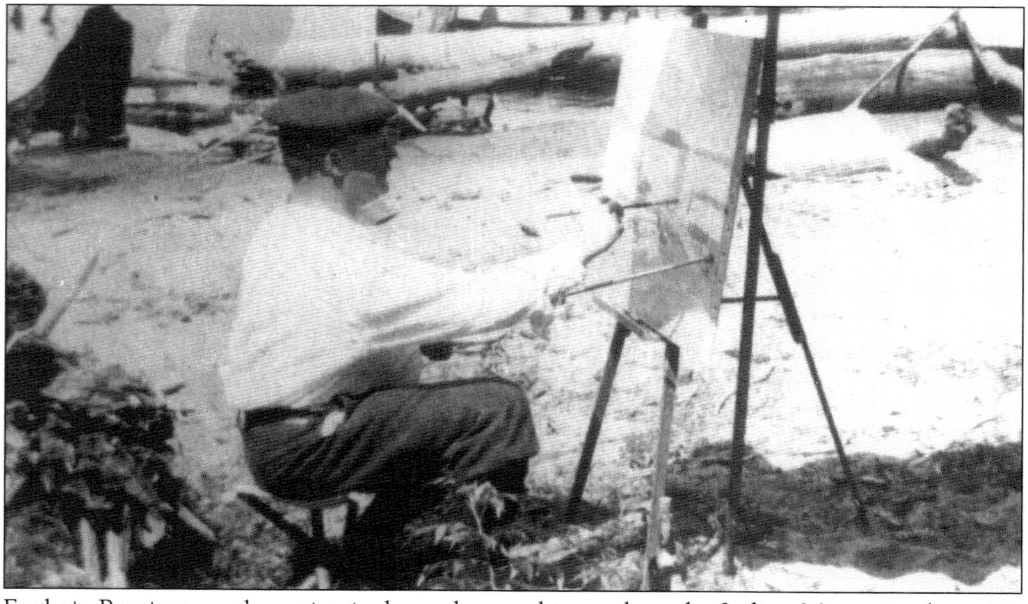

Frederic Remington, the artist, is shown here at his easel on the Indian Mountain shore. He visited friends on the lake every summer between 1889 and 1900 and is known to have done preliminary sketches for the first illustrated edition of Henry Wadsworth Longfellow's *Song of Hiawatha* while there in 1889. (Courtesy of the Frederic Remington Art Museum.)

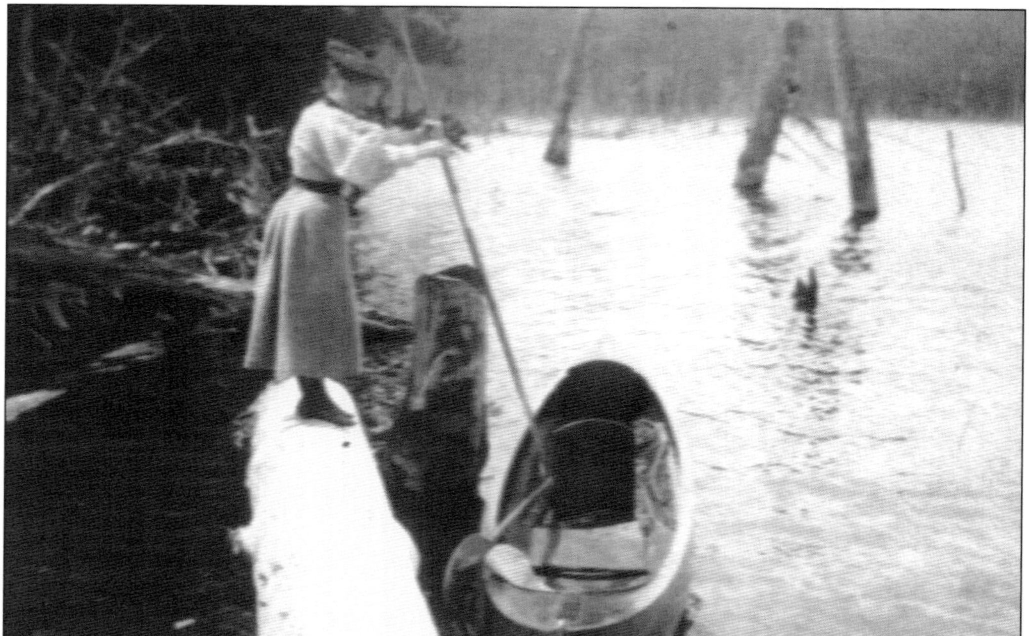

Remington was born in Canton in 1861. He and his wife, Eva, enjoyed friendships with several Canton families who owned camps on Cranberry Lake in the Great South Woods, as the Cranberry Lake area of the Adirondacks was known. In 1889, the trip from Canton took a full day. Eva is shown here coaxing a guide boat to shore. (Courtesy of the Frederic Remington Art Museum.)

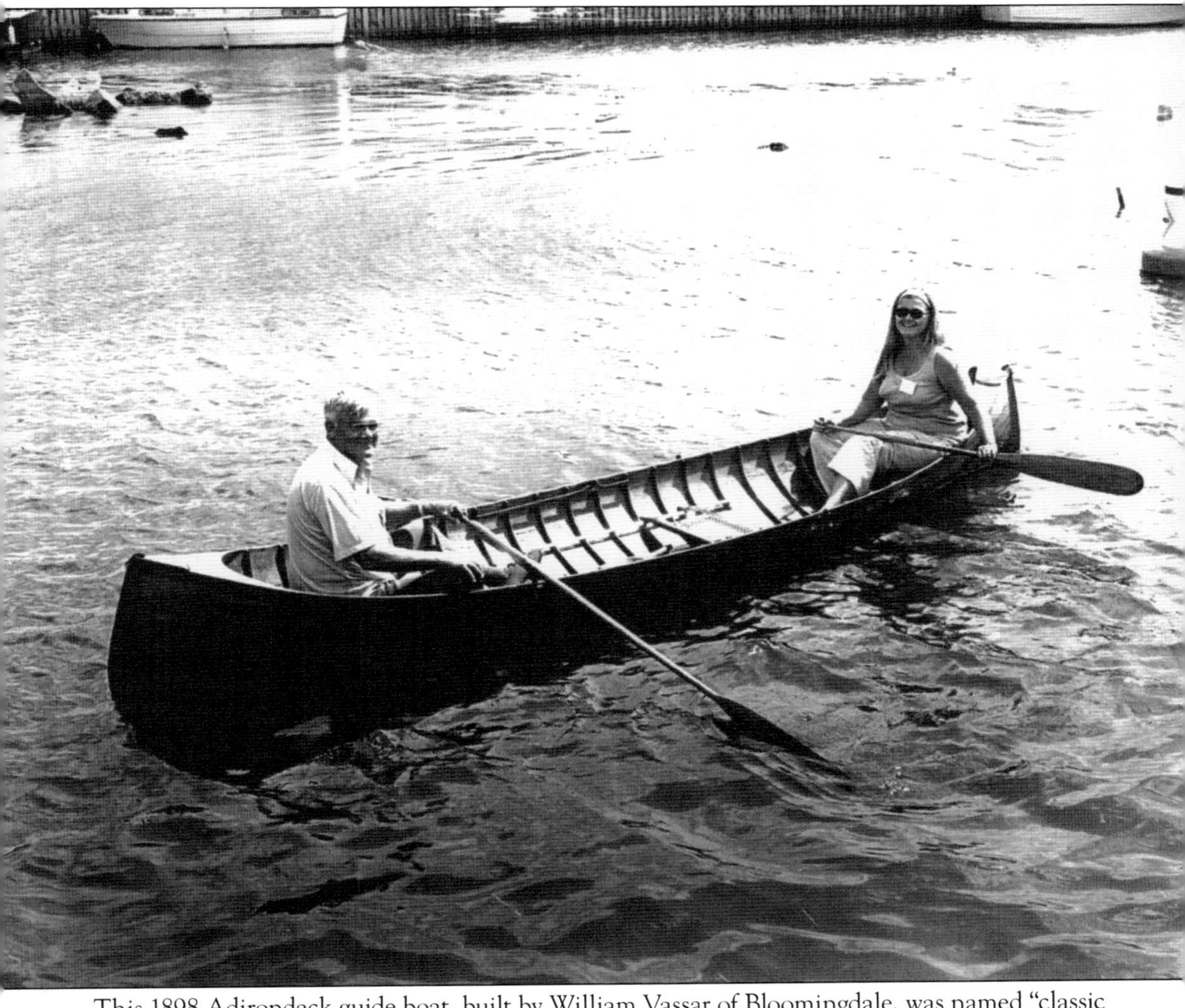

This 1898 Adirondack guide boat, built by William Vassar of Bloomingdale, was named "classic boat of the year" at Clayton's 11th annual antique boat show in 1975. Gilson Slater (left) purchased it in 1945. His daughter Barbara Slater (right) said the boat was used "almost daily" on Cranberry Lake until she gave it to the Adirondack Museum in Blue Mountain Lake in 2005. (Courtesy of Barbara Slater.)

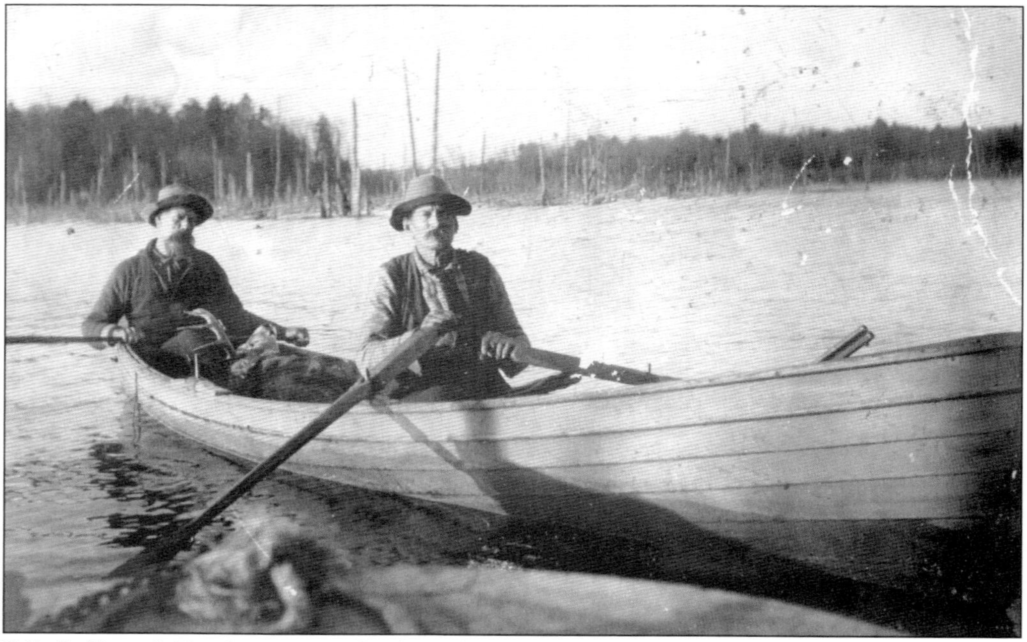

Bill (left) and Floyd "Has" Rasbeck, Adirondack guides in the Cranberry Lake area, are shown here in their guide boat. Has and artist Frederic Remington undertook a trip down the Oswegatchie River from the Cranberry Lake Dam intending to reach Ogdensburg. They did not succeed, but a story about the trip appeared in *Harper's Monthly* in August 1893. They were paddling a J. Henry Rushton canoe called *Necoochee*. (Courtesy of the Adirondack Museum.)

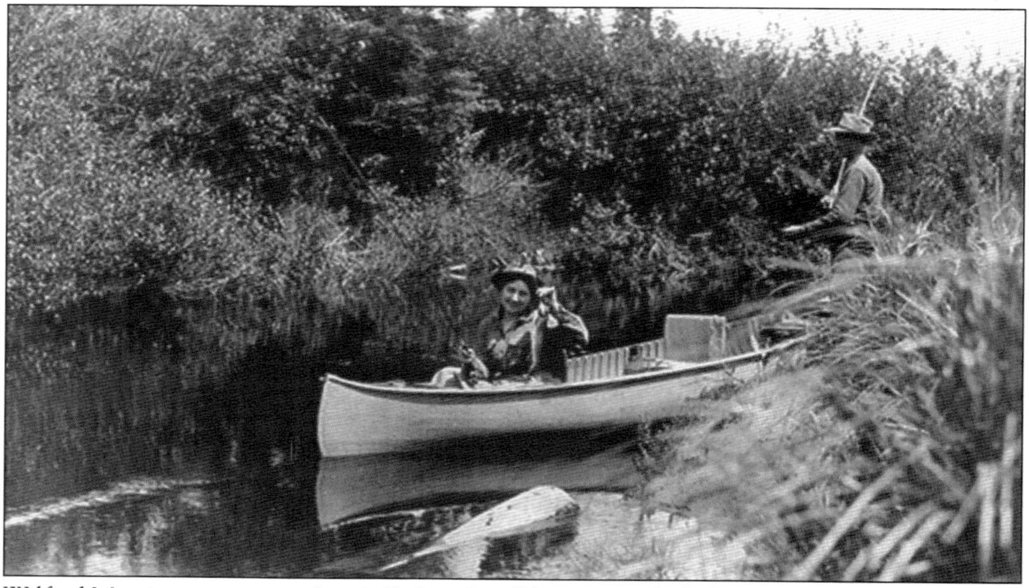

Wilfred Morrison was a popular, skilled, and well-known guide for hunters and fishermen in the early 20th century. Stories told about him usually relate heroic or misguided adventures in the woods with groups of hunters. This undated photograph of two people in a guide boat shows Wilfred Morrison (right) fishing with Marian Todd, who has just caught a nice trout. (Courtesy of Margaret Parker.)

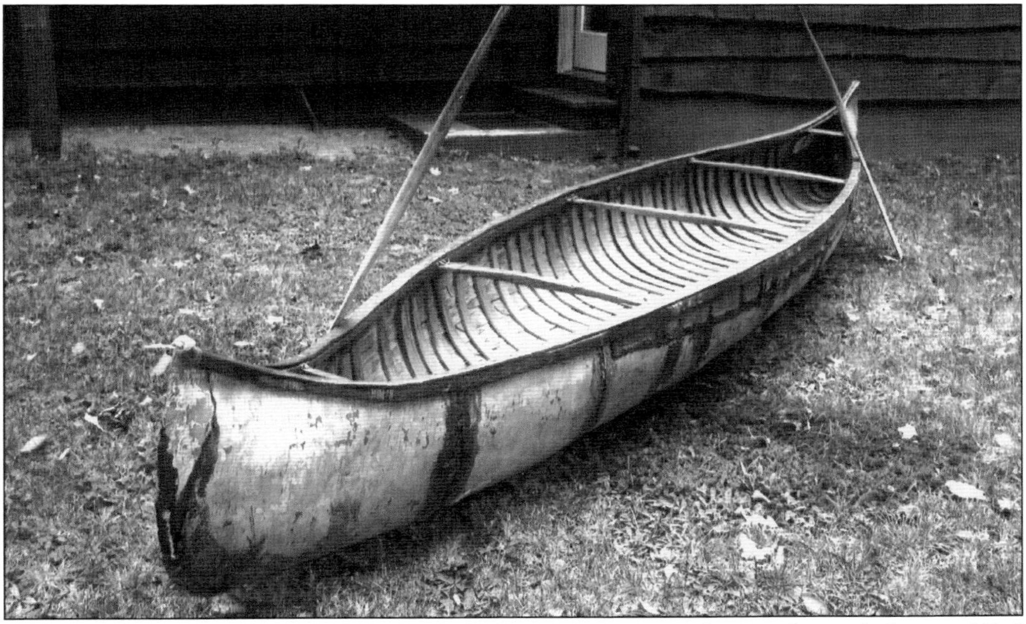

In 1959, 24 feather-light but sturdy birch bark canoes were made to order and then paddled by members of a tribe of Cree Indians from Quebec for a "canoecade" on Lake Champlain to commemorate the trip of Samuel de Champlain and his Algonquin Indian allies on the lake in 1609. These canoes were produced by stripping large pieces of birch bark, which were weighted with stones in the middle, then folded up on the sides and held in place by stakes. Spruce roots were used for sewing; spruce gum was melted and used for patching. Kermit Remelé, faculty member at the Wanakena Ranger School, purchased one after the event. Above is the canoe. Below, Remelé is showing the birch bark canoe at the Cranberry Lake Boat Show in 2006. (Courtesy of Mary Ann Remelé.)

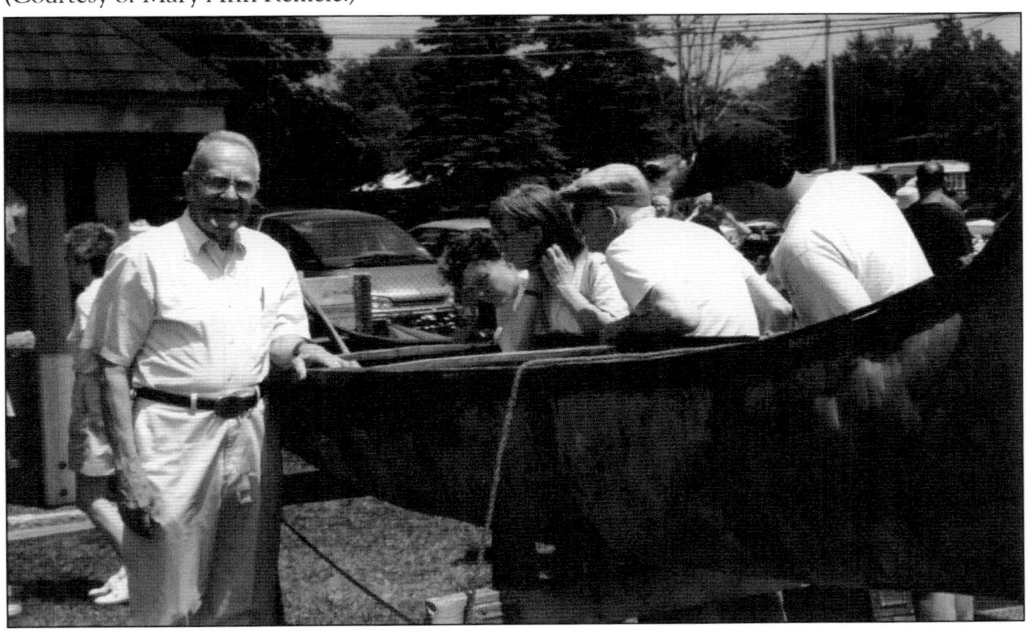

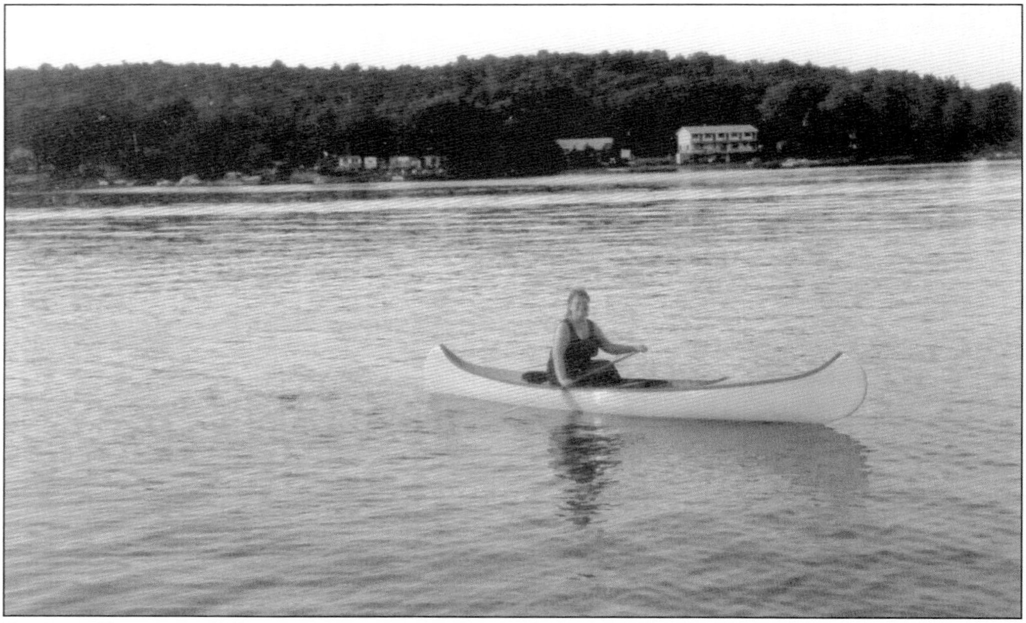

Barbara Slater is paddling a "courting canoe" made in 1917 by Charles River. One did not buy a courting canoe; one fitted up the canoe to go courting, often with cushions or other luxurious appointments. The passenger (presumably the woman) was seated in the stern, leaning against a backrest facing the paddler (presumably the man). (Courtesy of Barbara Slater.)

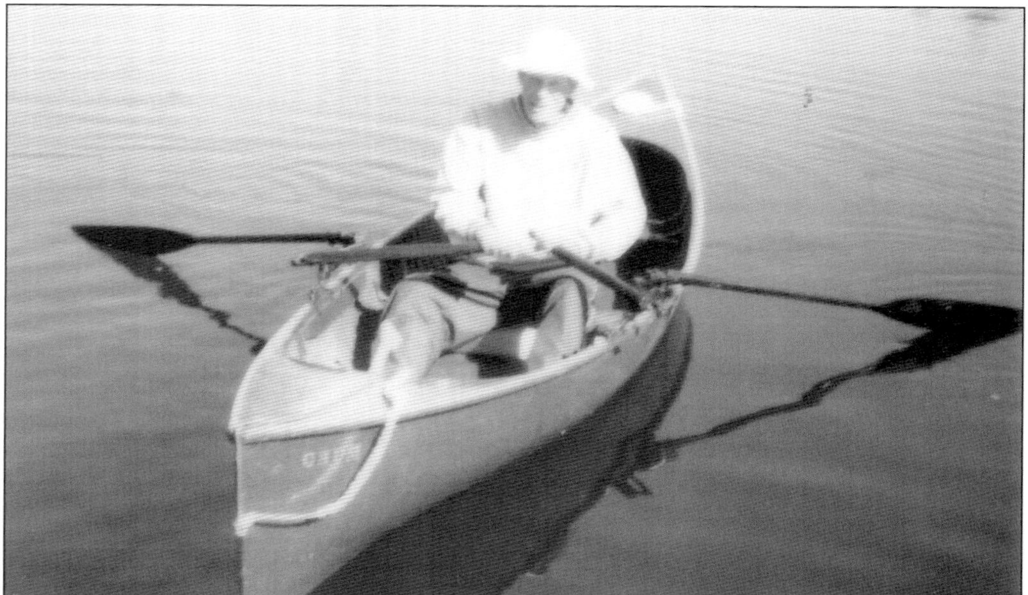

Clarence "Feets" Shelton is rowing one of J. Henry Rushton's St. Lawrence skiffs, named *Gram*, for his grandmother Harriet Shelton. It has special Lyman's patented bow-facing rowing gear. These forward-facing oars were made for Harriet to help her see where she was going. Rowers continue to be fascinated by the concept, and there is still at least one commercial manufacturer. (Courtesy of Clarence Shelton.)

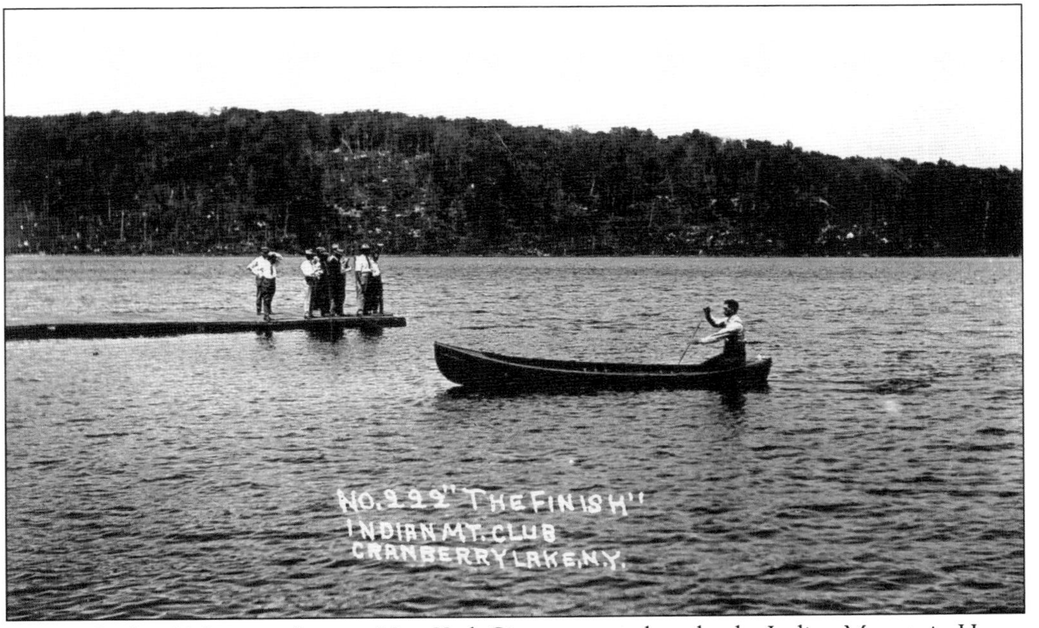

In 1911, Richard Mortimer Jesup, a New York City magnate, bought the Indian Mountain House from Mrs. George Nunn and organized the Indian Mountain Club, which lasted until 1917. In that period, the club was a lush hotel operation with tournaments and races organized for guests. Its enormous dock, shown here, jutted 80 feet into the lake. The hotel burned in 1926. (Courtesy of Susan Smeby.)

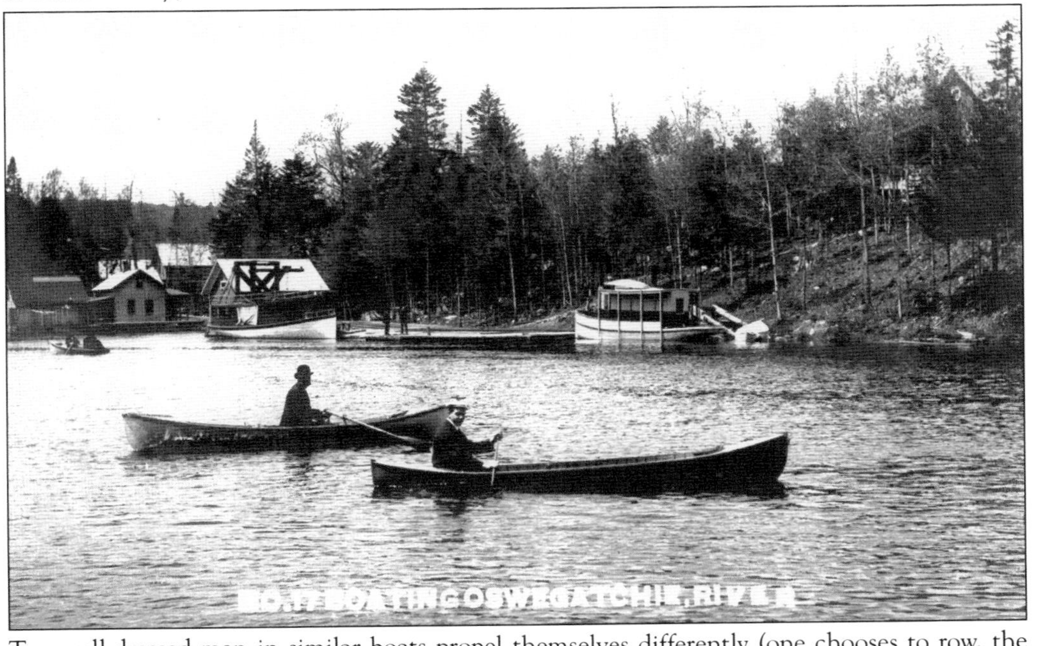

Two well-dressed men in similar boats propel themselves differently (one chooses to row, the other to paddle) along the Oswegatchie River near Wanakena around 1910. The docks in the center of the picture are on the site of the present town beach. The Hotel Wanakena is behind the trees on the upper right. (Courtesy of Peter VandeWater.)

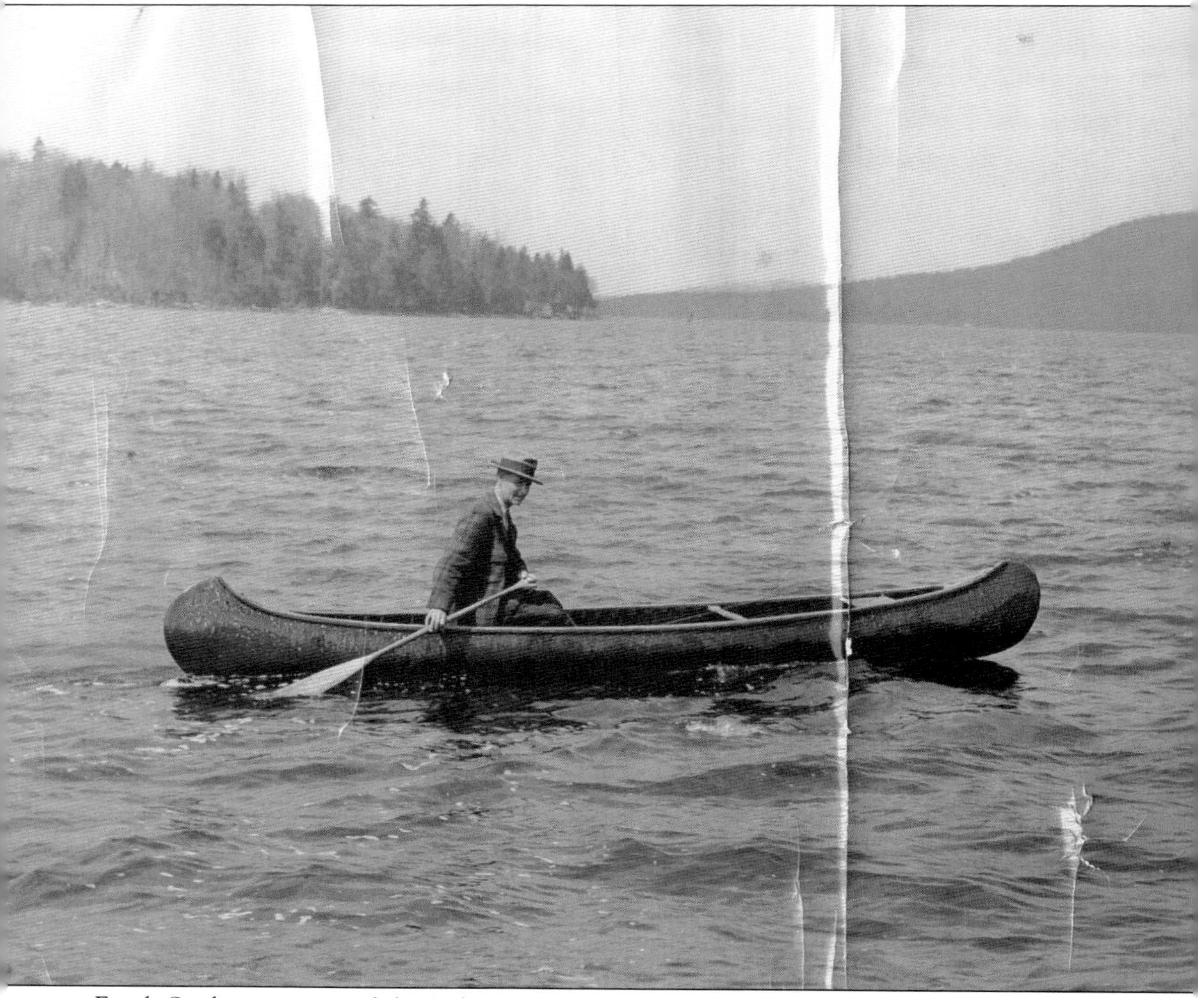

Frank Starkey was one of the Indian Mountain Club's best guides. He earned enough in his career to buy several acres of land bordering Chair Rock Flow just east of the Indian Mountain Club land. There in 1924, he built a primitive log cabin, setting the logs vertically instead of horizontally. He lived there until his 70s, the hermit of Chair Rock Flow. The cabin is still there. (Courtesy of Jeanne Reynolds.)

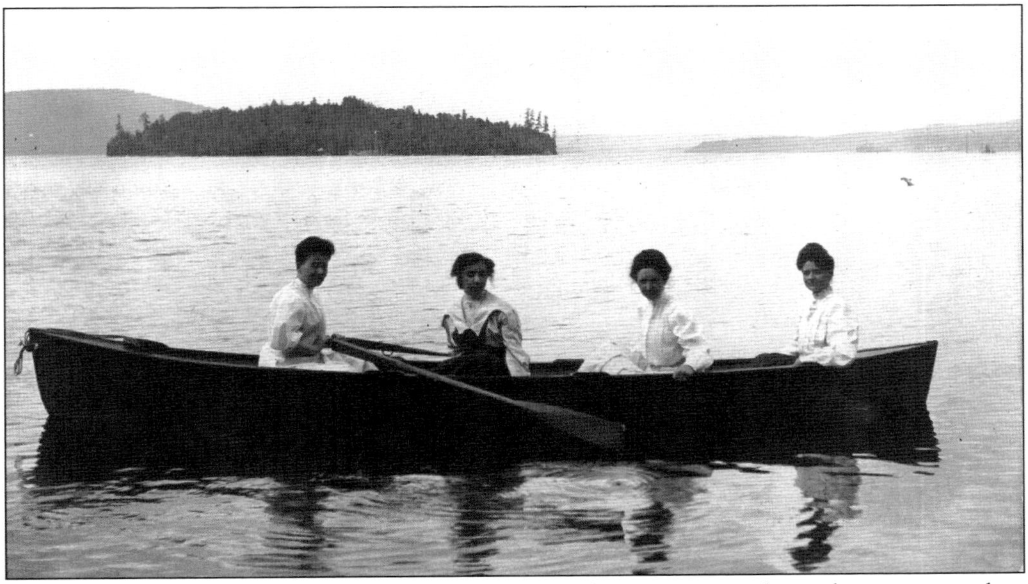

Four well-dressed unidentified ladies pause prettily with oars at rest to have their picture taken in an 1890s rowing skiff. They are in the Nunn's Inn waterfront area at the head of Cranberry Lake. Buck Island is in the center background. Bear Mountain is to the upper left. (Courtesy of Peter VandeWater.)

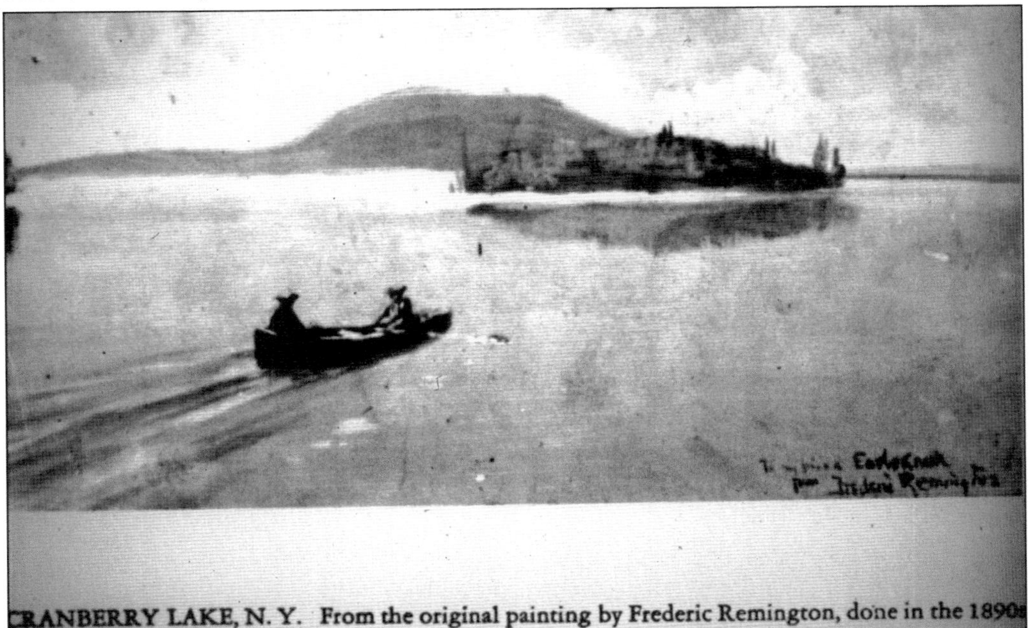

The subject is Cranberry Lake, with Buck Island and Bear Mountain, a scene familiar to anyone who ventures to the head of the lake. It is 7 inches by 13.5 inches and was painted in oil on a wood shingle, sometime in the 1890s, by Frederic Remington, internationally known chronicler of the American West. He inscribed it to his friend Earle Knox and signed it. It later came into the possession of Judge Irving G. Vann of Buck Island. Remington, born in Canton, visited Cranberry Lake often. (Courtesy of Albert Fowler.)

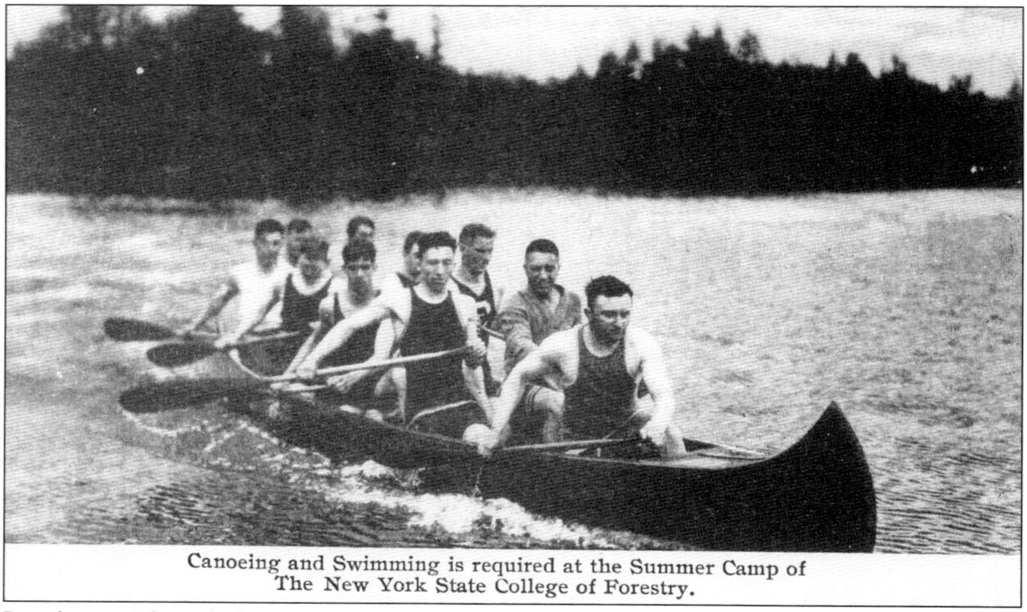

Popular in Adirondack summer camps, war canoes built teamwork. Here 10 paddlers from the College of Forestry summer camp at Cranberry Lake prepare for their race against the Ranger School students at Wanakena around 1915. The average war canoe was 25 feet long. With the strongest paddler in the bow, and pairs of rowers in the middle, a single paddler in the stern called the cadence. This war canoe still exists. (Courtesy of Peter VandeWater.)

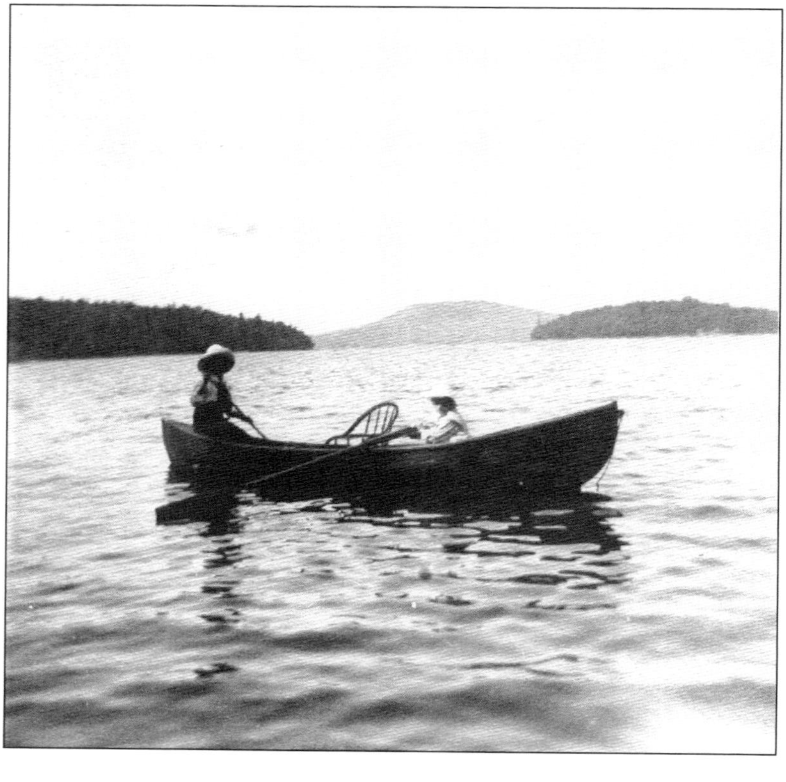

This is a rowing skiff with Adelaide Smith (left) paddling and Grace Smith rowing past Cole's Point (behind to the left) in the late 1890s. Bear Mountain is in the center (distant), and Buck Island is to the right. Of note are the empty chair in the middle and the combination of one person rowing and the other paddling. (Courtesy of Anna Fowler.)

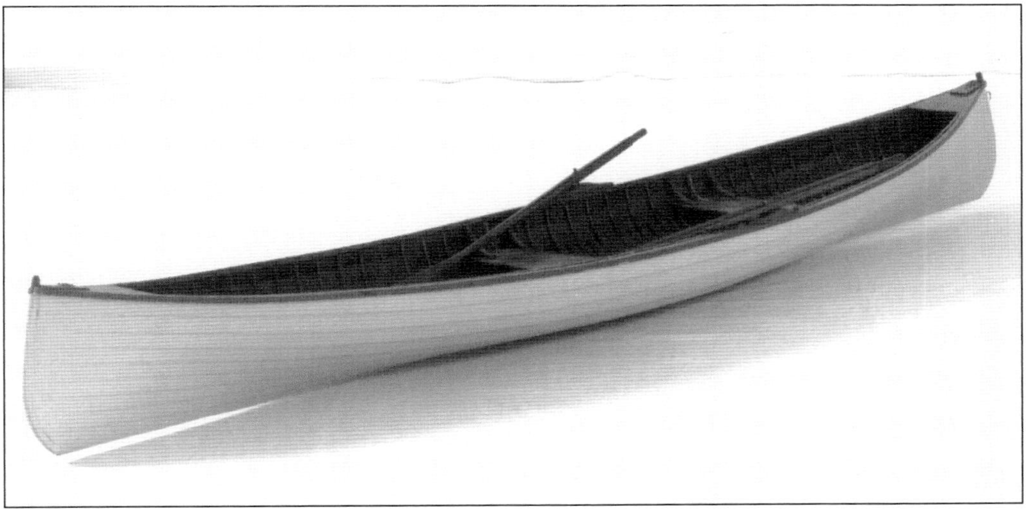

This pleasure rowboat was built by Herbert M. Sprague of Parishville in 1922. Known as a builder with an eye for the market, he added some features of the popular St. Lawrence skiff. It was purchased by Donald Spotswood's mother for his father's birthday. It was originally varnished inside and out and spent its life at a camp on Cranberry Lake. (Courtesy of the Adirondack Museum.)

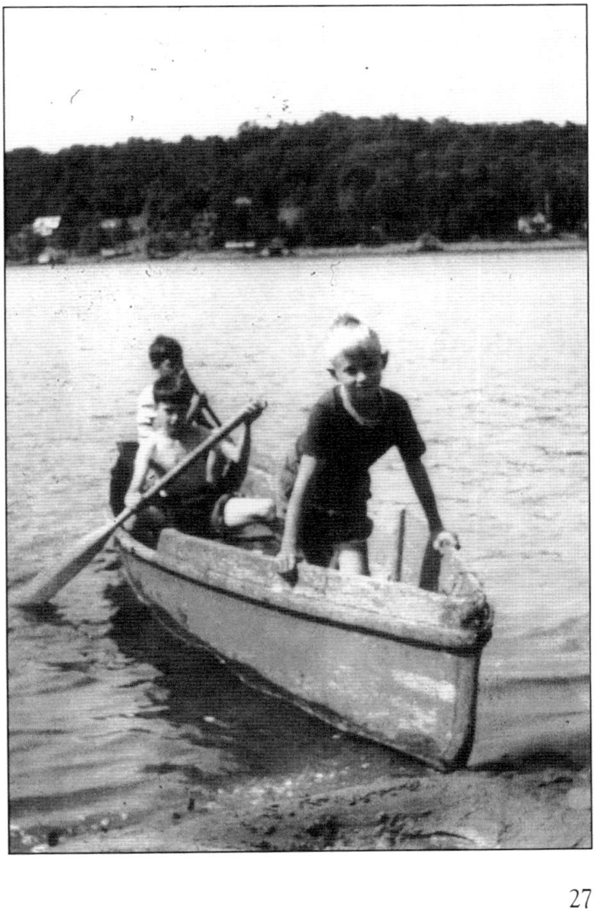

In the bow (right) of this wooden rowboat in 1938 is John MacAleese. His companions are Tom Tetreault (center) and Philip Tetreault. They are coming ashore at the Evergreen Hotel in Cranberry Lake. William MacAleese Sr. bought it in 1920. William MacAleese Jr. bought it from him in the 1930s. "Old Bill Mack" continued to live in the hotel and guide fishermen around the lake. (Courtesy of John MacAleese.)

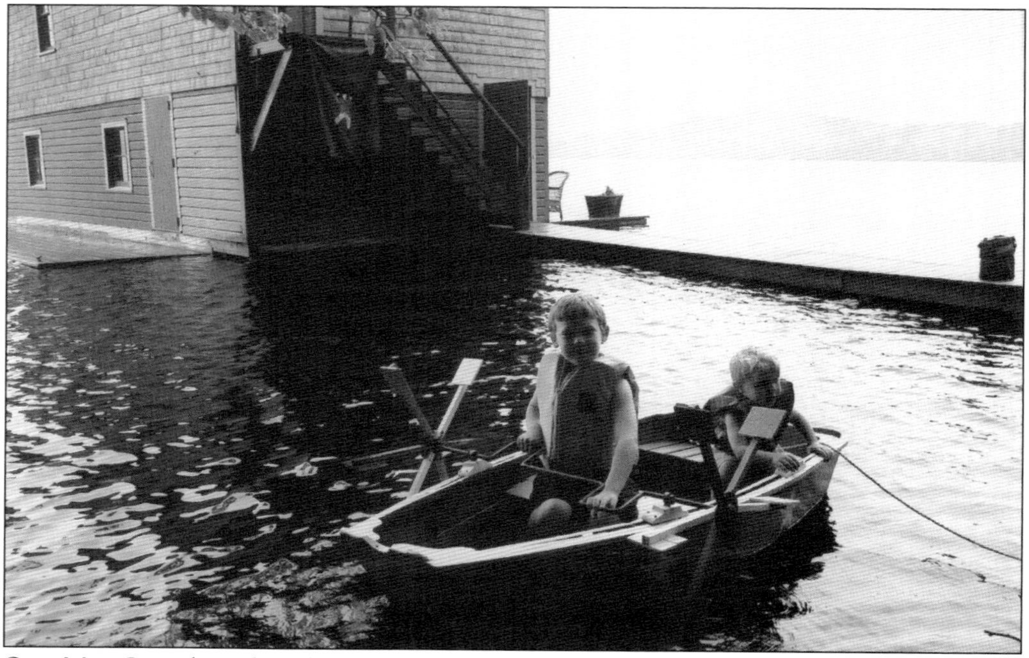

Otto Max Giraud purchased a red, white, and blue wooden paddleboat for his family in 1943. It is still in use and is currently being restored. It is 5 feet, 10 inches long with a hand crank in the center that turns the paddles. Leaning to the side will turn the boat. Pictured in 2002 are Charlie (age six) and Danny (age two) Jerome, sons of Amy Giraud Jerome. (Courtesy of Ernest Giraud.)

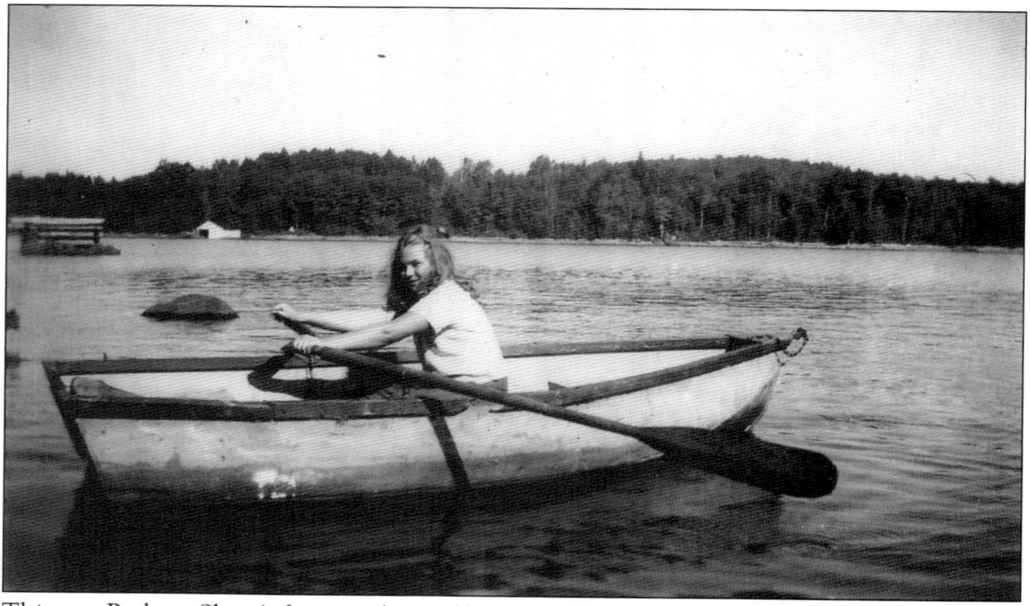

This was Barbara Slater's first new boat of her own. She received it from her grandfather, who lived in Saranac Lake, New York. It was made of tin with air chambers for flotation on either end. Later she purchased a 2.5-horsepower Evinrude motor to use on it with money she had saved. She appears delighted with "her" boat in this July 1947 photograph. (Courtesy of Barbara Slater.)

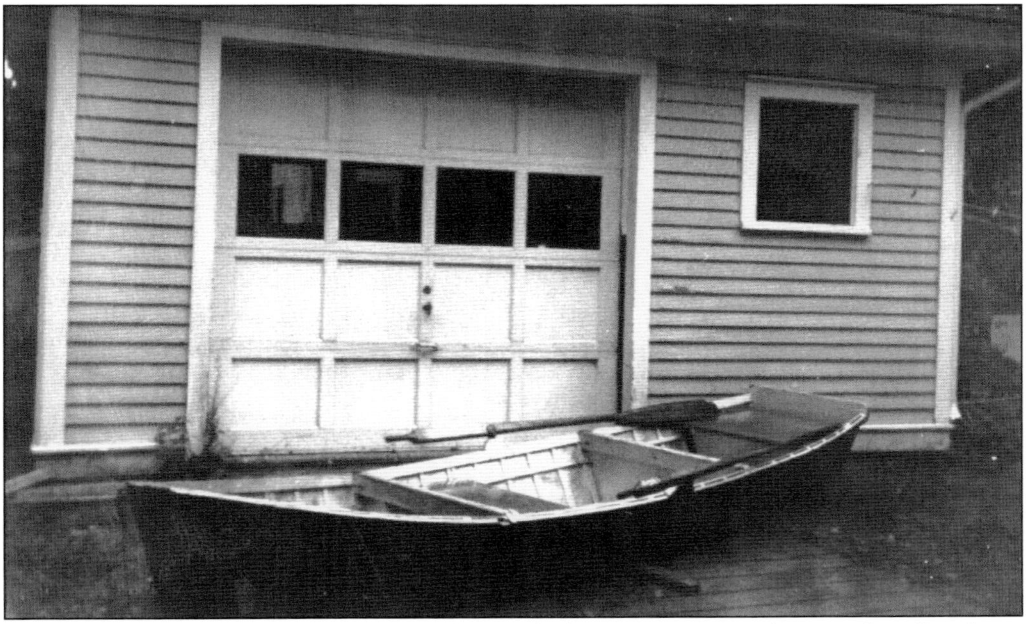

This is an unusual three-section metal rowboat. It had a canvas cover and was used on Cranberry Lake until 1983. The boat was made by Norton of Mexico, New York, before 1925. Lewis "Tui" Cook Jr. owned the boat. When fully assembled as shown above, it is about 3.5 feet wide and 14 feet long. The photograph below shows the boat in three sections, which made it easier to handle for storage. It is now in the Antique Boat Museum. (Courtesy of Barbara Slater.)

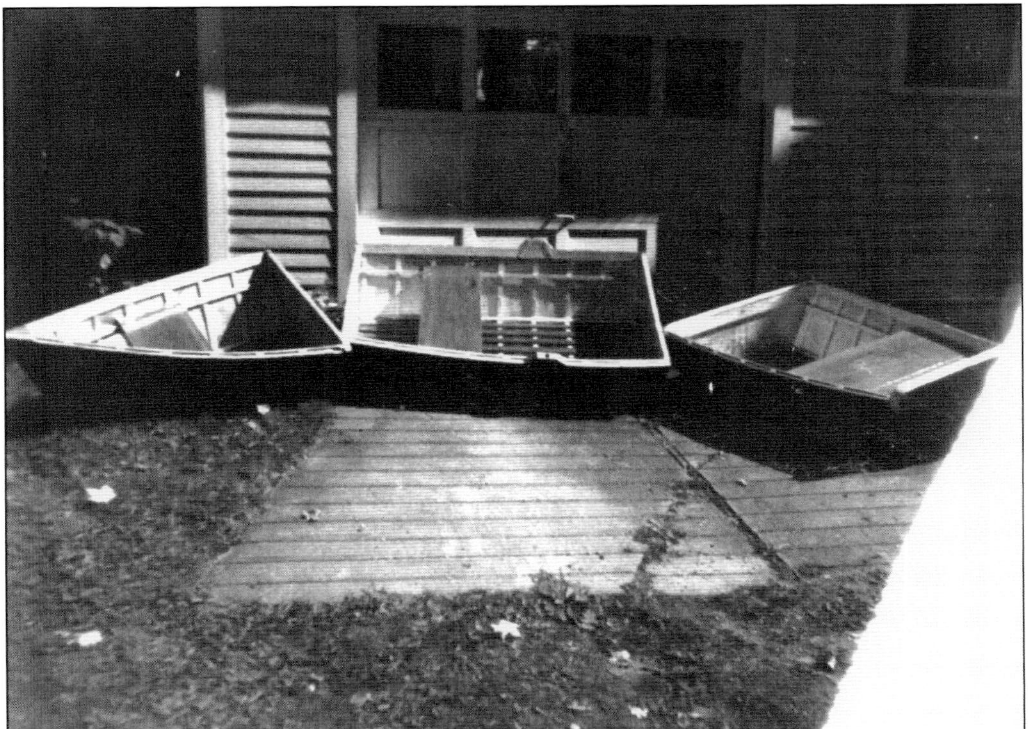

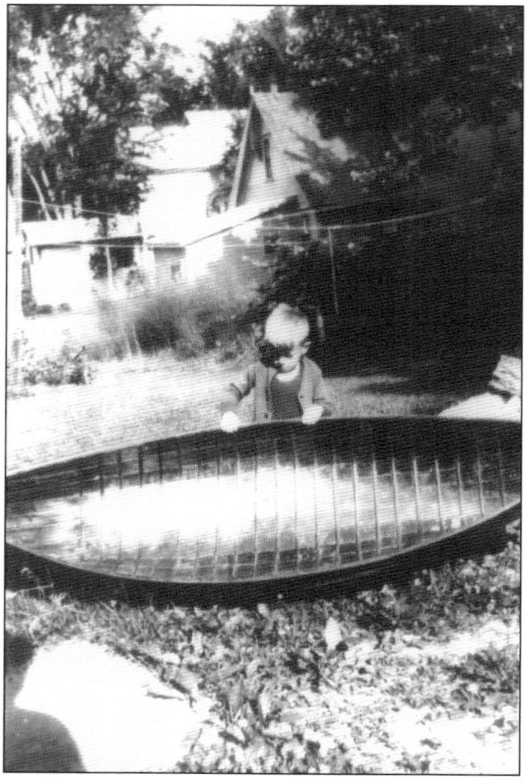

This photograph shows a young Lewis "Tui" Cook Jr. of Cranberry Lake in 1930 peering down into a tiny Nessmuk-type guide boat made of white cedar. It was only eight feet, three inches long and weighed in at 14 pounds. The oars were four feet long. It was designed to hold a person up to 150 pounds. (Courtesy of Barbara Slater.)

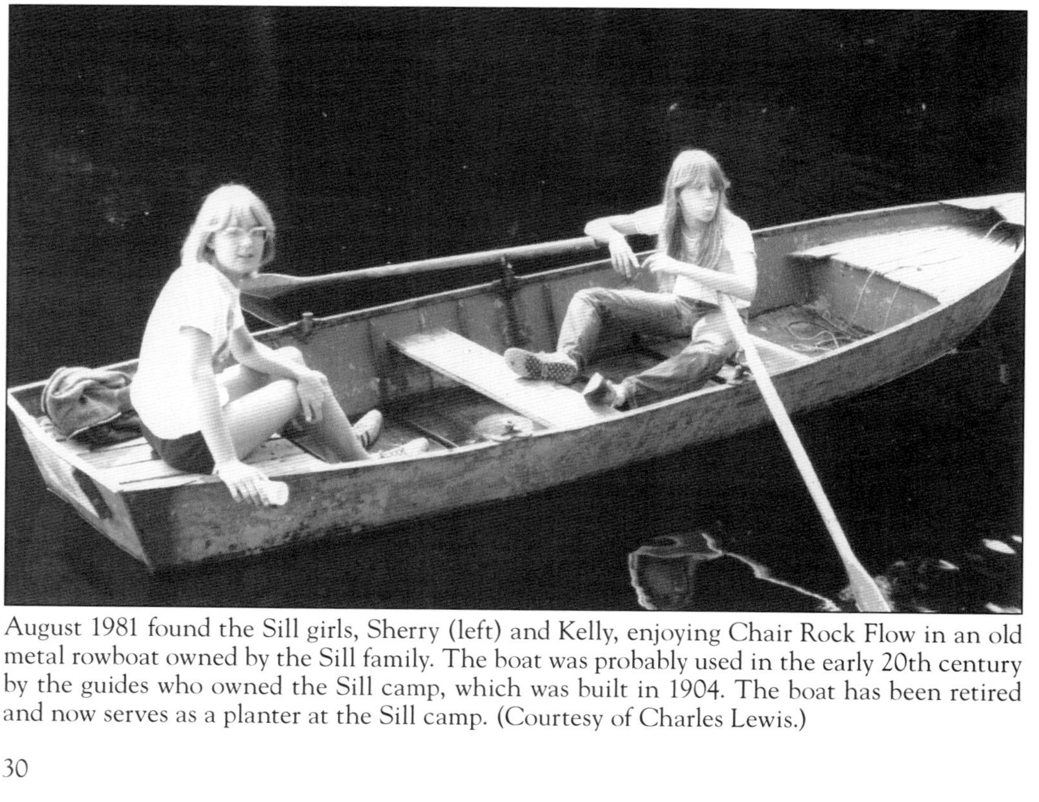

August 1981 found the Sill girls, Sherry (left) and Kelly, enjoying Chair Rock Flow in an old metal rowboat owned by the Sill family. The boat was probably used in the early 20th century by the guides who owned the Sill camp, which was built in 1904. The boat has been retired and now serves as a planter at the Sill camp. (Courtesy of Charles Lewis.)

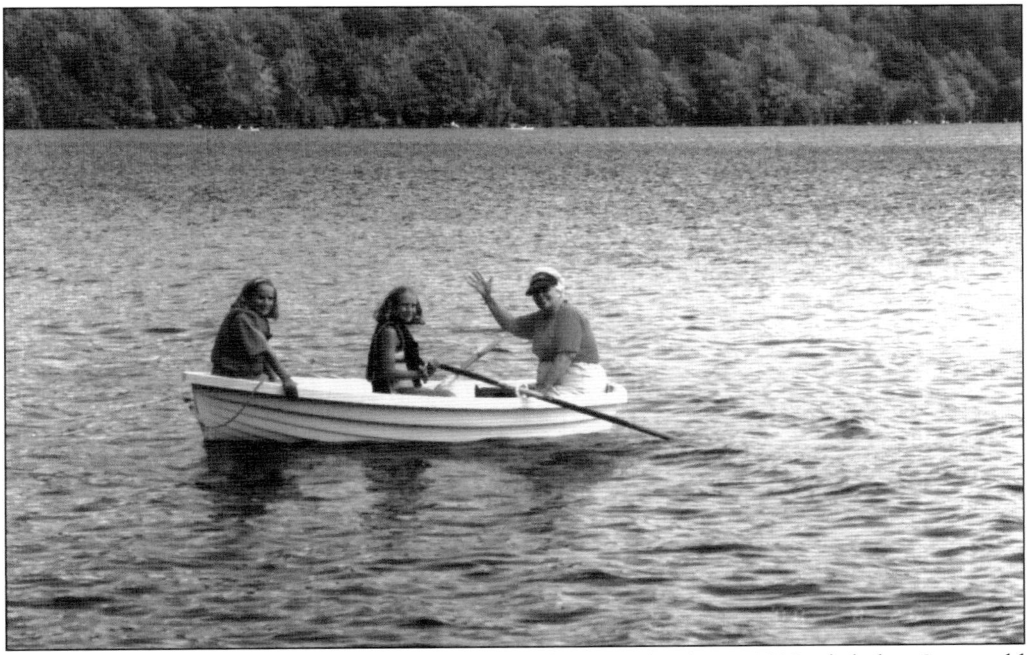

Nicole Wilder (center), 11 years old, rows this Walker Bay dinghy in 1998 while her 8-year-old sister, Alison (left), rides in the bow and neighbor Jan Thurston in the stern waves. The boat is eight feet long and about 10 years old. It is made of plastic, can be sailed, and is still in use. (Courtesy of Melissa Wilder.)

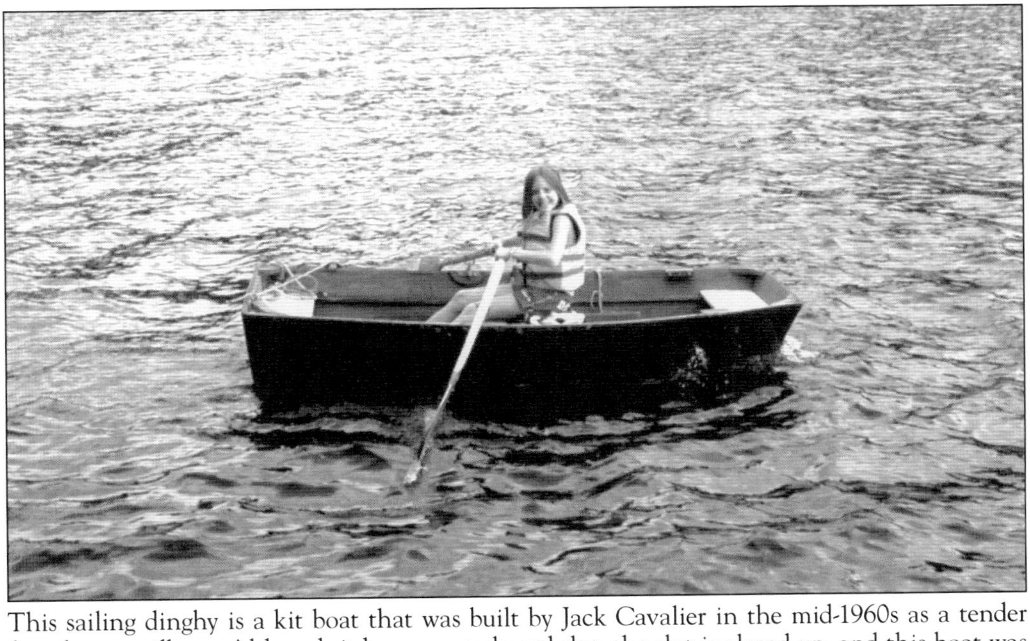

This sailing dinghy is a kit boat that was built by Jack Cavalier in the mid-1960s as a tender for a larger sailboat. Although it has a centerboard slot, the slot is closed up, and this boat was probably never used to sail. It has been at Cranberry Lake for six years and is being rowed by Alisa Rose Guevara. (Courtesy of Fred Guevara.)

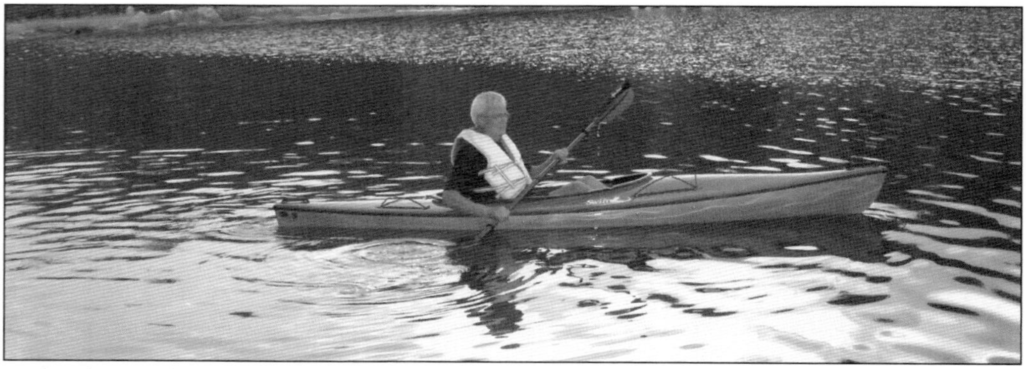

Technology in kayak design has improved to the point that Fred Guevara was able to purchase a lightweight Swift model weighing a mere 16 pounds from Saranac Lake Outfitters after trying it out at the 2006 Cranberry Lake Boat Show. (Courtesy of Fred Guevara.)

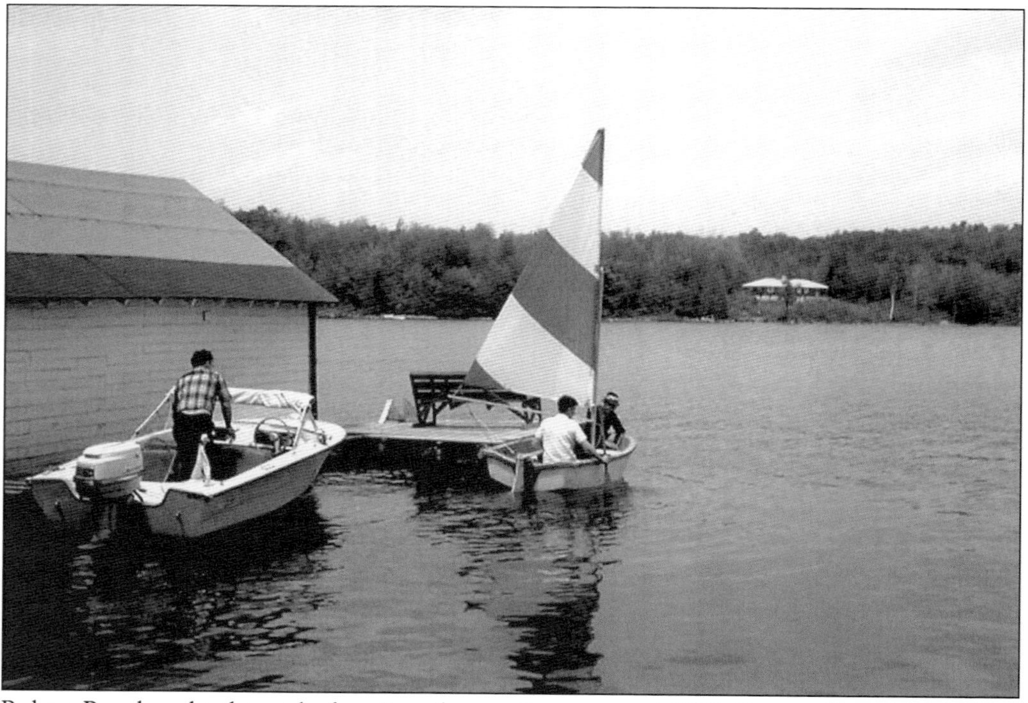

Robert Barr bought this eight-foot Styrofoam sailboat around 1965. His son, David (in stern at tiller), said he and his friends would have races for beer. "It wasn't very fast," he said, "and if you spilled gas in the boat, the gas would disintegrate the Styrofoam." It was "unsinkable" and could take a small outboard motor, he added. (Courtesy of David Barr.)

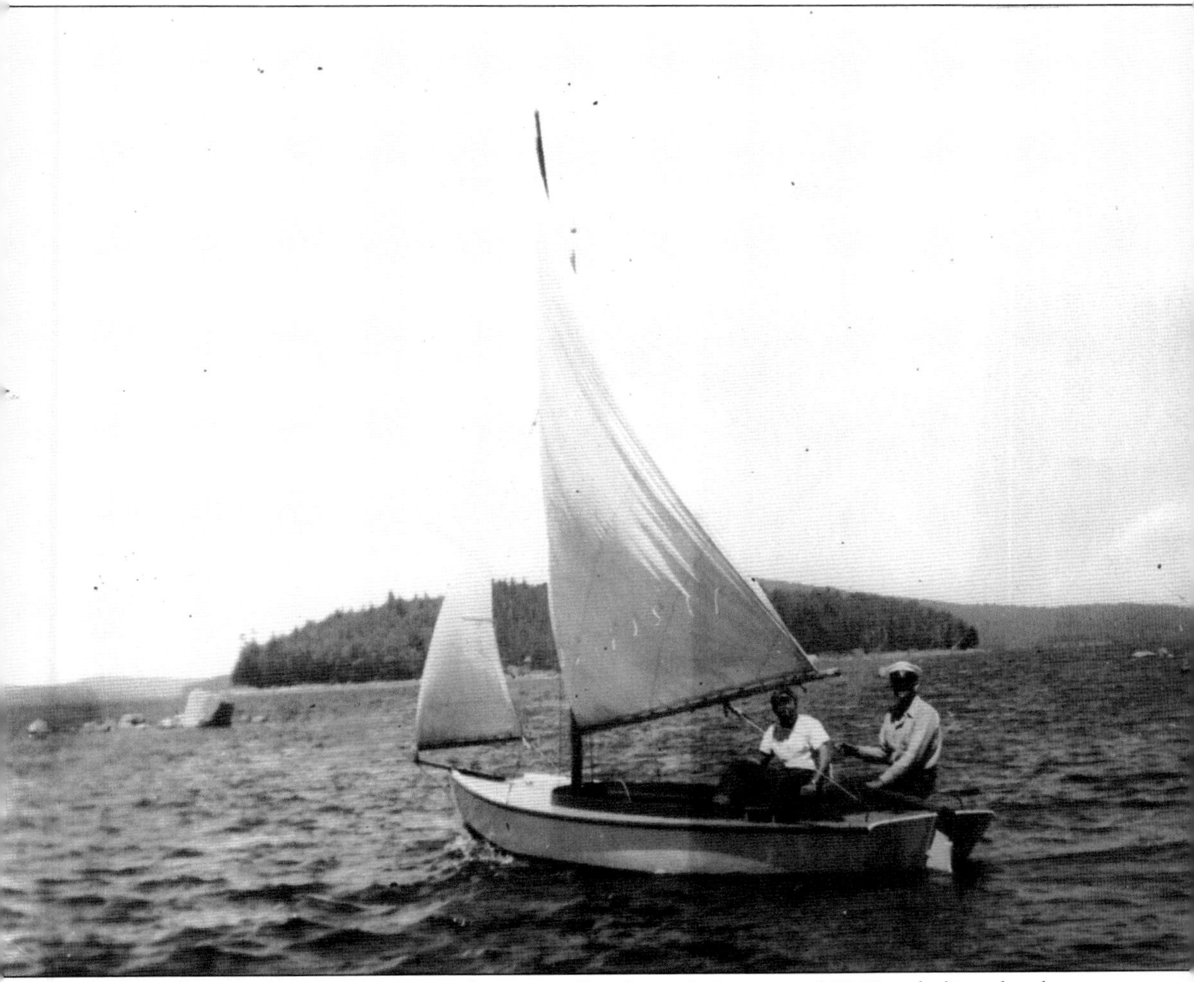

This sailboat, called *Sink or Swim*, shown on Cranberry Lake around 1940, is believed to be one of a kind. Bill Barlow (left) serves as crew, and Nelson Leavell wears the captain's hat. Buck Island is seen in the background. (Courtesy of Rod Leavell.)

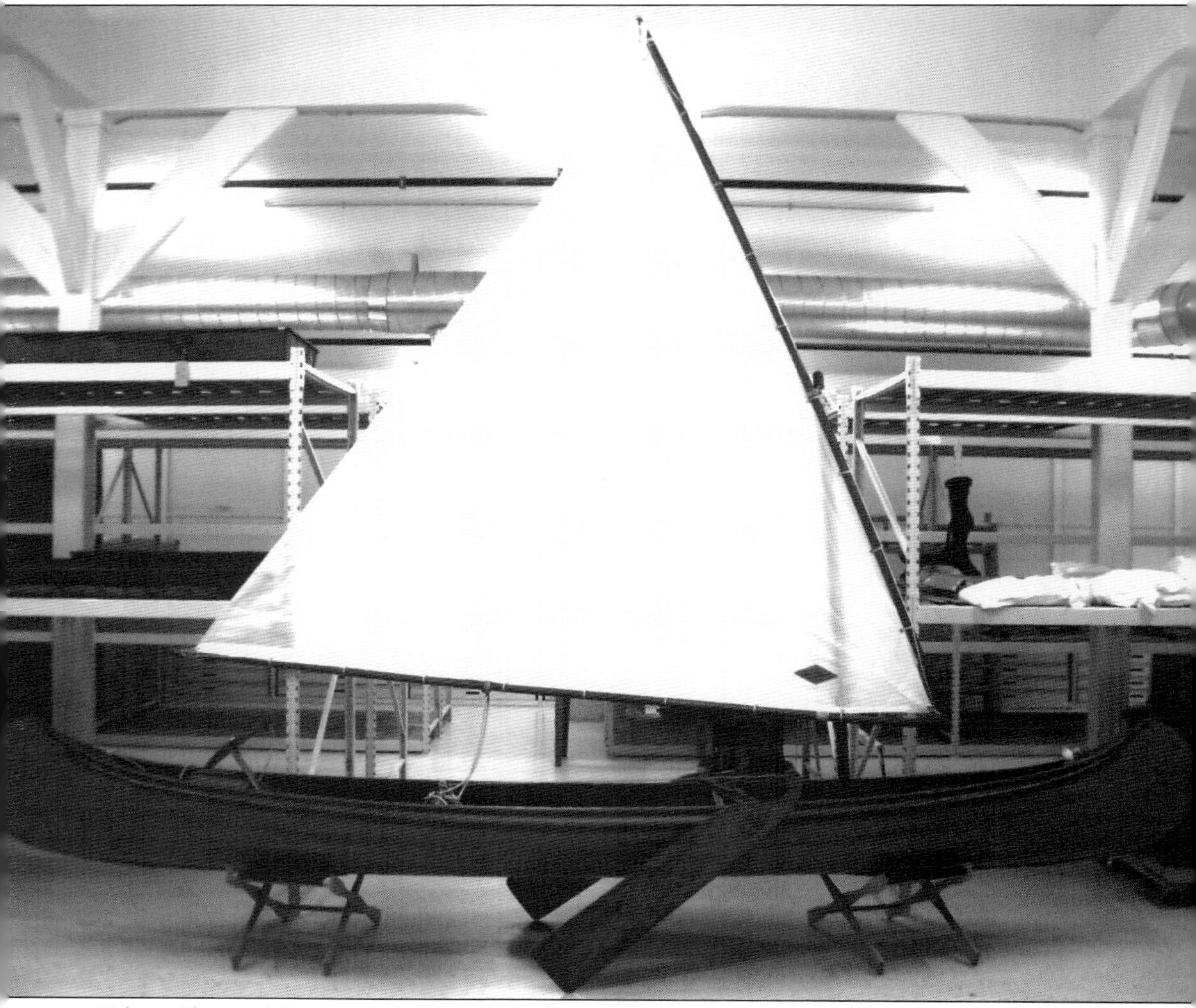

Gilson Slater of Cranberry Lake owned this 1936 wooden canoe rigged for sailing by the Old Town Canoe Company. It was painted red with a hull that was 16 feet by 40 inches. Slater's daughter, Barbara, sailed it regularly on the lake from 1954 until she donated it to the Adirondack Museum in 2001. (Courtesy of the Adirondack Museum.)

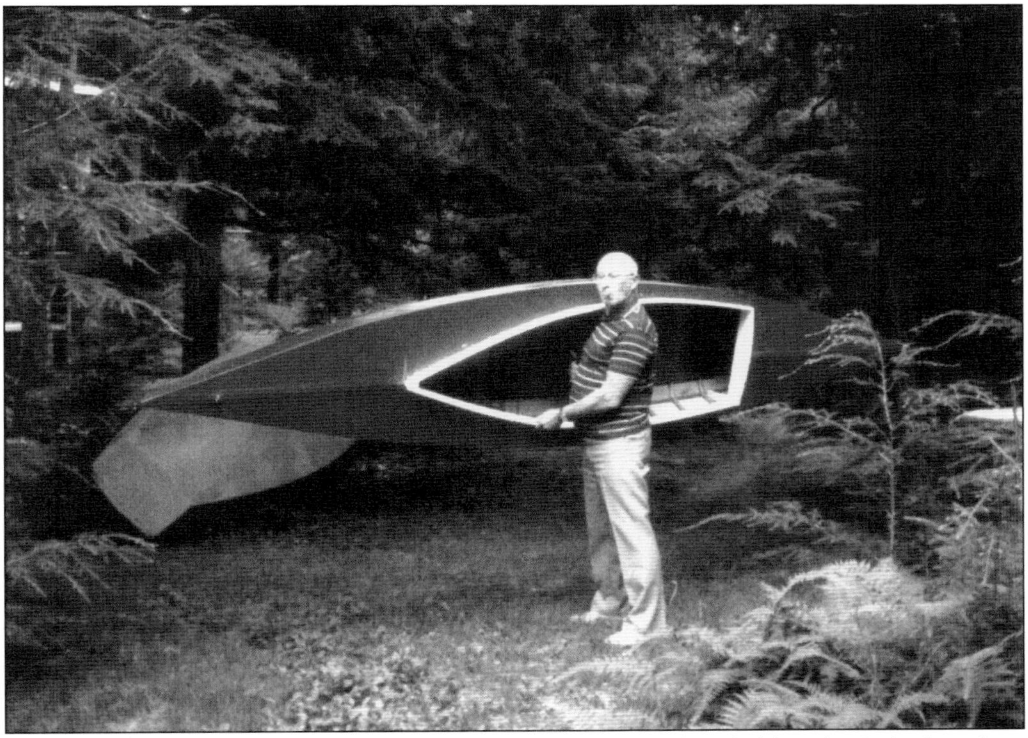

In 1935, Frank Bogart purchased a kit to build a homemade kayak (above). He built it from four-foot-long plywood pieces covered with airplane canvas and secured with airplane glue. He was about 18 years old at the time. Later he bought a second kit to add a sail, rebuilt it with new canvas, and put a pontoon on each side to use it for sailing (below). It is still seen on Cranberry Lake and is owned by Frank's brother, Gerald Bogart. (Courtesy of Gerald Bogart.)

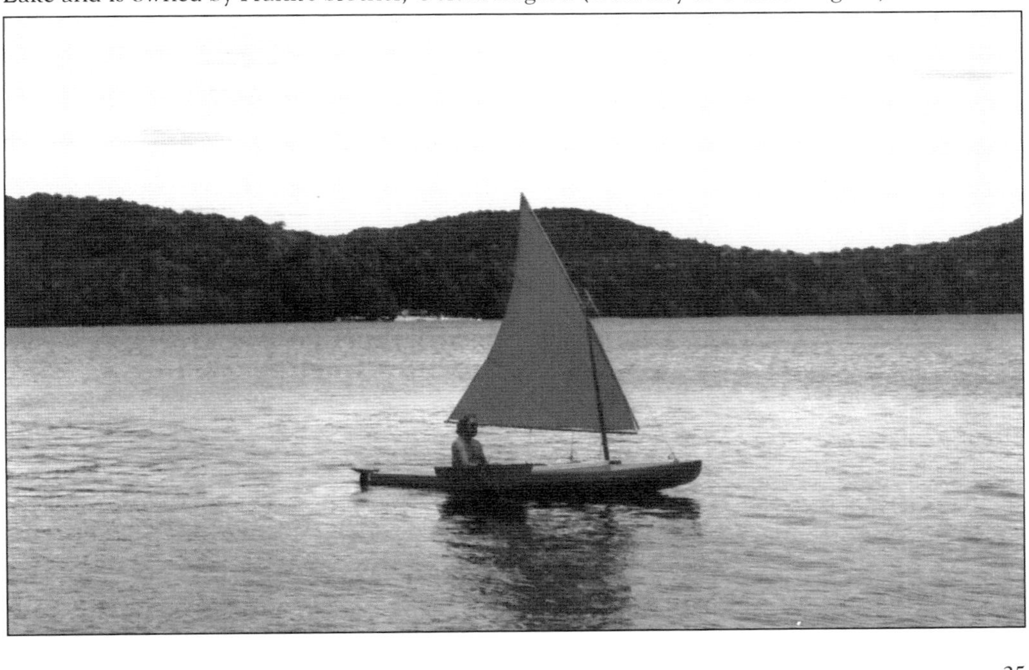

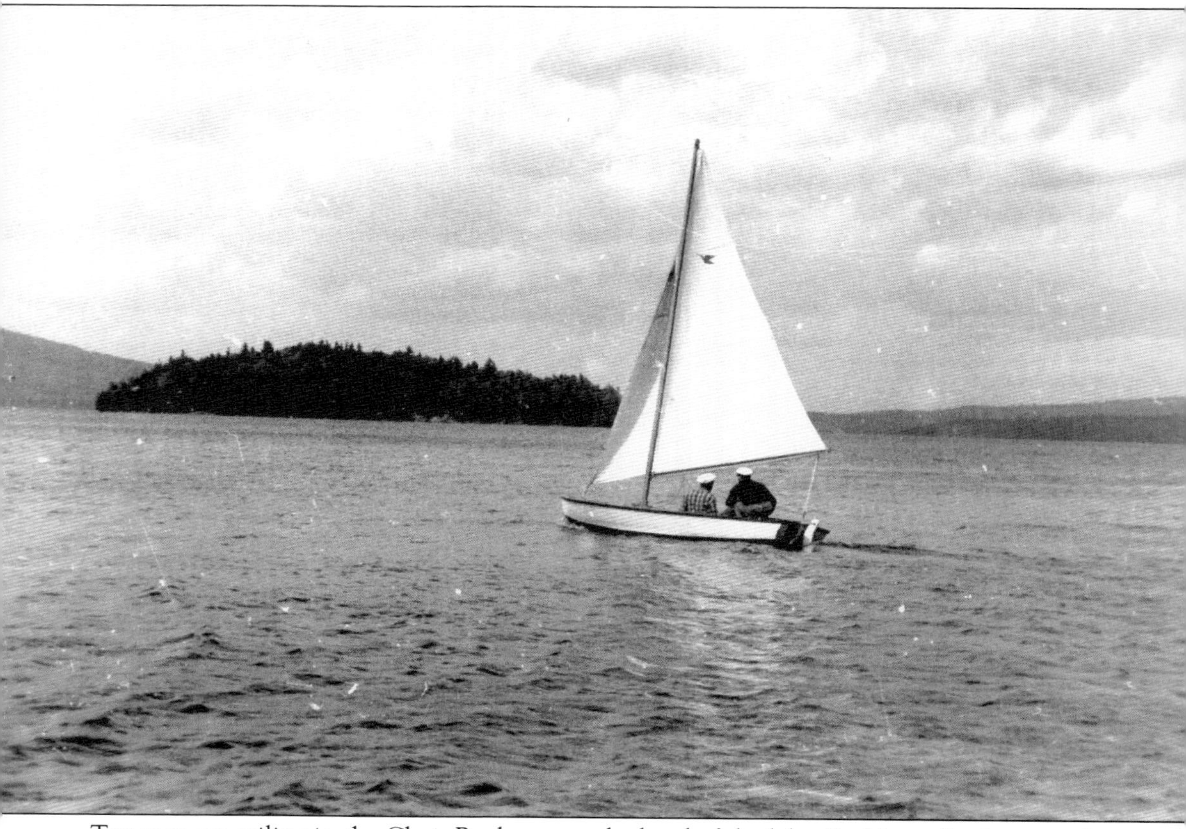

Two men are sailing in the Chair Rock area at the head of the lake. Rod Leavell, who owned a Snipe like this one, thinks it belonged to the Arnold family. Boat club minutes indicate Leavell won a race with his Snipe in 1948. (Courtesy of Anna Fowler.)

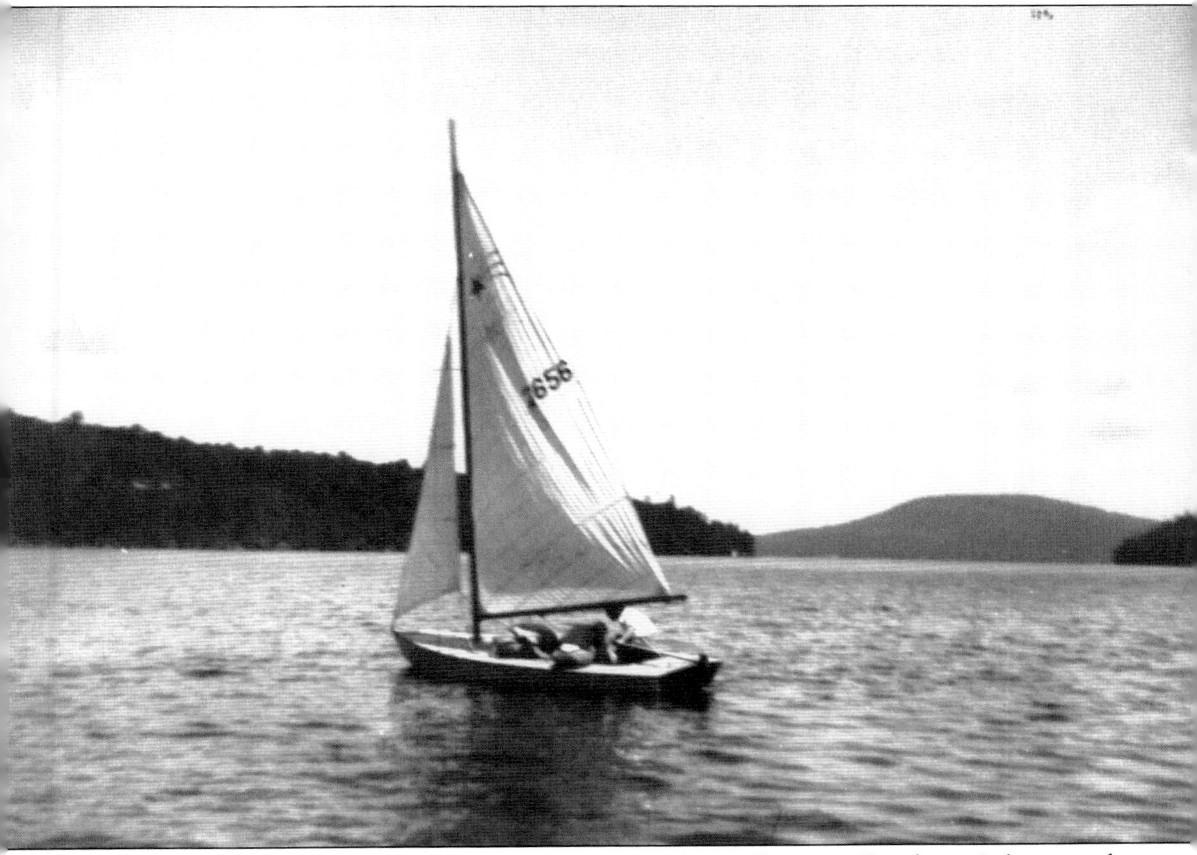

It is said that Grace Smith had the only Comet, a 16-foot sailboat, on Cranberry Lake around 1940. There were more Snipes than anything else. Here she is sailing away from Chair Rock with Cole's Point on the left and the edge of Buck Island to the right. Bear Mountain is in the background. (Courtesy of Anna Fowler.)

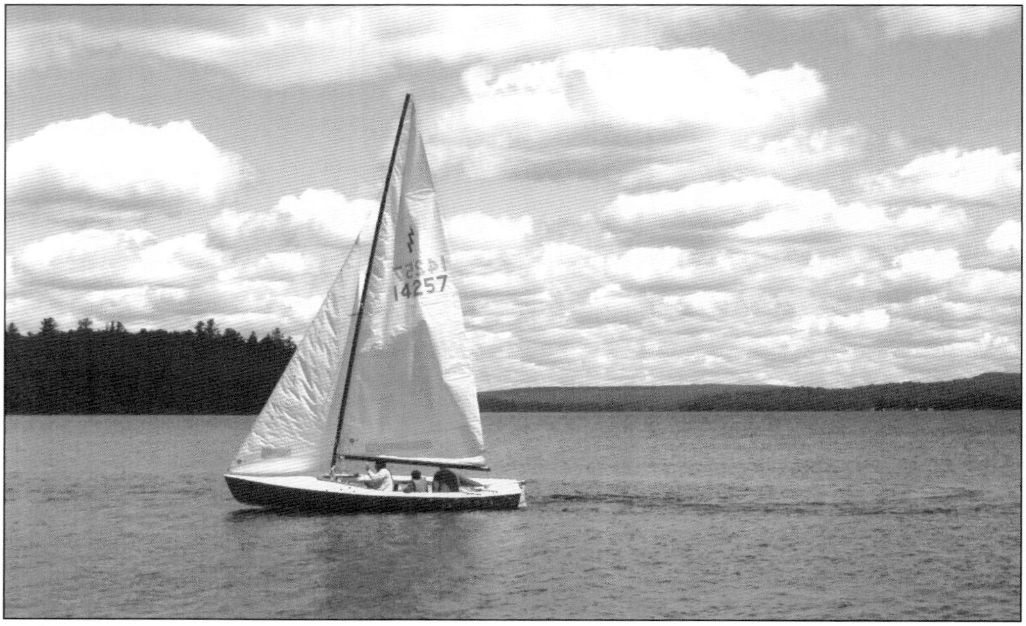

Sailboats grace Cranberry Lake today. One is the 19-foot *Lightning*, which was built by James Carson, a small manufacturer in Brick, New Jersey, in 1986. John Loganbuhl bought it from the original owner in 2006. Beneath the sails on the 26-foot mast are Loganbuhl (left), Michael Moore (center), and Connor Moore. The boat remains on South Bay, and it is used every summer. (Courtesy of John Loganbuhl.)

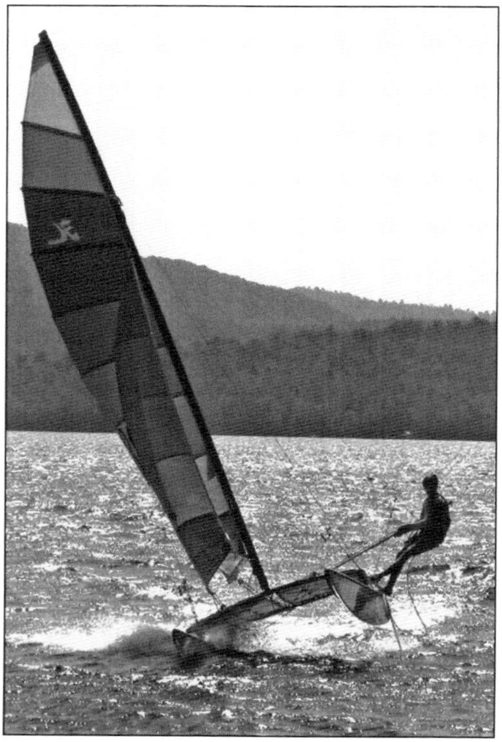

International competitor Michael Siau began his sailing career on Cranberry Lake. He first sailed on a Hobie Cat with his father as a toddler and continued to sail his father's boat from his grandfather's camp at Union Point whenever he could. At age 15, he bought his own Hobie Cat. He has raced in several states and in Canada, South Africa, France, and Fiji. (Courtesy of David and Shirley Smith.)

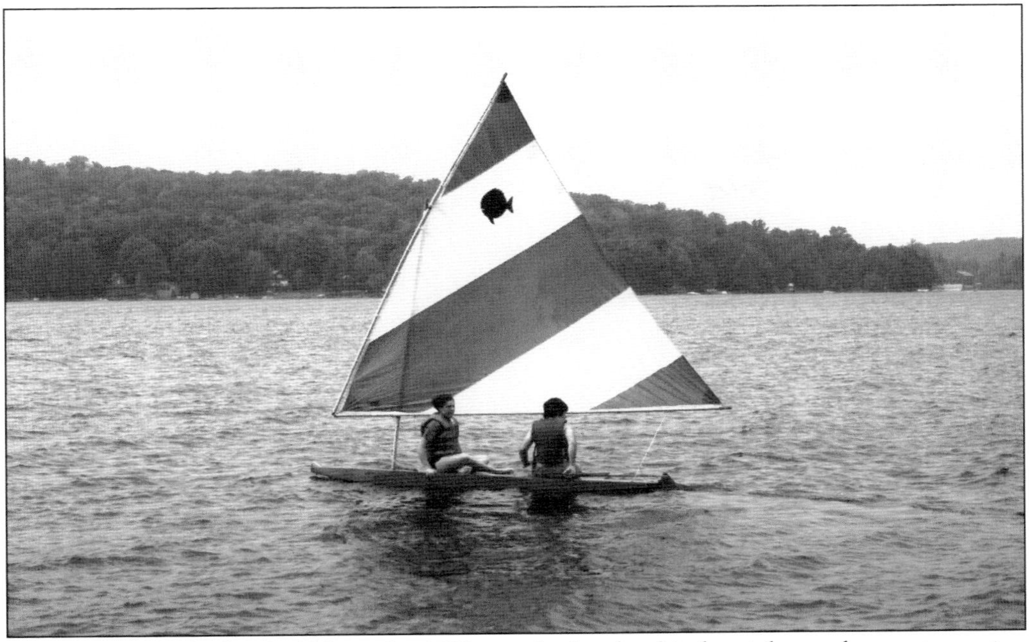

Bruce Covell built this Sailfish in the 1950s as a high school industrial arts class project using plans from *Popular Boating* magazine. It was launched at Higley Flow in Colton with local newspaper coverage. In the 1960s, Rudy Hayes, a local marina owner, helped him with repairs and refinishing. Sailing it on Cranberry Lake in 2004 are Abby White (left) and Matthew Covell. (Courtesy of Bruce Covell.)

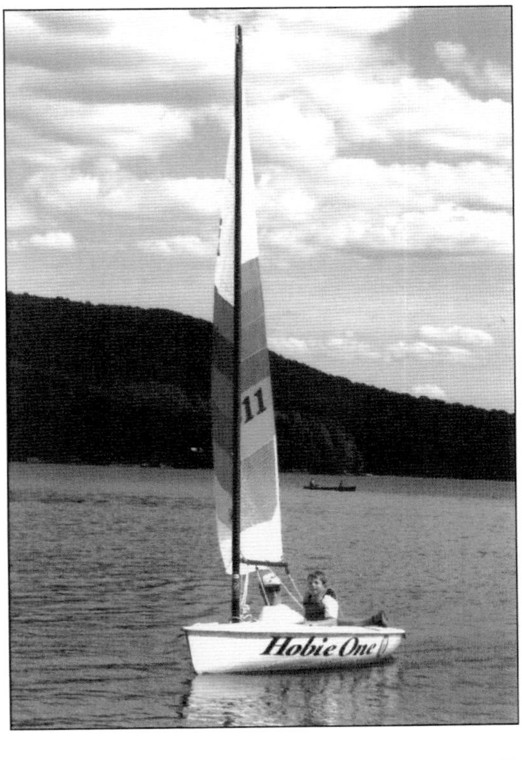

Out for a sail on his Hobie 1-12 called *Elena B.* is Eugene Carver (left) with his grandson Casey Hingtgen on the tiller. The sailboat was built in 1992 and is made of fiberglass. He bought it to teach his grandchildren how to sail. It is ideal for learning to trim and shape the sail. It is a very safe craft but would tip over, part of the learning experience. (Courtesy of Eugene Carver.)

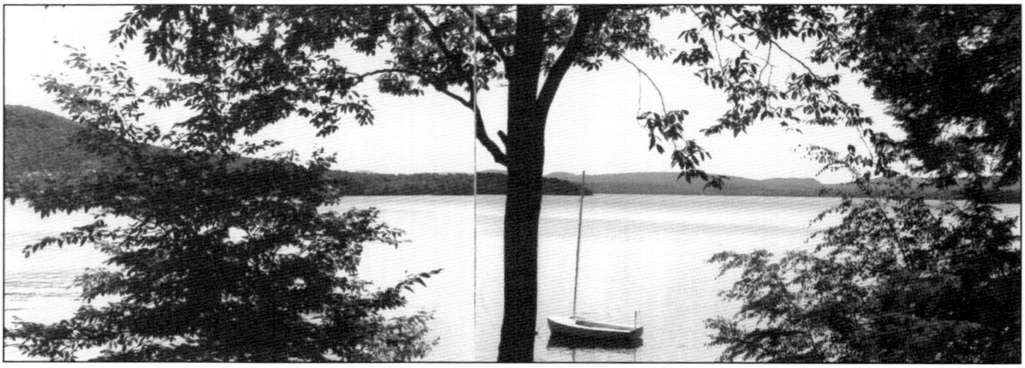

Robert Thurston's *Force Five* was an O'Day Javalin, shown here with sails down in front of his camp on Columbian Road. Sailboat records indicate that Thurston was active and involved in many races between when he purchased the boat in May 1974 and sold it in July 1976. Bear Mountain stands out on the far left. (Courtesy of Robert Thurston.)

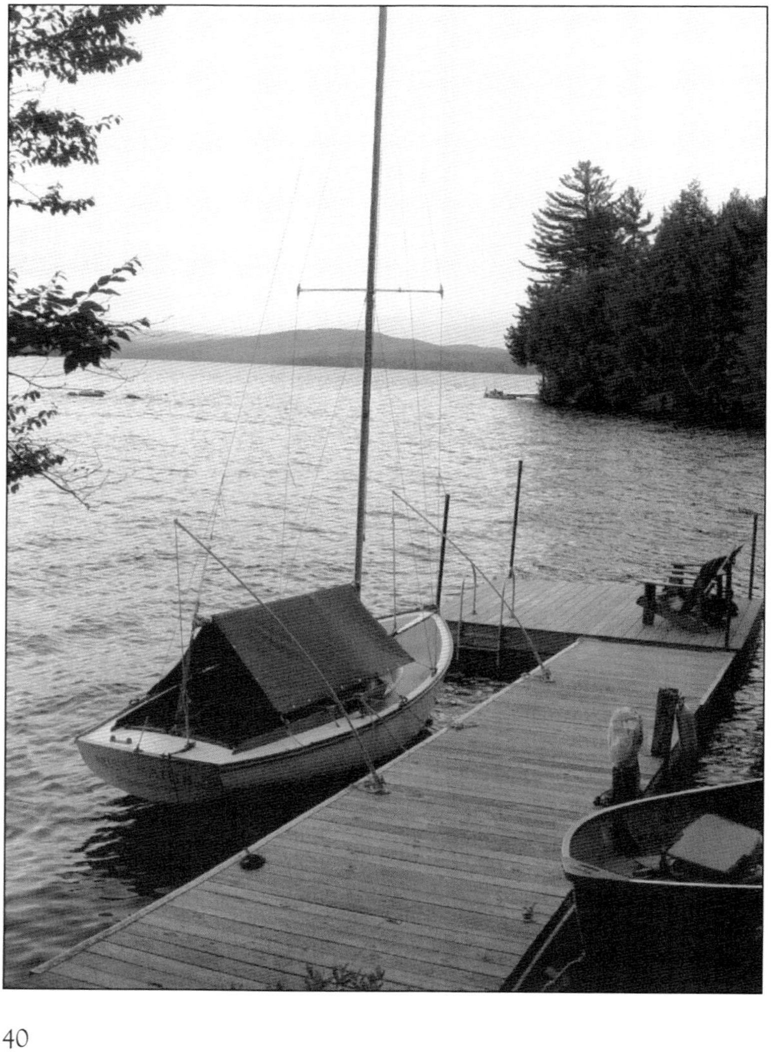

At the end of the day, Cranberry Lake is quiet. Boats are moored, and residents and visitors relax on their docks and porches. They may have spent the day rowing, paddling, or maybe sailing on this 1976 19-foot, fiberglass Cape Dory Typhoon. There is a lot of space for paddlers and sailors on Cranberry Lake. (Courtesy of Suzanne Liberty.)

Two

Workboats and Passenger Boats

In the beginning, in 1910, the Emporium Forestry Company's boats towed logs from Chair Rock Flow and other inlets to the railroad pier at Cranberry Lake village where a 16-mile stretch of the Grasse River Railroad connected to the New York Central Railroad's Childwold station. A visitor going the other way took the New York Central sleeper north, got off at Wanakena, and took a steamer down the Oswegatchie River to Cranberry Lake to stay for a week or a month. As lumbering declined, summer visitors built camps on the lake and turned into seasonal residents. Enterprising businesspeople built hotels. There was a greater need for transportation around the lake, to carry passengers, mail, groceries, and freight. At the start, in the early 1900s, the *Helen* and the *Wanakena* posted schedules and ran regular routes. Later individual hotels and enterprising businessmen offered boat services. From 1921 to 1940, George Shamp ran his mail boat, the *Grey Dawn*, on the lake and carried passengers. Then Spencer Howland took on the route with the *Grace*. Current residents who were children then remember the excitement of putting a flag on a pole to indicate they had outgoing mail, hearing the familiar engine sound, and watching as the shallow-draft boat made its way to the dock. There would be an exchange of news and gossip, a settling of accounts for groceries, and soon the *Grace* would be backing away. The State University of New York Environmental Science and Forestry (SUNY ESF) boat, named the *Forester*, today crosses the lake daily to its summer camp. The Emporium Marina provides barge services. Families have larger boats and no longer need public transportation. After Spencer Howland died in 1958, others provided delivery services. In 1967, Lucian (Lou) Plumley, retired director of the Ranger School, took over the mail boat route with the *Golden Goose*. Mail service ended in the 1980s, and today the *Golden Goose* hangs in a boathouse on Columbian Road. It "needs work."

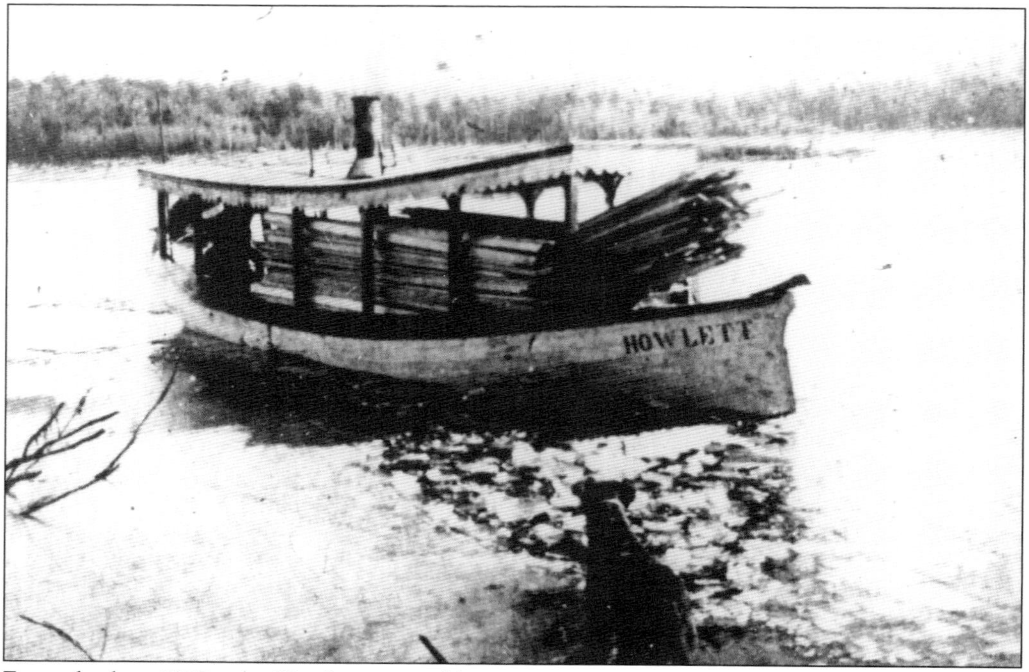

From the late 1880s, the *Howlett*, a wood-burning, steam-powered vessel, carried mail, lumber, and cargo around Cranberry Lake. Owned by Riley Bishop, it also transported passengers between Bishop's Hotel at the foot of the lake and Tramps Retreat, a large log cabin owned by brothers A. A. and Albert H. Howlett. Visitors included Frederic Remington, artist, and Irving Bacheller, writer. (Courtesy of the Adirondack Museum.)

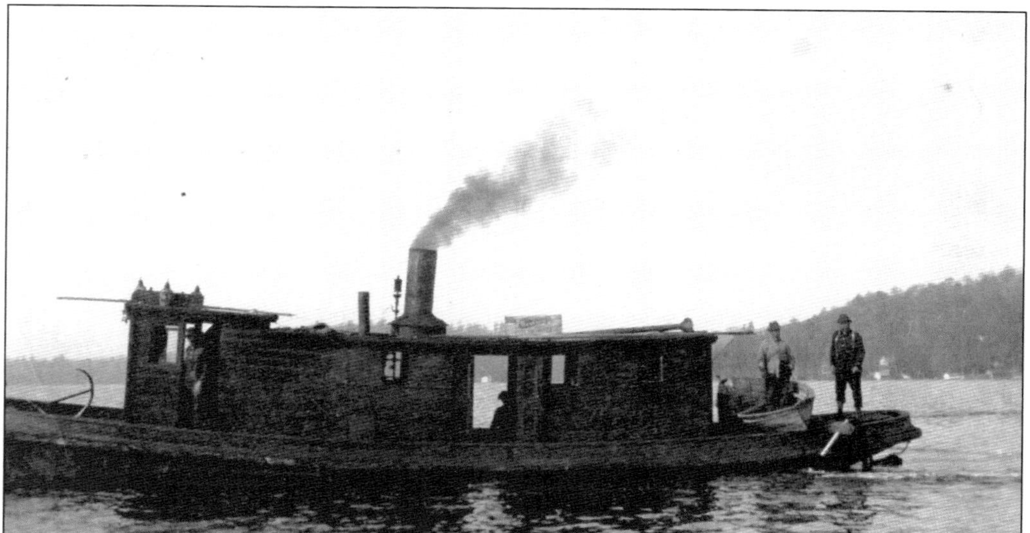

Between 1916 and 1919, the *Ironclad* towed floats of logs from the head of Cranberry Lake to the foot of the lake. A float was made of four large spruce boom sticks about 50 feet long, and a tugboat could tow as many as 10 at a time. Harte LaFountain, who directed International Paper Company's towing operations, used a towboat called the *Old Ironclad*, possibly this one. (Courtesy of the Adirondack Museum.)

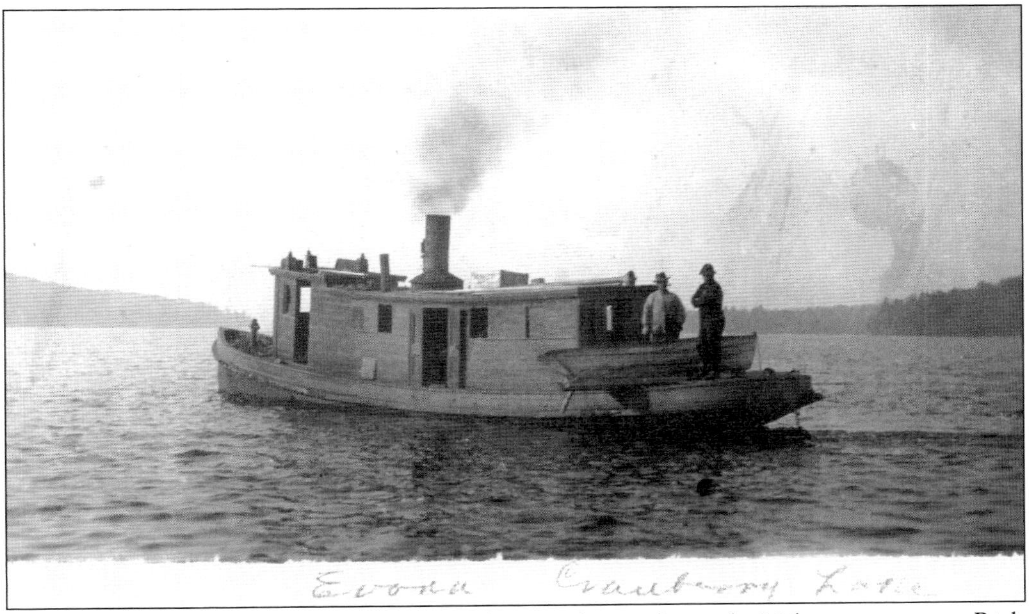

Three large lumbering operations on Cranberry Lake in the early 20th century were Rich Lumber Company, International Paper Company, and Emporium Forestry Company. Smaller companies were Bissell Brothers and the Abbott Company. Tugboats like the *Evona* sometimes took two days to tow a collection of sawlogs that extended for half an acre, circled by a log chain, the six-mile journey to the foot of the lake. (Courtesy of Adirondack Museum.)

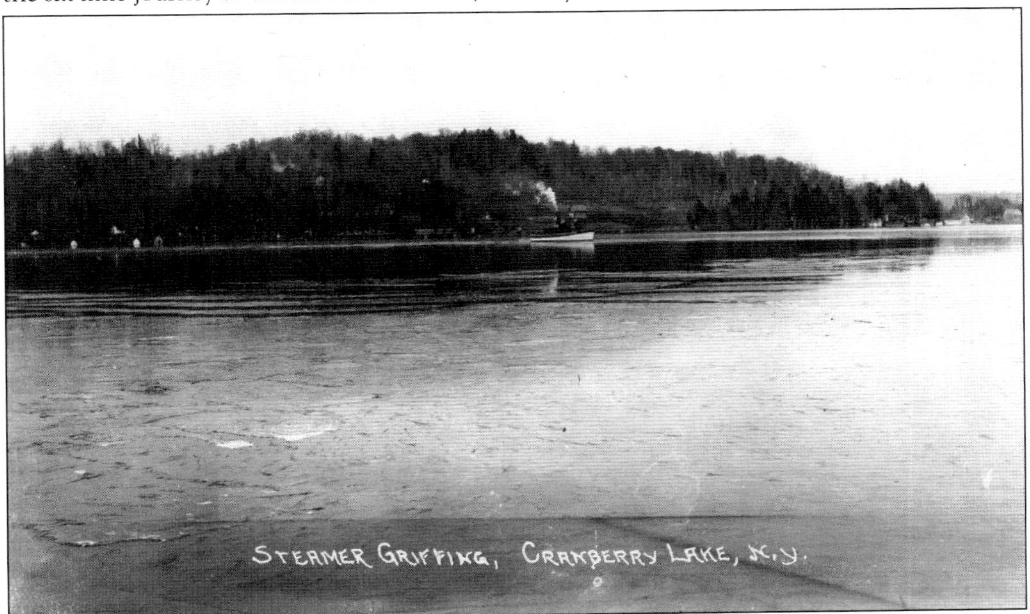

"Everything that was in the [lumber] camp had to be lugged in. Every day, they would go down to the landing wherever the boats landed and they would bring their supplies up. They could bring in the hay and grain and groceries and roofing paper, even the clothing—everything that you wanted," said Warren Guinup, early-20th-century lumber jobber at Cranberry Lake, about steamers like the *Gruffing*. (Courtesy of Susan Smeby.)

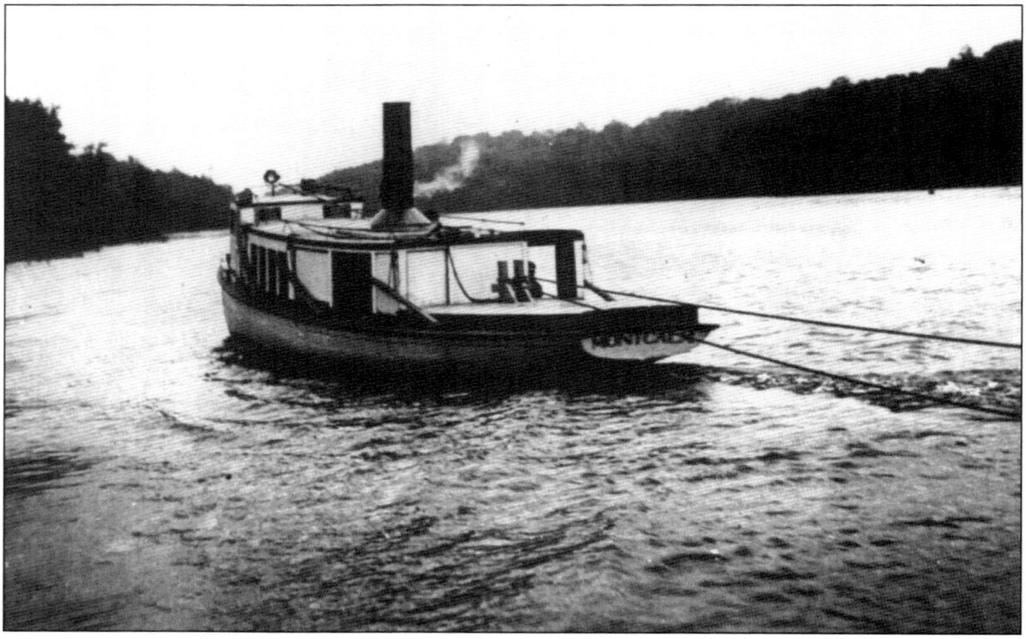

Known as the "little tug" *Montcalm*, this steam-powered tugboat is shown heading through the narrows near Wanakena. It was far from little in terms of its workload, towing logs and other boats in the early 1900s. Notice the strong towing cables fully extended. (Courtesy of Barbara Slater.)

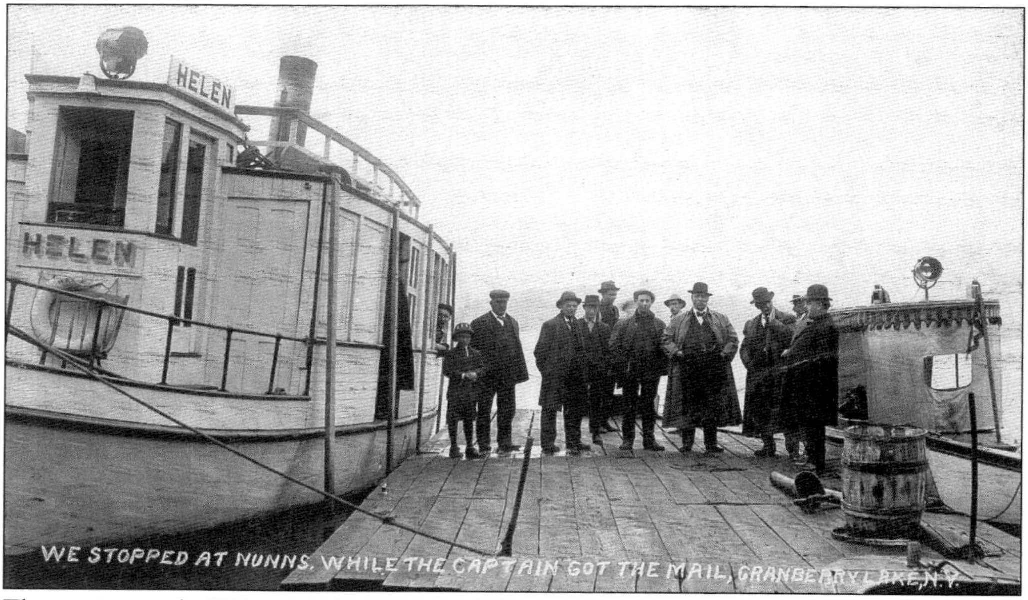

The caption reads, "We stopped at Nunns, while the captain got the mail, Cranberry Lake, N.Y." It shows a group of gentlemen waiting for the *Helen* on a foggy morning. The steam-powered *Helen* would stop at all the hotels and docks around the lake in the early 20th century, picking up and discharging mail, passengers, and freight. Nunn's Inn was at the foot of Indian Mountain. (Courtesy of Jay Edel.)

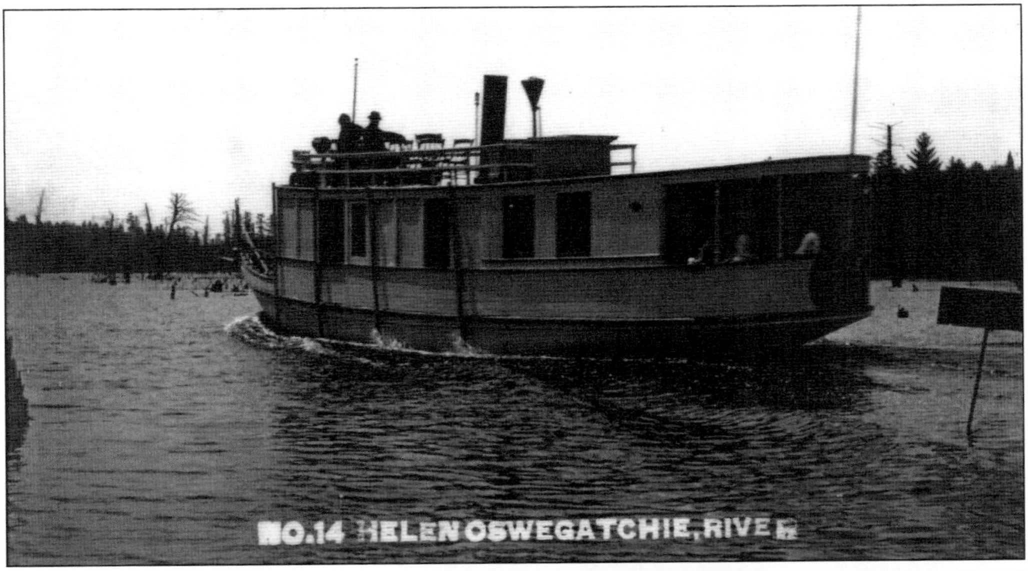

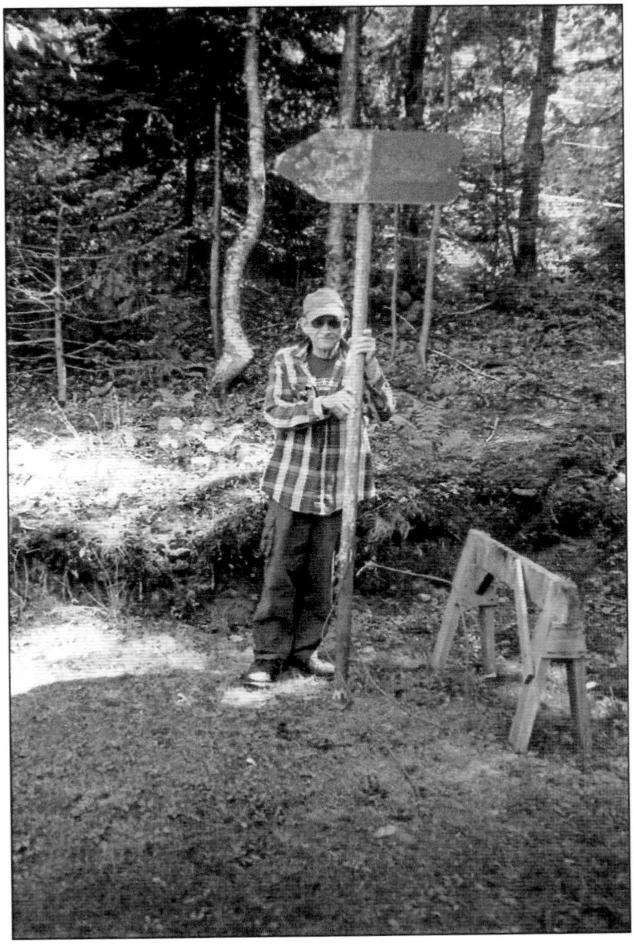

Passengers could ride atop the two-decked *Helen* (above) through the narrow Oswegatchie River from Wanakena to Cranberry Lake. There is a metal navigation buoy (lower right corner of photograph) to warn the captain away from a shallow area. Few examples of these navigation buoys remain today. Paul Peacock of Wanakena (right) stands next to a replica of an original buoy. It was made in 1958 at Benson Mines by welders Allen Thornton and Lyle Squires. William Vickers, former commodore of the boat club, was manager of the shop at the time. It is eight feet tall, painted white on the left-hand (arrow) side and red on the right-hand side. A quarter-inch hole in the rebar allowed for nailing or bolting it to a stump. The buoy is currently being restored. (Above, courtesy of the Wanakena Historical Association; right, courtesy of William Gleason.)

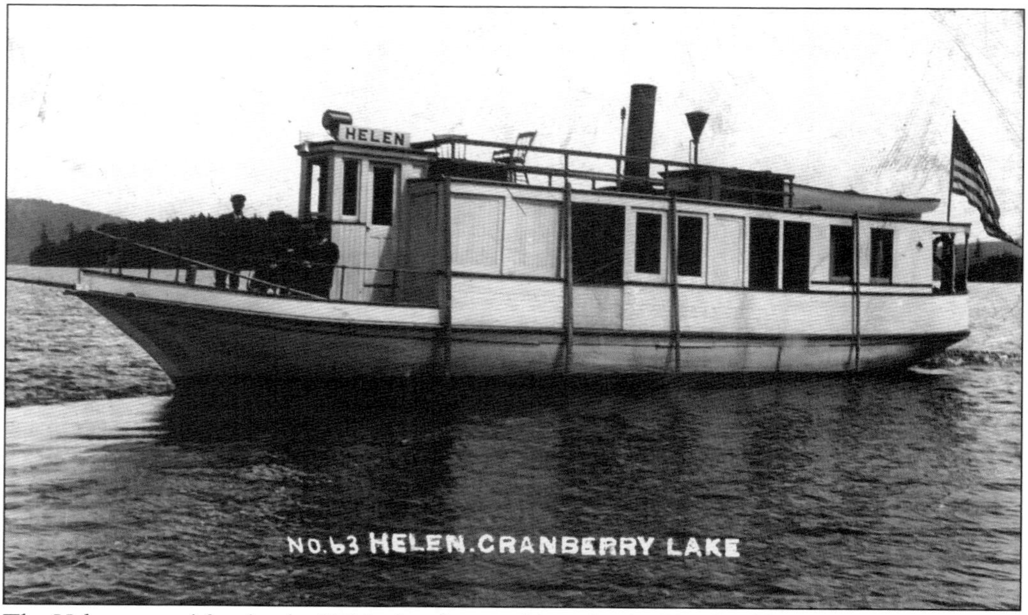

The *Helen*, owned first by the Wilder brothers and later by the Howland brothers, faced difficulty trying to stop at all the hotels and docks on the lake in the summer due to low water. Judge Irving G. Vann of Buck Island wrote to postmaster general George Cortelyou in 1906, "Service is irregular. . . . If mail could be left at one of the hotels as a distributing center that would be satisfactory." (Courtesy of Susan Smeby.)

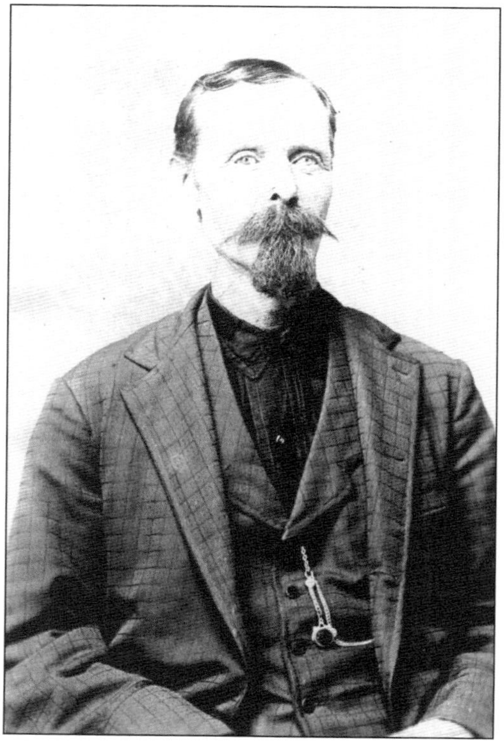

George Wells was a captain for the Cranberry Lake Transportation Company, which was owned by Frank Wilder at the time. Its boats, the *Helen* and the *Wanakena*, provided mail service between Cranberry Lake and Wanakena, with stops at hotels and docks along the way. There was mail service of some sort on the lake from 1903 until the service ended in the 1980s. (Courtesy of the Adirondack Museum.)

An advertising poster for the *Helen* from the period 1909–1911 indicates that those in Wanakena could take the steamer to and from dining spots at Nunn's Inn or Deremo's Hotel at the head of the lake. Charles E. Leach, manager of the line, was an early officer in the Cranberry Lake Motor Boat Club. (Courtesy of Jay Edel.)

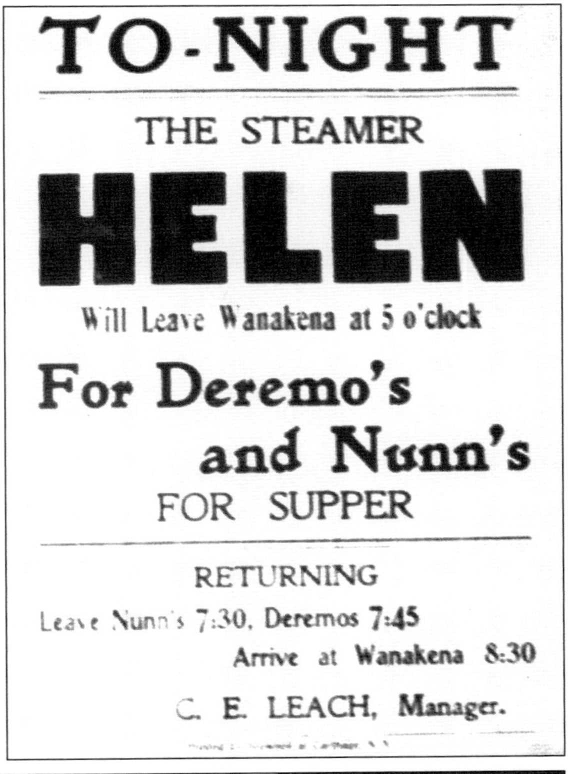

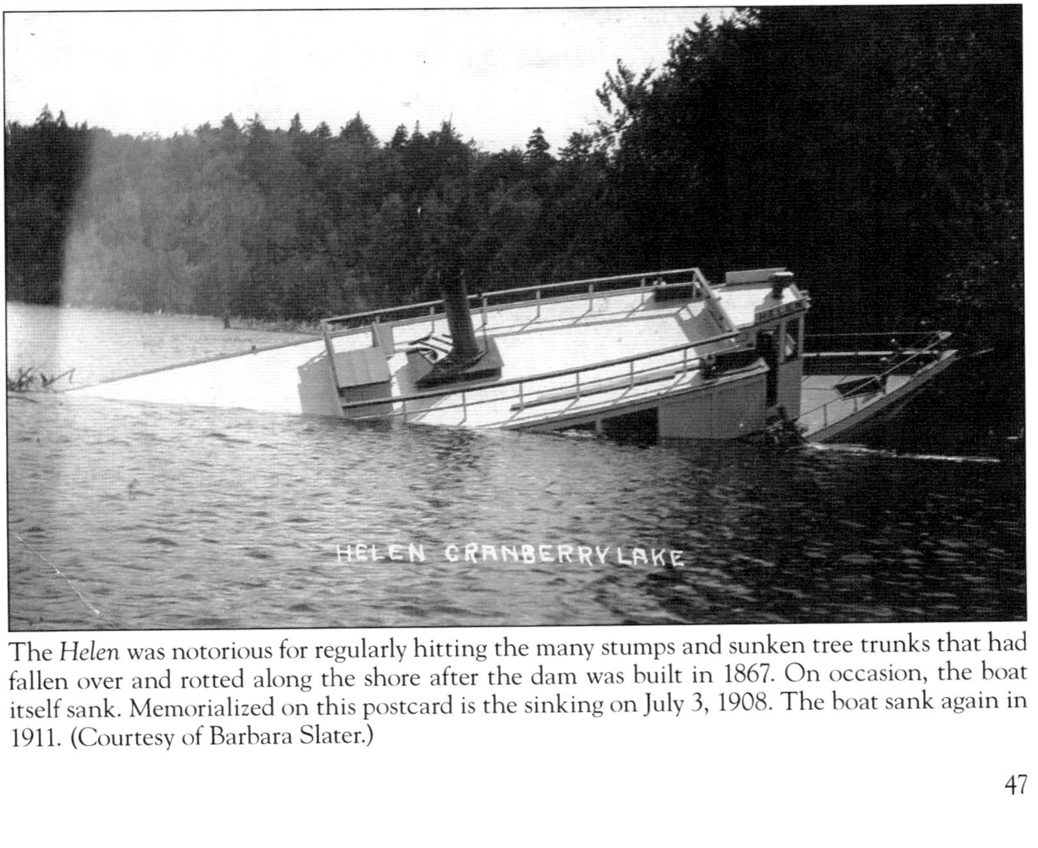

The *Helen* was notorious for regularly hitting the many stumps and sunken tree trunks that had fallen over and rotted along the shore after the dam was built in 1867. On occasion, the boat itself sank. Memorialized on this postcard is the sinking on July 3, 1908. The boat sank again in 1911. (Courtesy of Barbara Slater.)

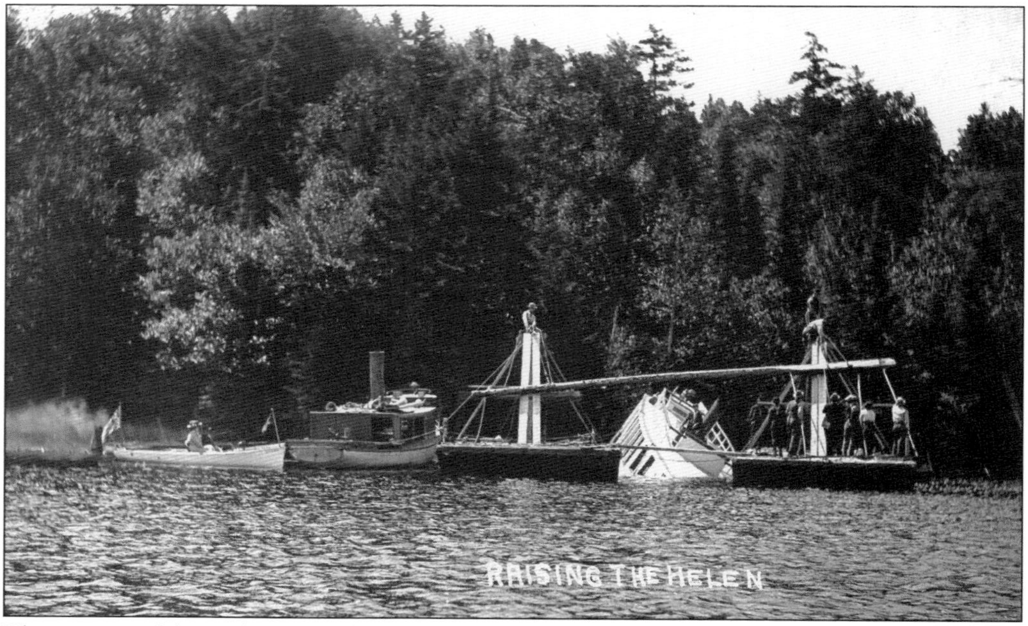

The owners of the *Helen* wanted to keep the steamer afloat and spent time and money to raise the vessel. Raising the boat (above) involved workers on a barge and a tugboat. A debonair couple in a motor launch looks on. Below, some well-dressed gentlemen, possibly the owners, join the work crew to pose for a picture. Three of the men hold giant pry bars to exert pressure to tip the boat up. The card indicates that this raising was related to the 1908 sinking. (Above, courtesy of Barbara Slater; below, courtesy of Jay Edel.)

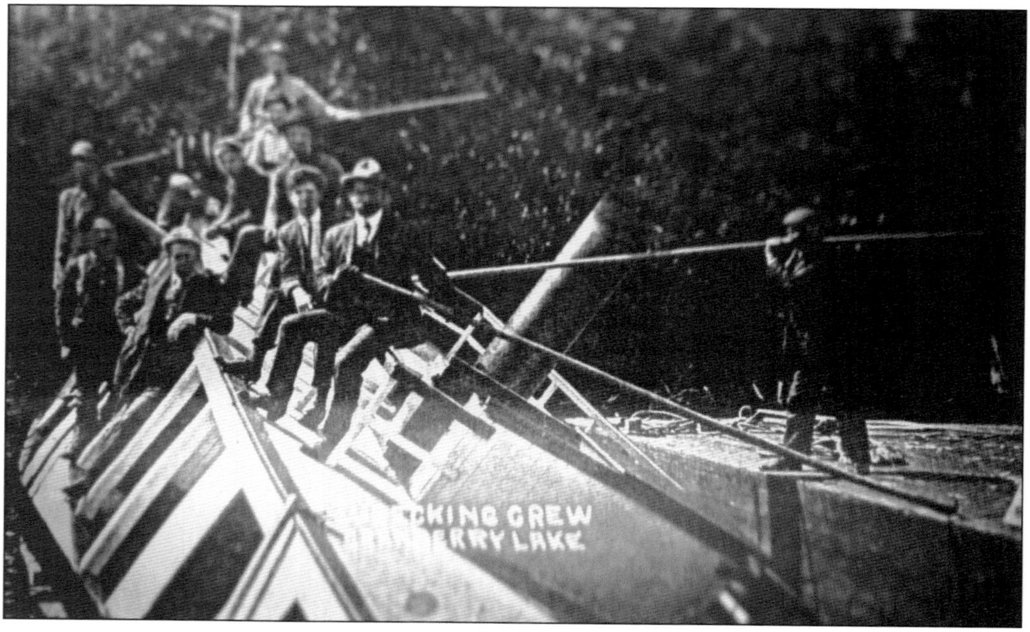

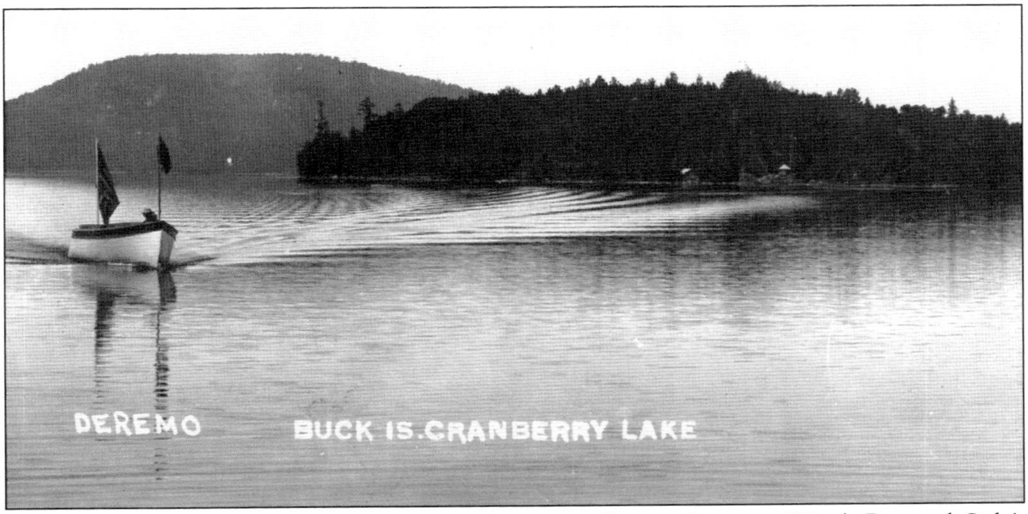

Ed Deremo built his hotel, Deremo's, in 1903 on a small point between Witch Bay and Cole's Point. He cut the big timbers used for construction from nearby banks and built a business catering to the summer tourist trade. His inboard motor launch, the *Deremo* (above with Buck Island behind), served as a water taxi to deliver guests to the hotel. It was 35 feet long, with a large three-cylinder engine, and could be fitted with a top supported by wooden poles. Seats ran around the entire boat, so it could carry 20 or more people. The group pictured below, on July 29, 1907, were among the last guests. The hotel burned to the ground on November 2, 1907, and was not rebuilt. The Indian Mountain Club purchased the launch and renamed it the *IMC*. (Courtesy of Susan Smeby.)

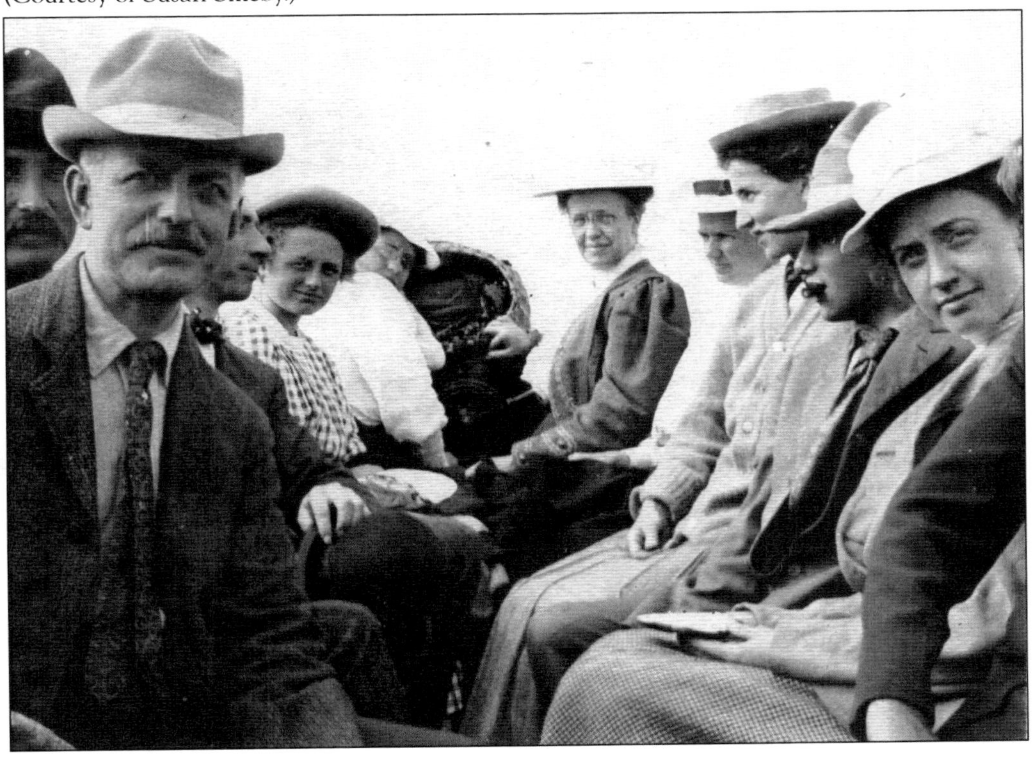

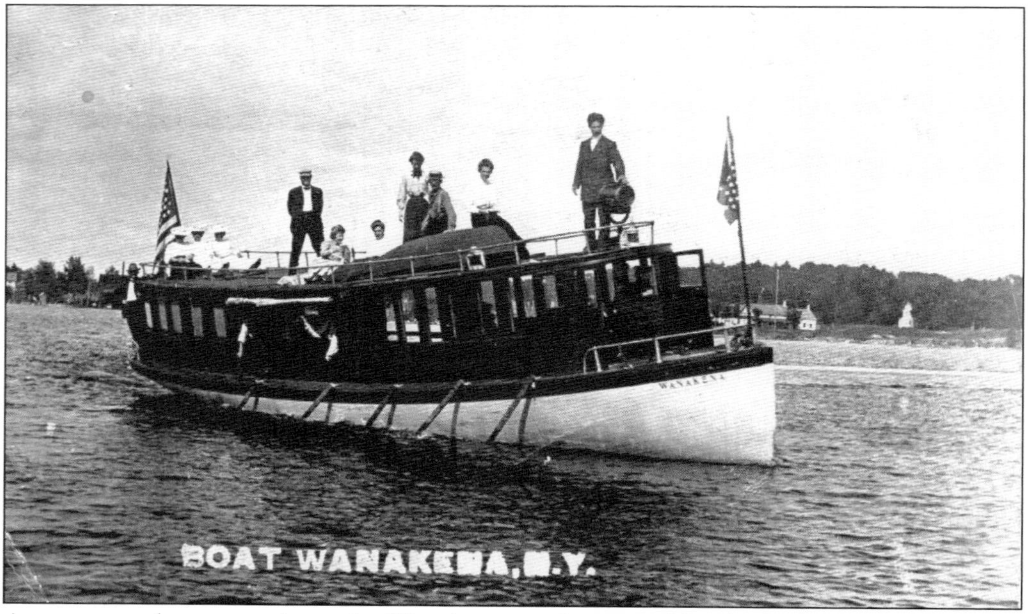

A gas-powered passenger boat, the *Wanakena* was first owned by the Rich Lumber Company, then sold to Fred Howland of the Cranberry Lake Transportation Company in 1913. It was 61 feet long with a 9-foot beam and delivered mail, passengers, and groceries around the lake. It could carry 125 passengers, and the crew consisted of a pilot, a purser, and an engineer. The *Wanakena* burned around 1930. (Courtesy of Susan Smeby.)

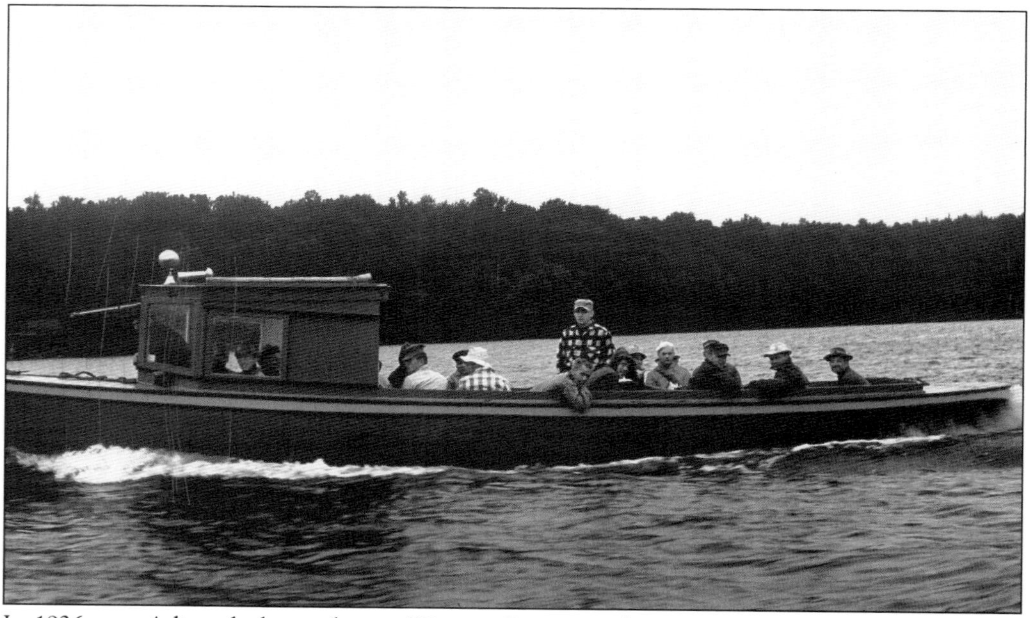

In 1936, two Adirondack woodsmen, Warren Guinup and Ivan Bancroft, built the *Grey Ghost* for the College of Forestry sophomore summer camp at Barber Point from a mail-order kit. It was painted battleship gray, measured 35 feet long with an 8-foot beam, had a small roof over the pilot, and carried a tremendous load of miscellaneous articles and all the students who could pile on top. (Courtesy of Jeanne Reynolds.)

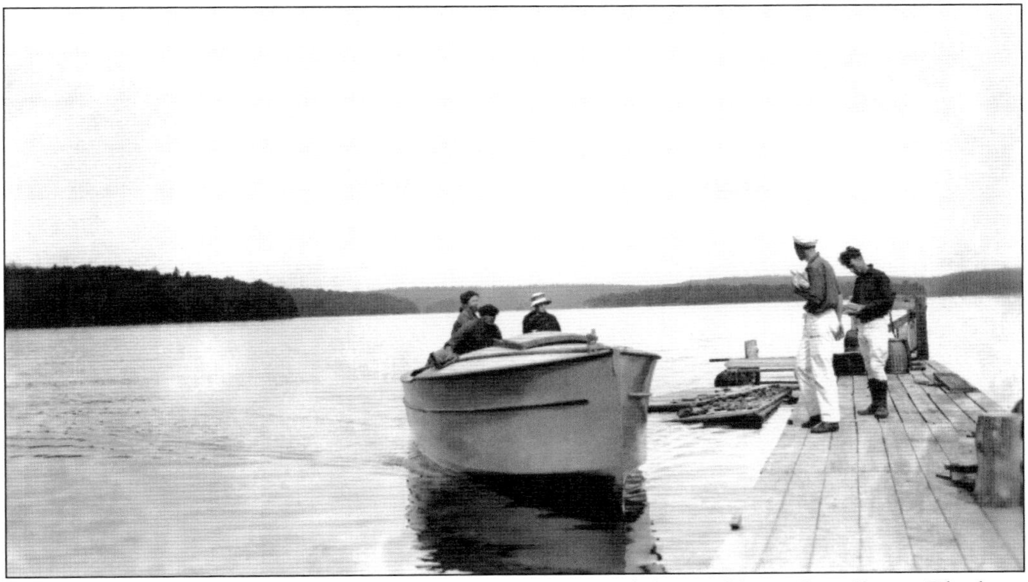

From 1921 to the 1940s, George Shamp of Buffalo operated the mail boat *Grey Dawn*. The boat was 30 feet long with a 10-foot beam. This 1922 photograph by a Mr. Turpin (above) shows the boat landing at the College of Forestry summer camp dock at Barber Point to pick up and discharge passengers and mail. A second photograph, taken in 1922 by W. E. Sanderson, shows Shamp at the wheel leaving the College of Forestry summer camp dock. He and the *Grey Dawn* provided mail service until Spencer Howland took over the service with his own boat, the *Grace*. (Courtesy of the F. Franklin Moon Library, SUNY ESF.)

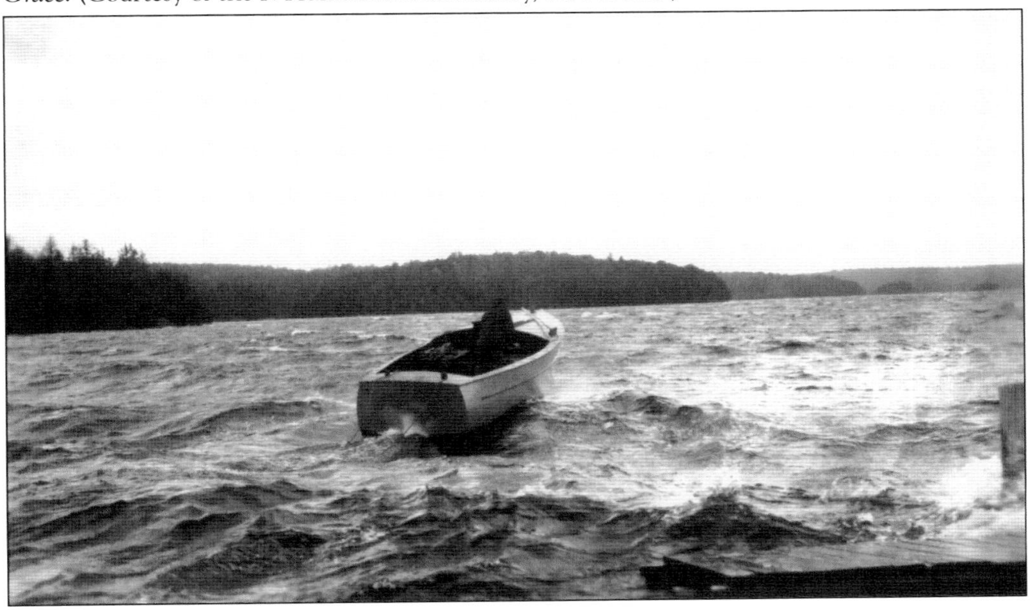

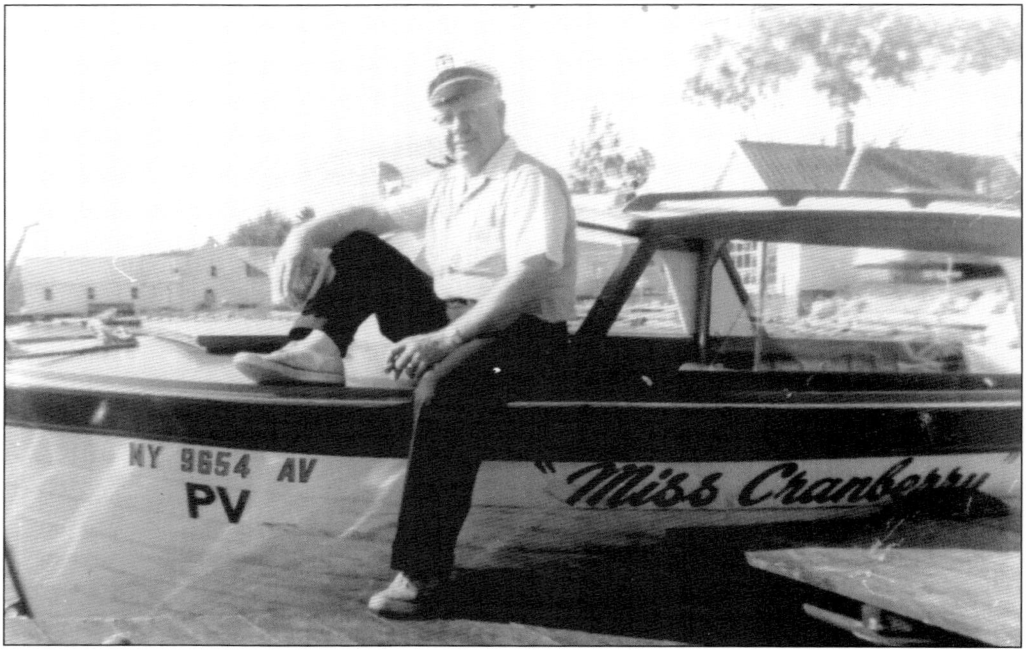

D. Kellogg "Doc" Morgan waits with the *Miss Cranberry* in 1958. In the 1960s, the enterprising Cranberry Lake Inn offered tours of the lake on this boat. Adults paid $1.50 each for an 80-minute tour "to see this beautiful remote wilderness area from the water." Morgan also provided water taxi services and carried mail for Cranberry Lake residents until 1967. (Courtesy of Bobbie Pascoe.)

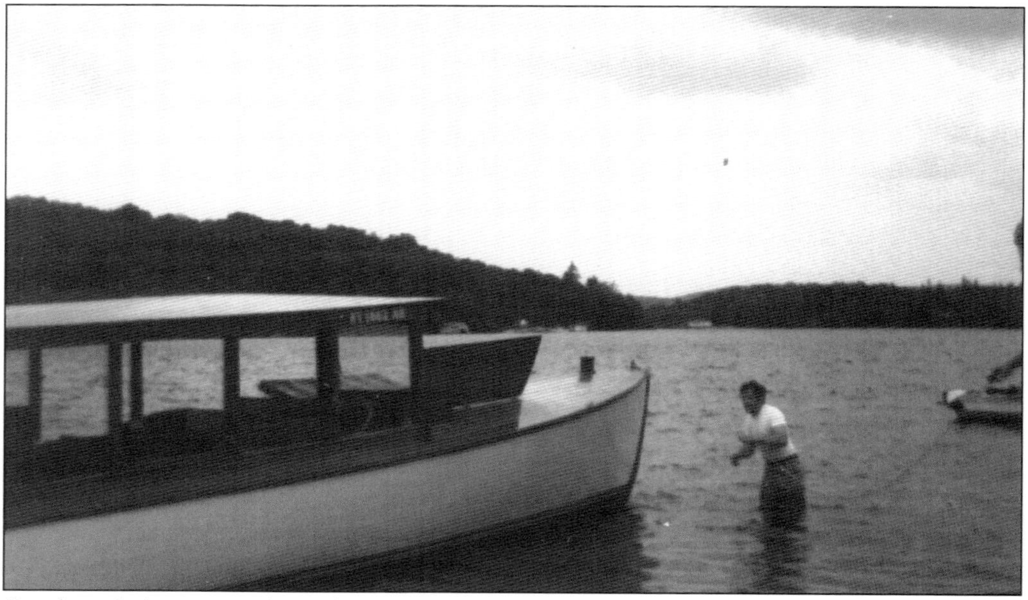

Cranberry Lake was popular with tourists in the 1970s, and the *Signet* provided them an opportunity to take a guided tour of the lake. Protected from the sun, but with a view of the surrounding mountains, they were comfortably accommodated in Robert Sherman's fine-appearing touring boat. Jeanne Reynolds, Cranberry Lake historian, provided the commentary for many trips. (Courtesy of Jeanne Reynolds.)

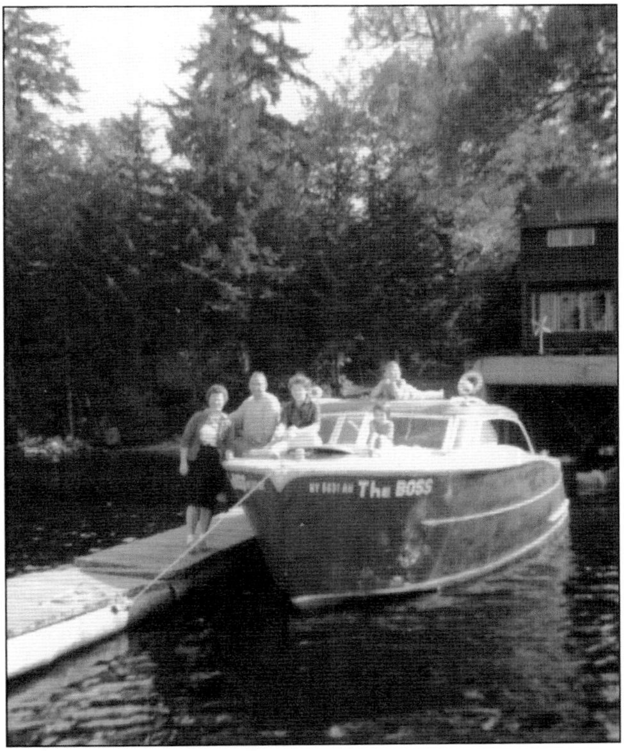

The Boss was a metal boat, weighing 10 tons and able to carry 16 passengers. It had a 115-horsepower engine. It was purchased and repainted with a distinctive blue bottom (right) by Kenneth Boss in the 1960s. He used it to ferry guests to and from Chair Rock, where he and his wife, Kathleen, operated a lodge and rental cabin business. They began by serving dinners to guests and soon found others making reservations and needing transportation. Kenneth (below with boat) later painted the boat white with distinctive red letters. He died in 1966, but Kathleen continued to run the business until 1977. (Courtesy of Lyle Boss.)

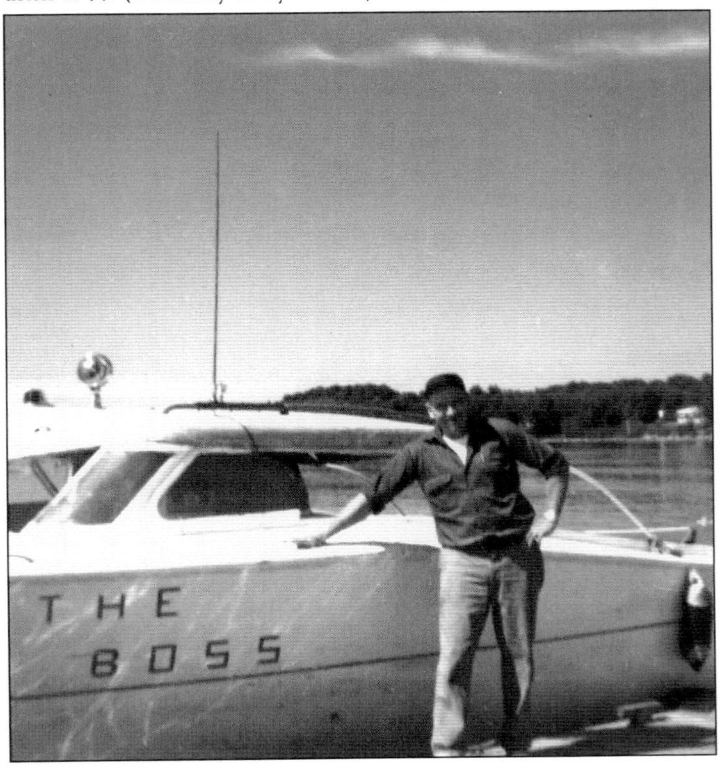

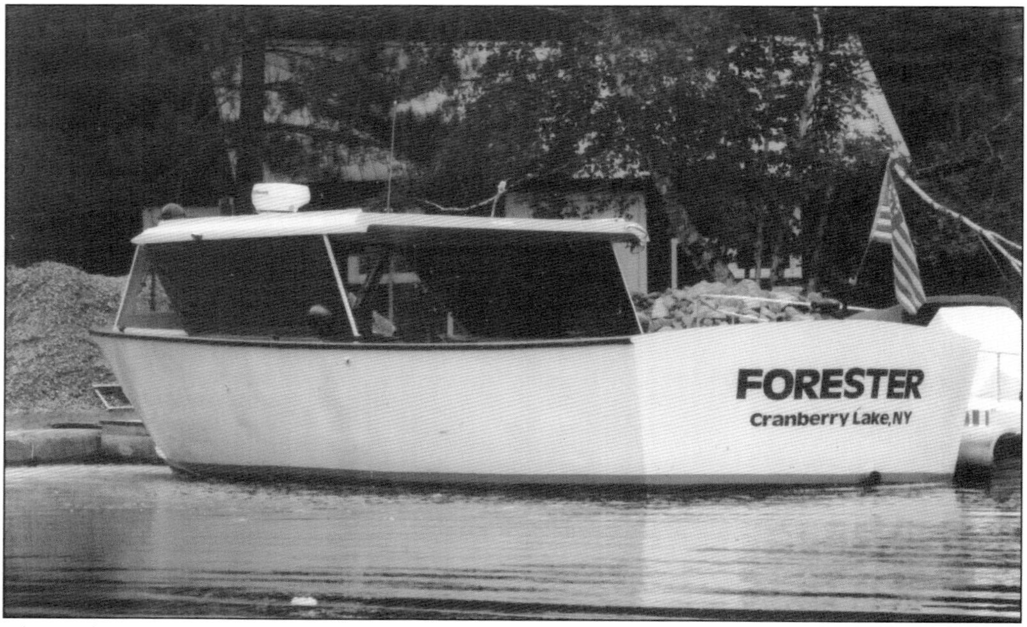

The 32-foot steel *Forester* today carries 28 passengers to the SUNY ESF summer camp. It carries large loads of academic supplies and groceries and also takes students to Janack's Landing for class trips to Cat Mountain and West Flow trailhead for classes. The camp boasts 20 other motorized boats, which haul smaller but similar loads, 15 aluminum canoes, and 2 26-foot wooden war canoes. (Courtesy of Ellen Giraud.)

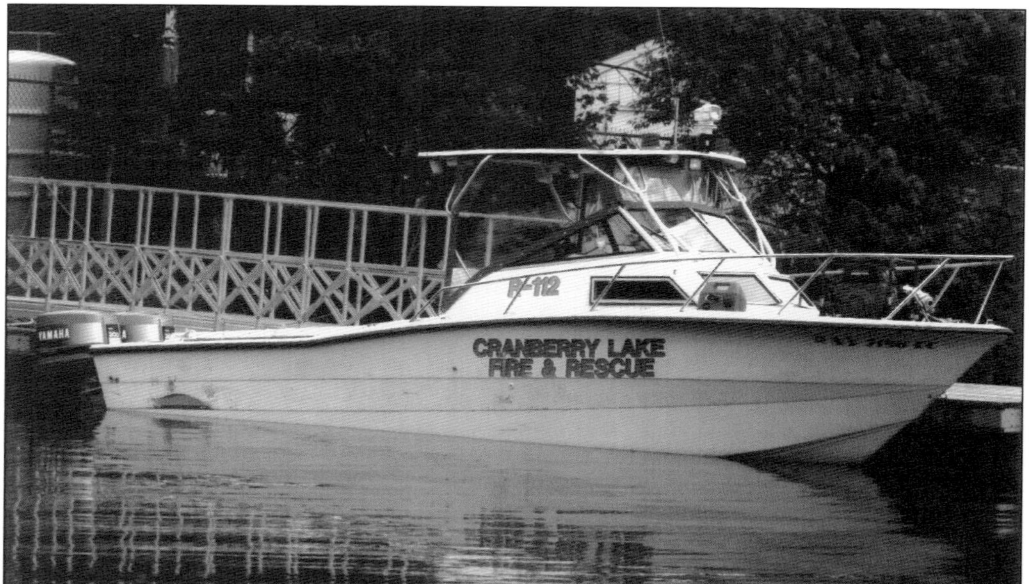

The Cranberry Lake Fire and Rescue boat is berthed near the Cranberry Lake Dam. It is a 25-foot Hydrosport, a sportfishing boat built in 1985 and purchased by the Cranberry Lake Fire Department in 1993. The boat is made of Kevlar over fiberglass and includes twin Yamaha engines of 200 horsepower each that were added in 1985. A newer boat will soon replace this one. (Courtesy of Ellen Giraud.)

Three

Pleasure Boats and Sport Boats

In the beginning, people who wanted to be on the water paddled a canoe. By 1907, they could buy a motorboat or even build one. The technology of the internal combustion engine was simple, plans were readily available, and the motor could be fitted to various existing boats. Herbert Keith, in *Man of the Woods*, tells the tale of a few Wanakena mechanics at the Rich Lumber Company machine shop in 1908 who built a "flat-bottomed boat with provision for a small propeller to turn and not extend below the bottom of the boat. The bottom had a tunnel in it to protect the propeller from logs and rocks." They ordered a one-cylinder engine from Truscott Boat Manufacturing Company in St. Joseph, Michigan. When Wilfred Morrison, a local guide, saw the contraption, he called it "the beast" and declared it "the most destructive device ever invented by man to ruin fishing on the upper Oswegatchie and other rivers." But powerboats had already caught on. At first, anglers used them to get to their fishing holes. In 1909, five seasonal residents, organized by Rev. J. Foster Wilcox, formed the Cranberry Lake Motor Boat Club to encourage camaraderie and oversee the rapidly growing sport of motorboat racing. National firms such as Chris-Craft marketed inboard motorboats that were affordable and were widely available in the Adirondacks by the 1930s. Overlapping that development was the perfection of the outboard motor in the 1920s. Ole Evinrude was its first widely successful developer. Hallie Bond, author of *Boats and Boating in the Adirondacks*, credits his wife, Bess, with capturing the public's imagination with her advertisement for their first outboard, urging, "Don't Row! Throw the Oars Away!" In 1959, the New York State legislature created a division of motorboats to address an increasing concern with the problem of "too many boats." As camps were built along the lakeshores, and every camp had a boat or two, congestion and use issues arose. They are still present, but the players are changing. Jet Skis, pontoon boats, and sleek kayaks share the water. Paddlers are back.

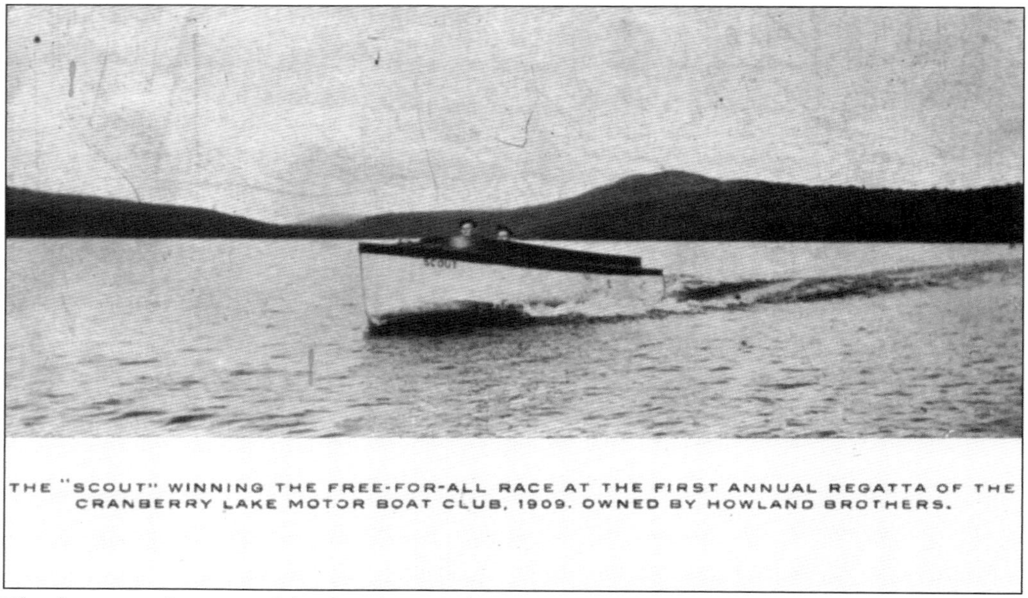

The first annual regatta of the Cranberry Lake Motor Boat Club brought out many motorboats to race, and many spectators to watch, in that summer of 1909. The *Scout*, owned by the Howland brothers, who also owned the workboat *Wanakena*, won the free-for-all race. That was the main race of the day, held at the end of the afternoon. (Courtesy of Marilyn Molnar.)

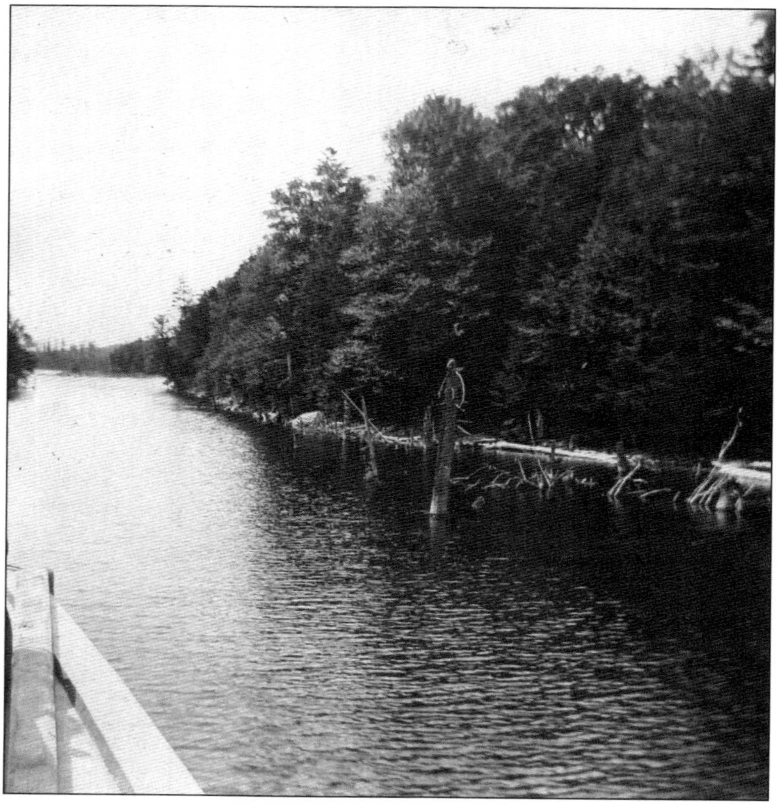

The pleasure motorboat offered ease and novelty when traveling longer distances on the lake. Speed was not always possible, however, when traveling to or from Wanakena in 1910. This unidentified motor launch is passing through the narrows near Yale Point on the Oswegatchie River. The small opening, shallow areas, and stumps meant both recreational boater and steamer had to slow down here. (Courtesy of Susan Smeby.)

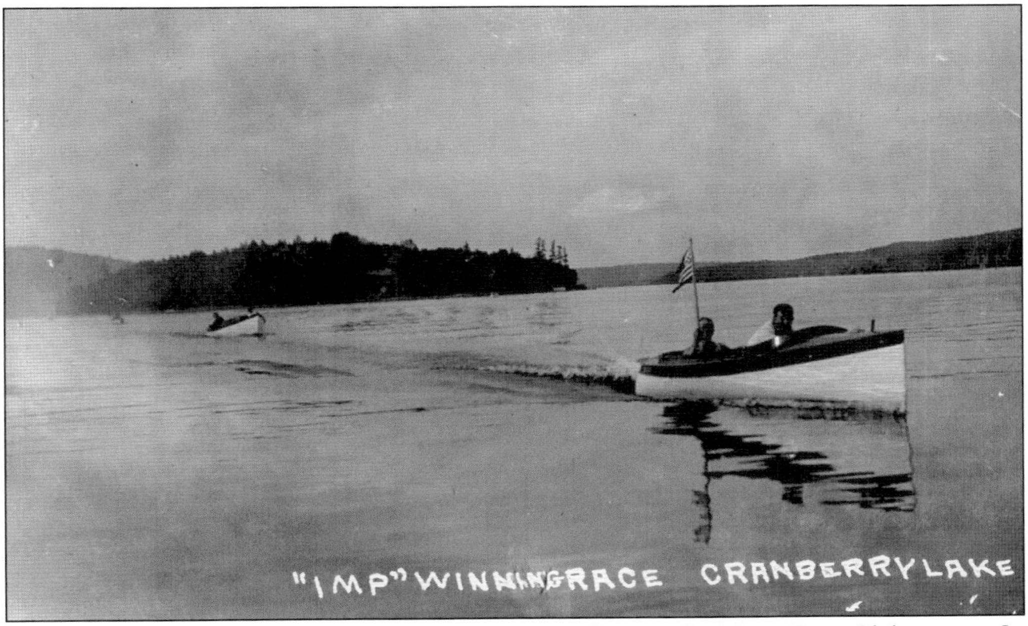

The motor launch *Imp* won its race in the 1909 Cranberry Lake Motor Boat Club regatta. In the boat are Theodore Rautenberg Sr. (left, holding flag) and Theodore Rautenberg Jr. (driving). T. H. Rautenberg III now has the trophy. The *Imp* also won in the eight-mile class in 1913. (Courtesy of Eugene Carver.)

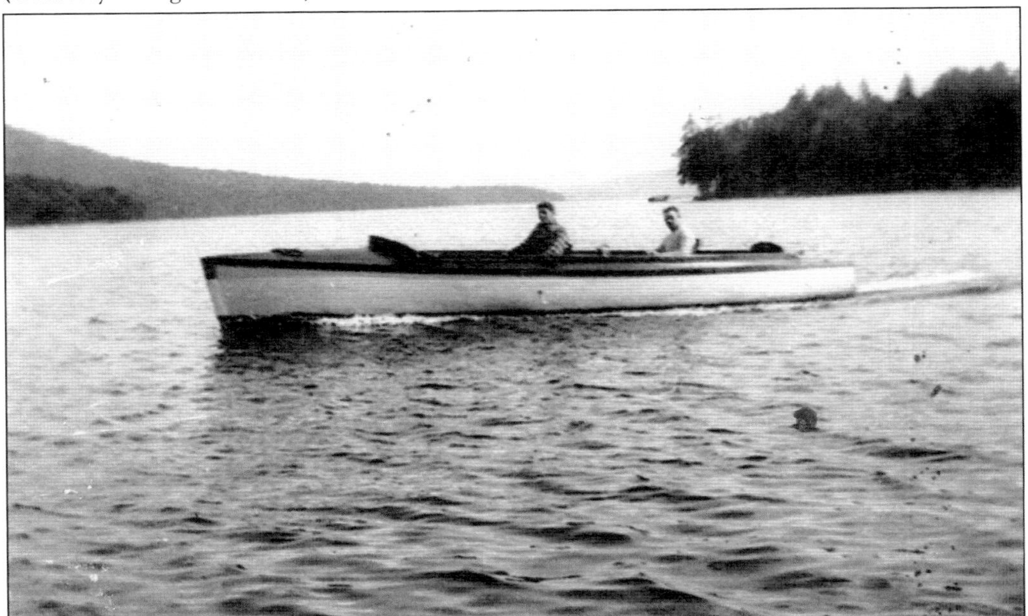

The *Diana*, in Matilda Bay around 1924, was about 20 feet long with a four-cylinder, gas-powered Ford engine and was steered from the side at midship. On board are T. H. Rautenberg (left) at the helm, Howard C. "Totsie" Hoople Jr. (middle, small and barely visible head), and Howard C. "Tot" Hoople. Rautenberg was fleet captain of the Cranberry Lake Motor Boat Club in 1915. (Courtesy of Eugene Carver.)

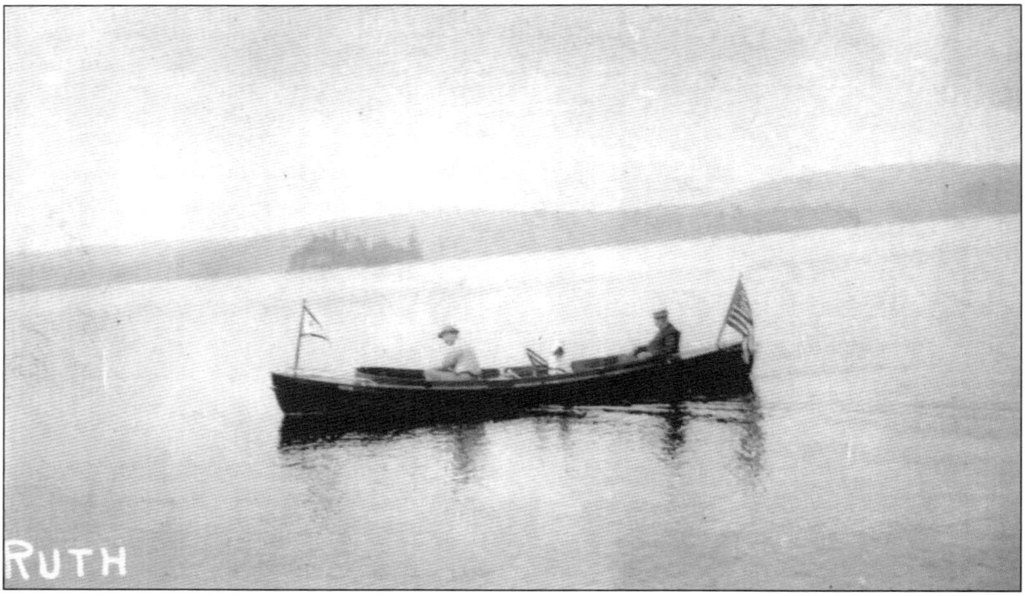

This *c.* 1909 photograph of the motor launch *Ruth* looks as if it could be in a modern magazine article related to safety issues. Powerboating was a tranquil affair in the early years, and boats did not go very fast, but taking a small child on a lake in a skiff chair (center) would raise eyebrows today. None of the passengers could be identified. (Courtesy of Eugene Carver.)

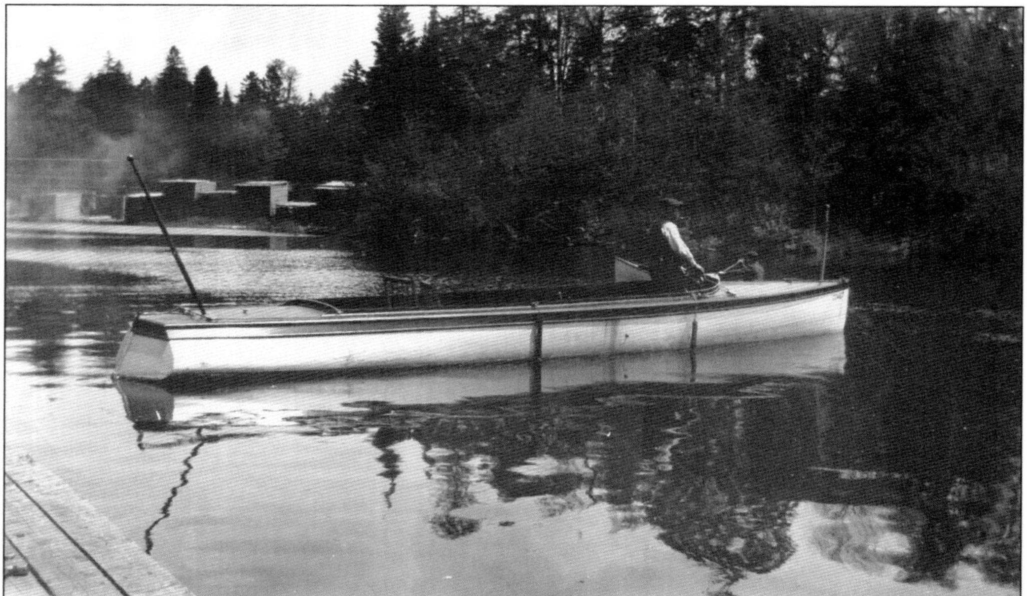

The *Comet* was the fastest boat on the lake for several years. It was built around 1910 by the Rich Lumber Company. Its 40-horsepower, four-cylinder, three-port Roberts gasoline engine could reach 40 miles per hour. It won the 1913 six-mile free-for-all race for the third time with a time of 17 minutes and 23 seconds, permanently retiring the prized Commodore's Cup. (Courtesy of Susan Smeby.)

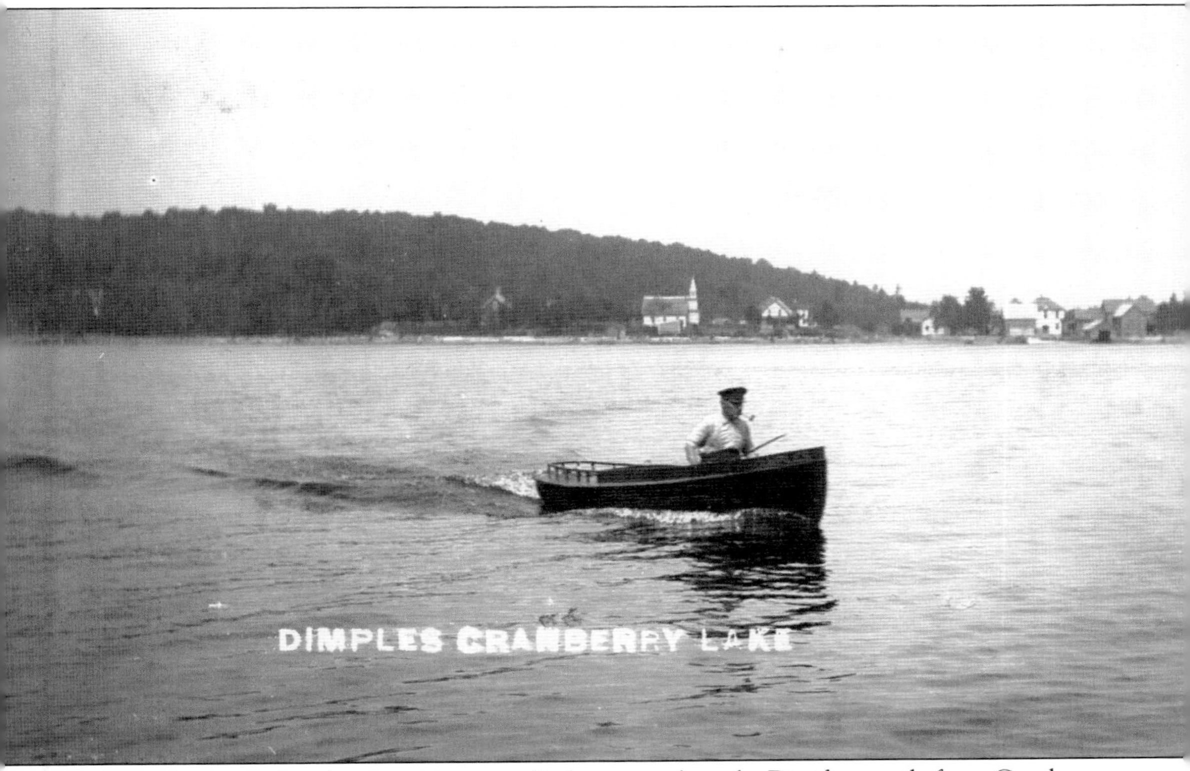

Capt. Charles E. Leach pilots his one-cylinder motor launch, *Dimples*, south from Cranberry Lake village. In the center behind him is the Community Presbyterian Church building, which today is a summer home for the Western Adirondack Presbyterian Church. Leach was an officer in the Cranberry Lake Motor Boat Club at its founding in 1909. He was also the office manager for the steamship *Helen*. (Courtesy of Peter VandeWater.)

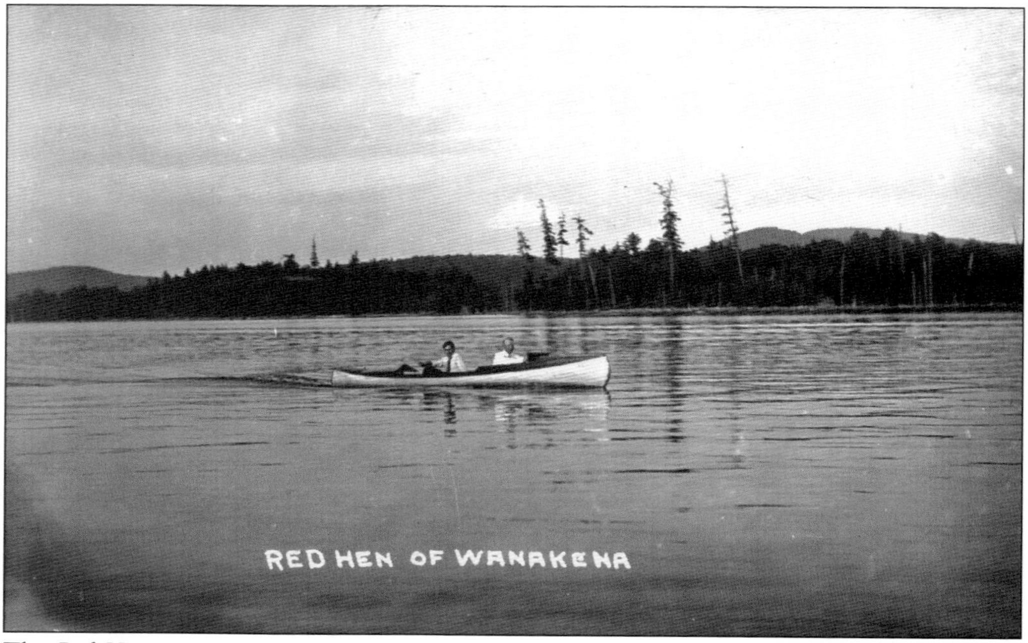

The *Red Hen* was owned by W. M. Babcock of Wanakena. It ran in the 12-mile race of the Cranberry Lake Motor Boat Club regatta in 1911. It entered again in 1913. However, an alert reporter for the *Watertown Daily Times* noted that while the *Red Hen* appeared to be winning that race, it had to drop out when its rudder fell off. (Courtesy of Susan Smeby.)

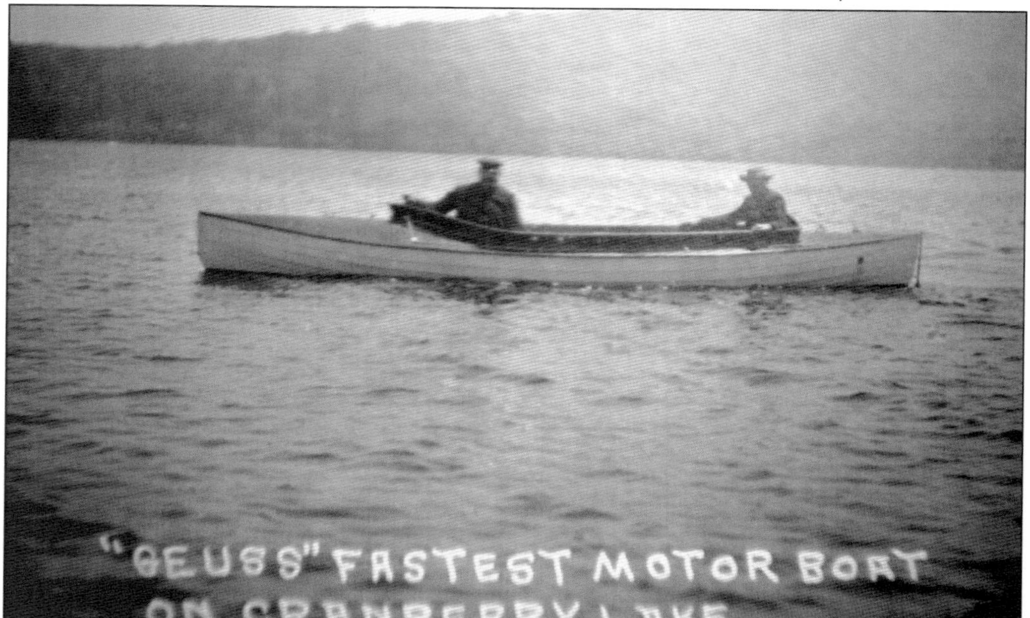

Promoted as the fastest boat on Cranberry Lake, the *Geuss* raced against the *Red Hen* in the 1911 Cranberry Lake Motor Boat Club regatta. It participated in the 12-mile race and was owned by E. N. Leibout of the Indian Mountain Club at Cranberry Lake. The postcard caption implies that the *Geuss* won the race. (Courtesy of Susan Smeby.)

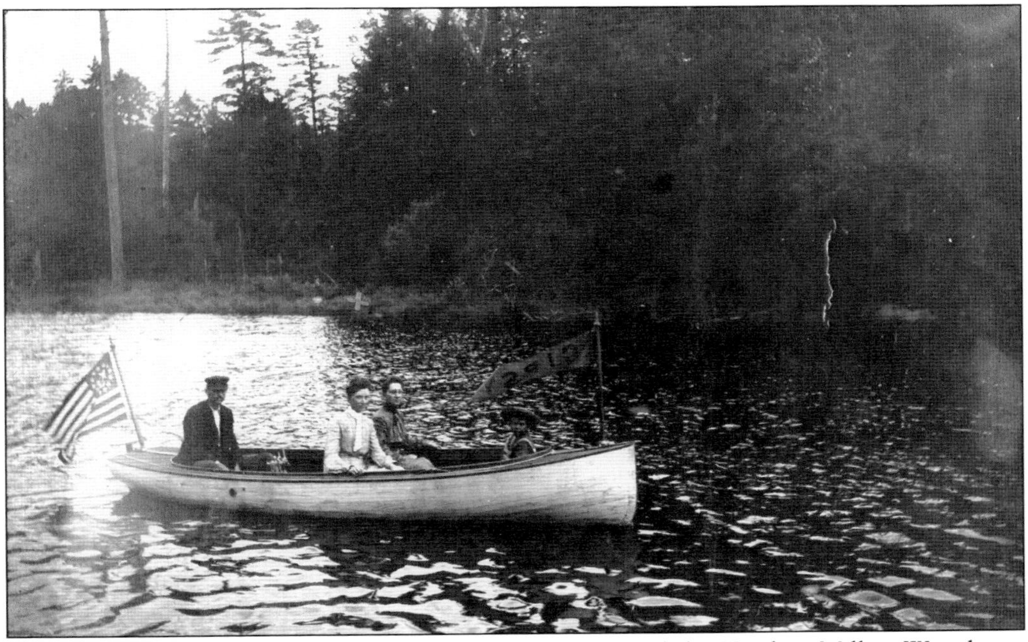

The *Gipsey* probably belonged to Henry Ventres, who owned the Heading Mill in Wanakena, which made hardwood barrelheads for cooperage manufacturers. This boat was listed on the program to race in the 1911 regatta. A note on the back of the photograph reads, "Our launch the Gipsy [*sic*]. Mary, Henry-Lawrence [?] and myself. It is run by gasoline engine—goes 10 (ten) mi. an hour." (Courtesy of Susan Smeby.)

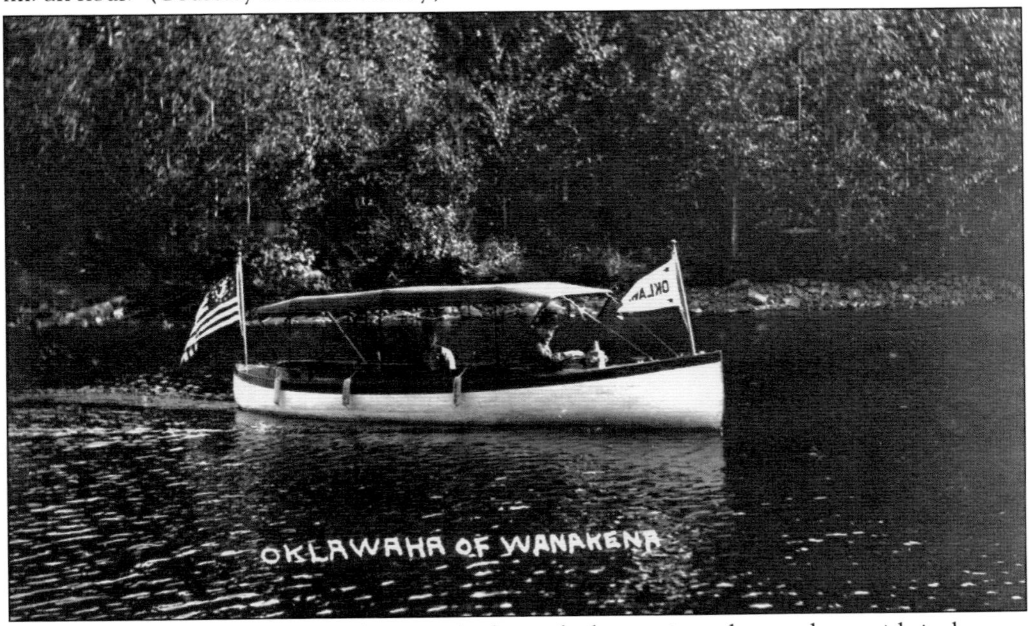

The tour boat *Oklawaha*, often photographed in a dock area, is under way here with its banner flying. The canvas top protected passengers from sun and rain. The owner of this launch is believed to have been either Patrick Ryan or George Schlieder, operators of Ryan and Schlieder Lath Mill in Wanakena in the early 1900s. (Courtesy of Susan Smeby.)

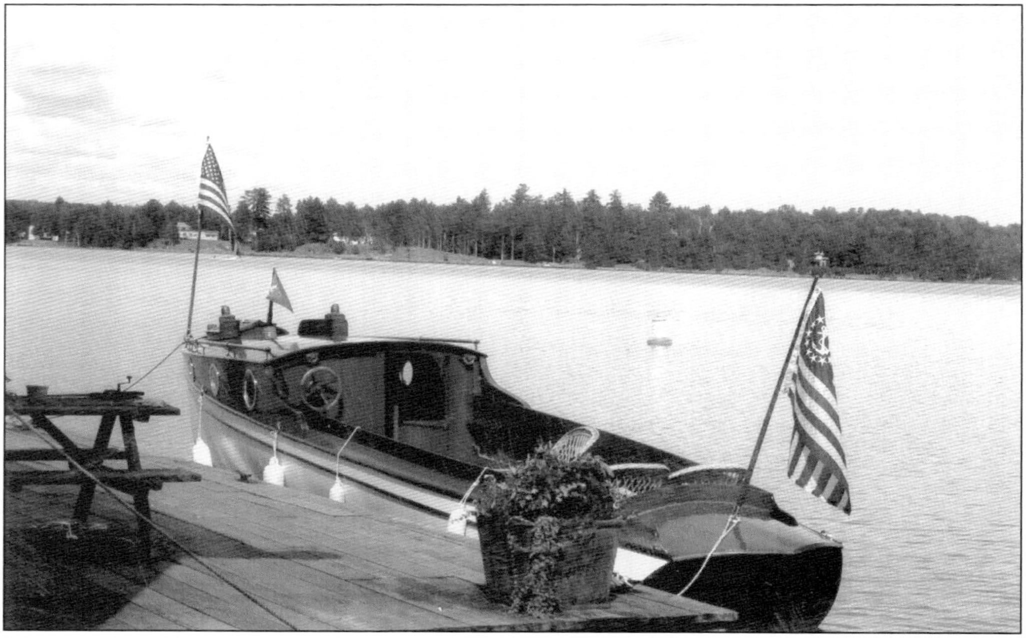

The *Luella* is a 31-foot wooden day cruiser built by Fay and Bowen in Geneva, New York, between 1912 and 1914. Ernest Giraud, its present owner, spent several years restoring it. The oldest boat active on Cranberry Lake in 2008, it leads the annual boat club parade each year. The *Luella* is featured on the Cranberry Lake Boat Club centennial postage stamp issued in 2009. (Courtesy of Ernest Giraud.)

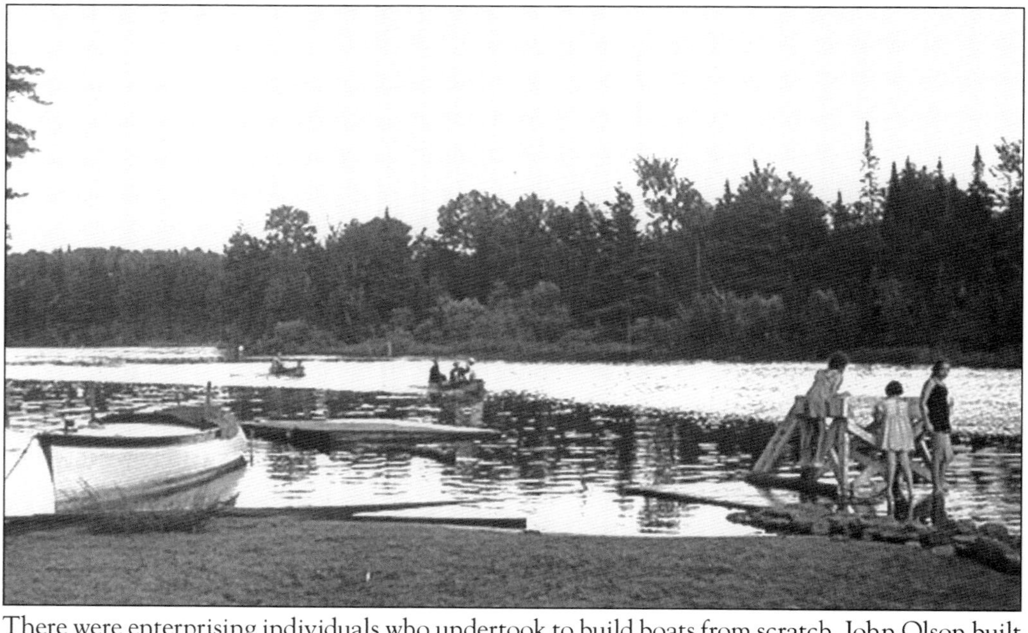

There were enterprising individuals who undertook to build boats from scratch. John Olson built this one, tied on the shore of the Oswegatchie River, in his garage on Second Street in Wanakena around 1920. Olson came to the small village in 1902. According to local lore, he built a number of other boats for people in Wanakena during that period. (Courtesy of Helen Olson.)

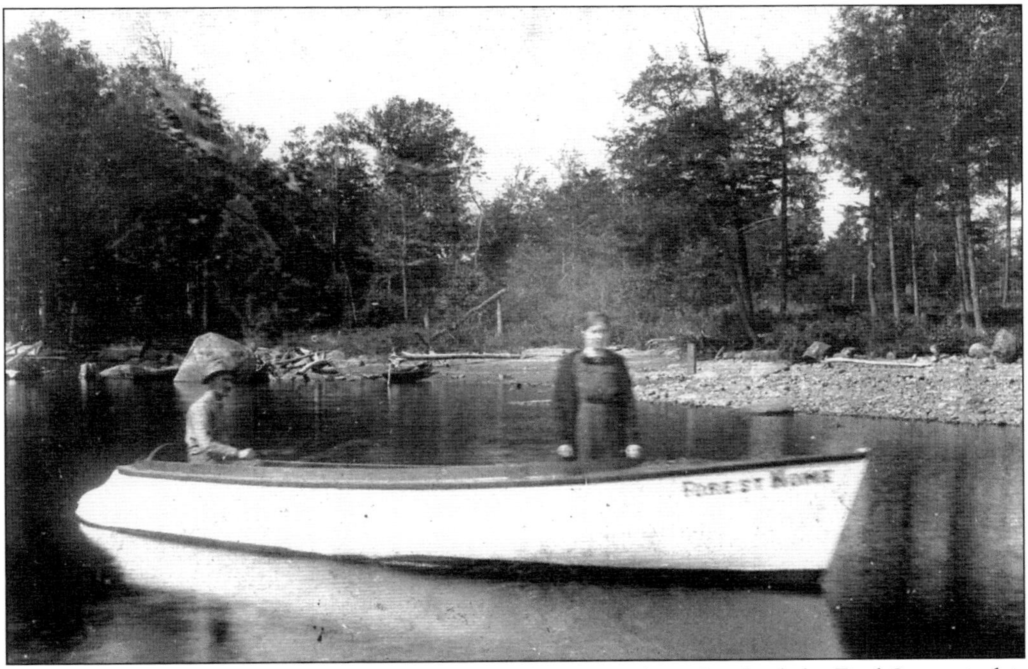

The *Forest Home* (above) is the first of two wooden motor launches built by Fred Smart in his carpentry shop in Lacona for use at his home of the same name on Cranberry Lake. Above, James Welch and Muriel Sprague pause near the camp at Deremo Point in 1909. The second *Forest Home* was built by Smart in 1931. It had a canvas top. Pictured below is a group of campers from Tanager Lodge on Upper Chateaugay Lake arriving for a visit at Forest Home. Tanager Lodge, a summer camp for children, was started by Fay Welch in 1925 and is operated today by his son Tom Welch. (Courtesy of Norman Widrig.)

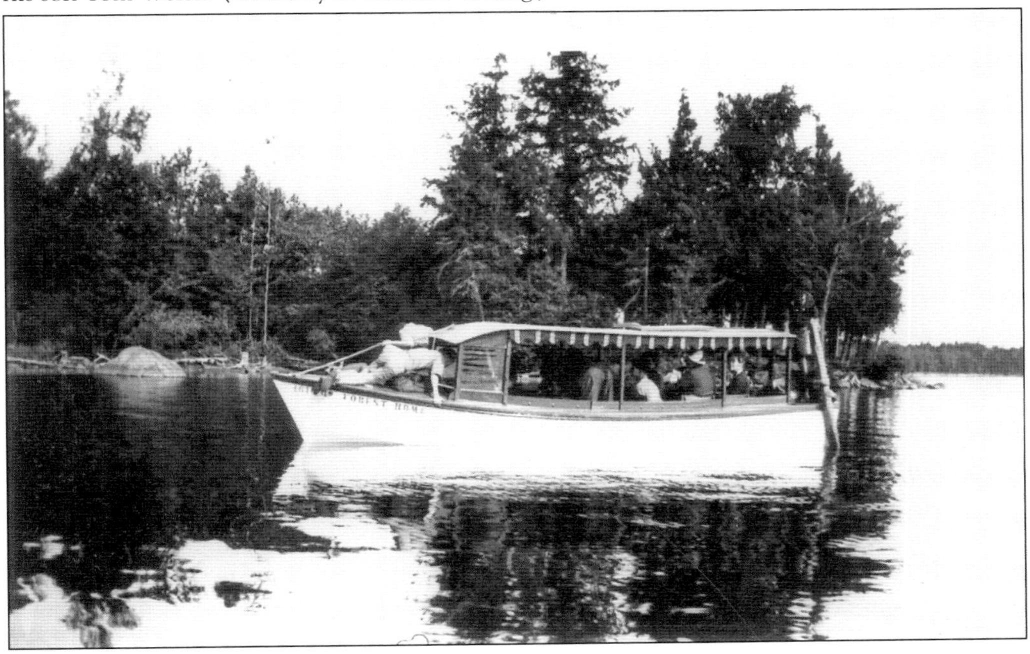

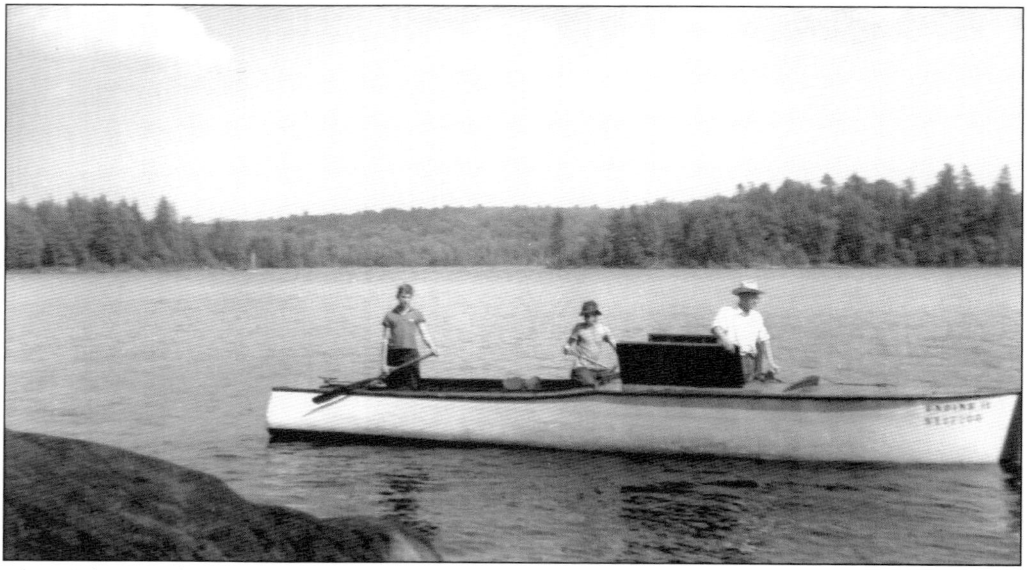

The 27-foot *Undine*, with its three-quarter-inch cypress hull, was built in Skaneatales in 1918. It was the only boat that transported residents of Buck Island to the foot of the lake until the 1960s. Its six-cylinder engine had a top speed of about 15 knots. The trip took 45 minutes. In the boat are, from left to right, unidentified, Sam Bragdon, and Channy Bragdon. (Courtesy of Julie Higgins.)

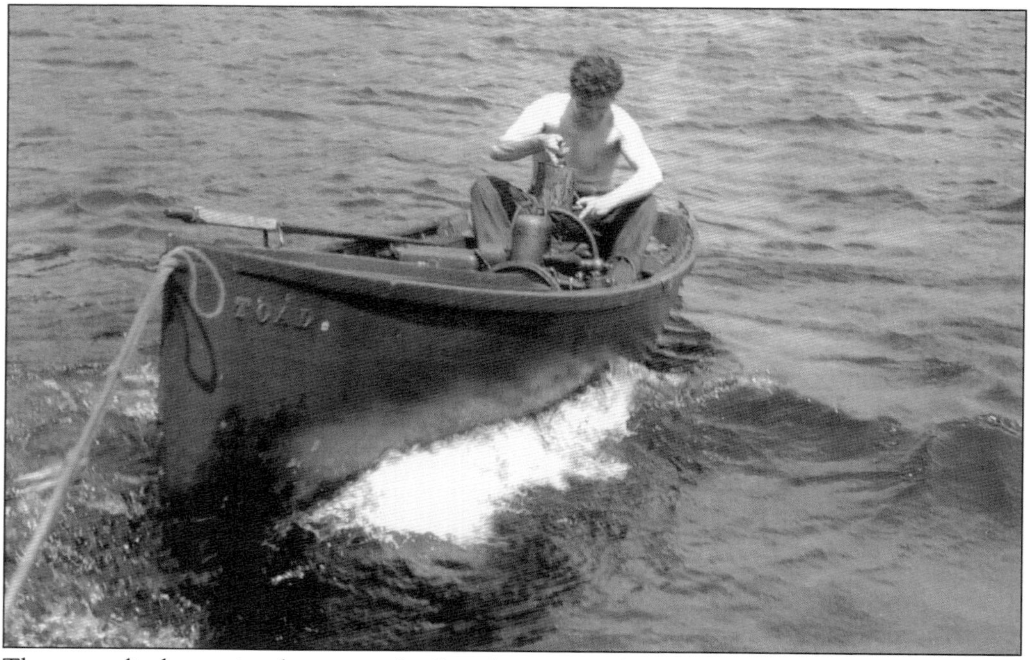

The one-cylinder engine, known as the "one-lunger" or "the beast," was made by Truscott Boat Manufacturing Company in St. Joseph, Michigan. It can be seen in the middle of the *Toad*, which is being towed up Cranberry Lake. It allowed a flat-bottomed boat to go into shallow water. William Giraud sits in the stern of the 20-year-old launch in this 1940s photograph. (Courtesy of Ernest Giraud.)

The *Mac*, named for William MacAleese Sr., in the boat, was a 1920s inboard motorboat with a throttle on it. MacAleese once headed the highway commission. This group supervised construction of the iron bridge over the Oswegatchie River below the Cranberry Lake Dam in 1905. The bridge, no longer used for automobiles, remains intact and is now a popular walking, biking, and fishing spot. (Courtesy of Jeanne Reynolds.)

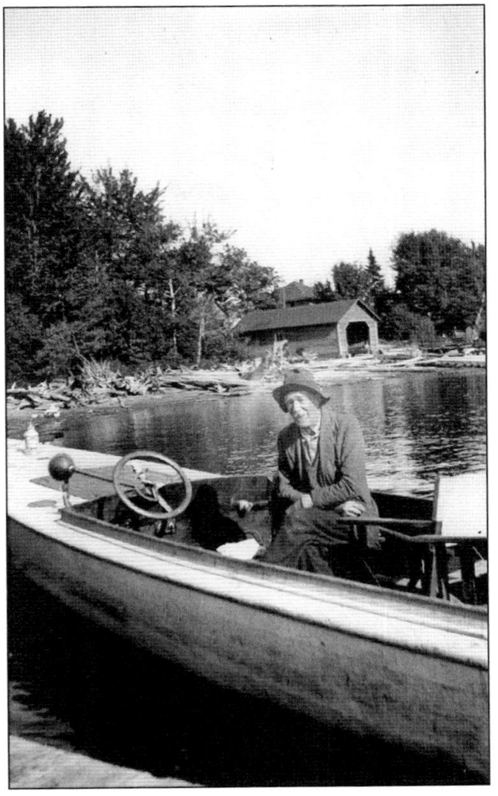

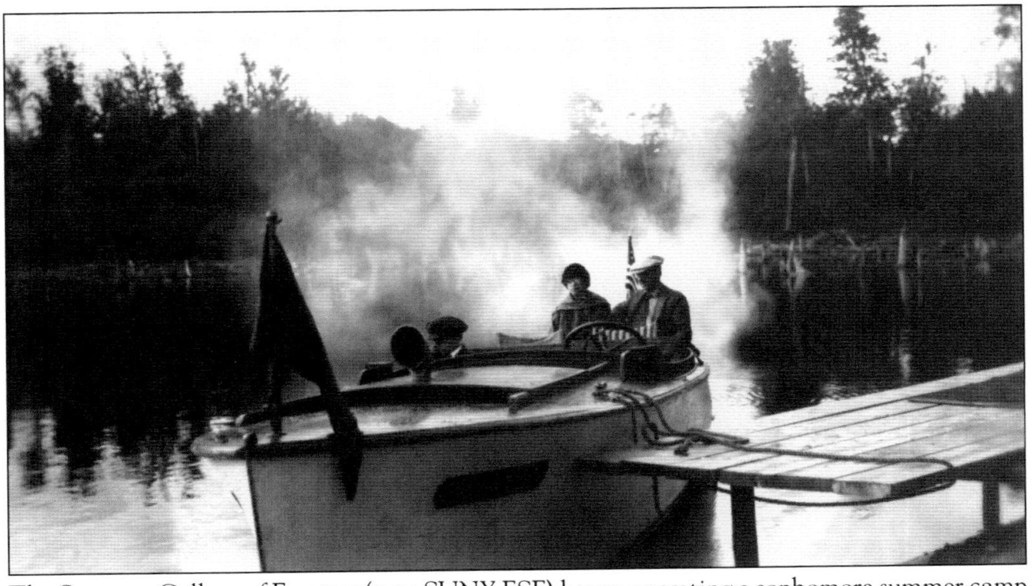

The Syracuse College of Forestry (now SUNY ESF) began operating a sophomore summer camp at Barber Point in 1913. Mrs. Moon, their son, Franklin, and Dean Franklin Moon are seen arriving at the summer camp dock in the *La Truda* for a visit around 1929. Dean Franklin Moon was a director of the Cranberry Lake Motor Boat Club. (Courtesy of F. Franklin Moon Library, SUNY ESF.)

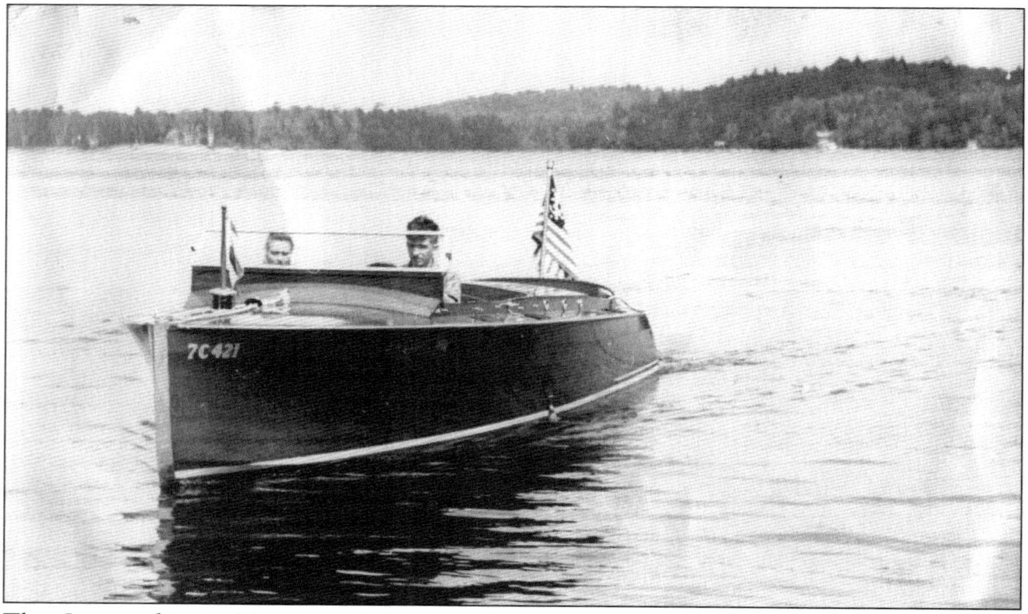

The *Oswegatchie*, or "Ossie," a 1927 Chris-Craft once owned by the McNally family on the St. Lawrence River, was purchased by Dr. L. E. Sutton of Syracuse. Then a plastic surgeon, he had worked at the College of Forestry sophomore summer camp on Cranberry Lake as an assistant cook in 1914. He became a seasonal resident in 1940. This 26-foot speedboat had double carburetors, making it a frequent race winner on the lake. In the image above, Helen and Richard Sutton (driving) are in the boat. Below, Dr. Sutton is seen reading by the boat at the village dock in Cranberry Lake. Given's Dock is immediately to the right, and the Cranberry Lake Dam is to the far right rear. (Courtesy of Jeanne Reynolds.)

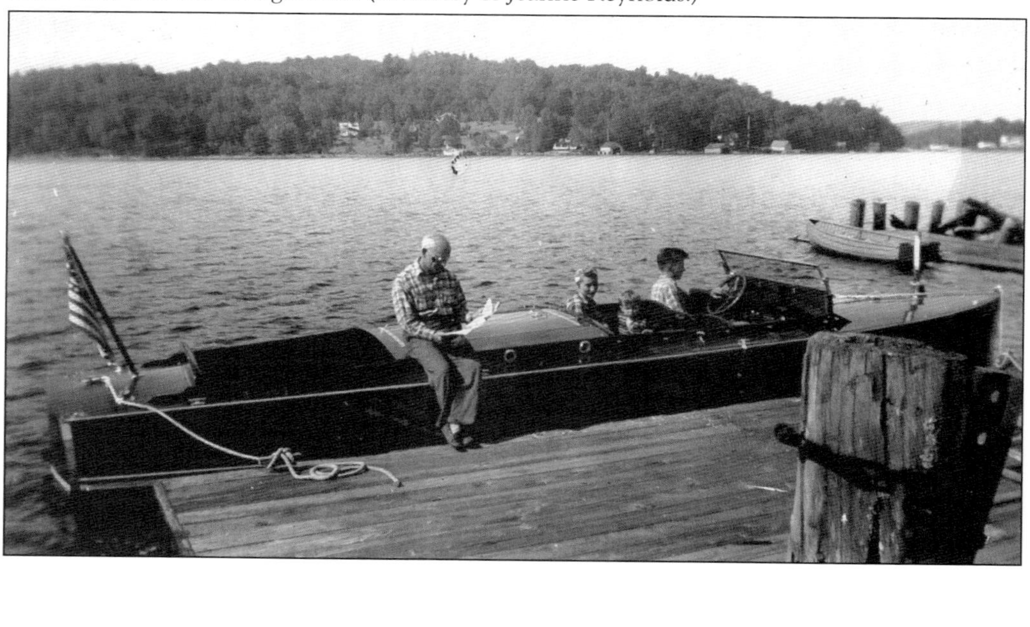

A typical summer afternoon on Cranberry Lake in 1938 might have found Charles Sleicher taking some kids out for a quick spin. But at other times, this runabout could be found participating in the regatta races against the likes of the *Fox*. Both were among the fastest boats on the lake. It is typical of the kind of speedboat on the lake at this time. (Courtesy of Harry K. Sleicher.)

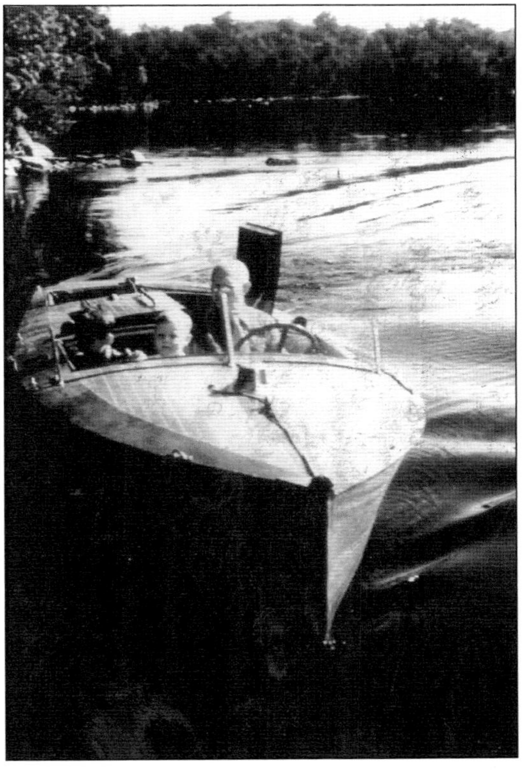

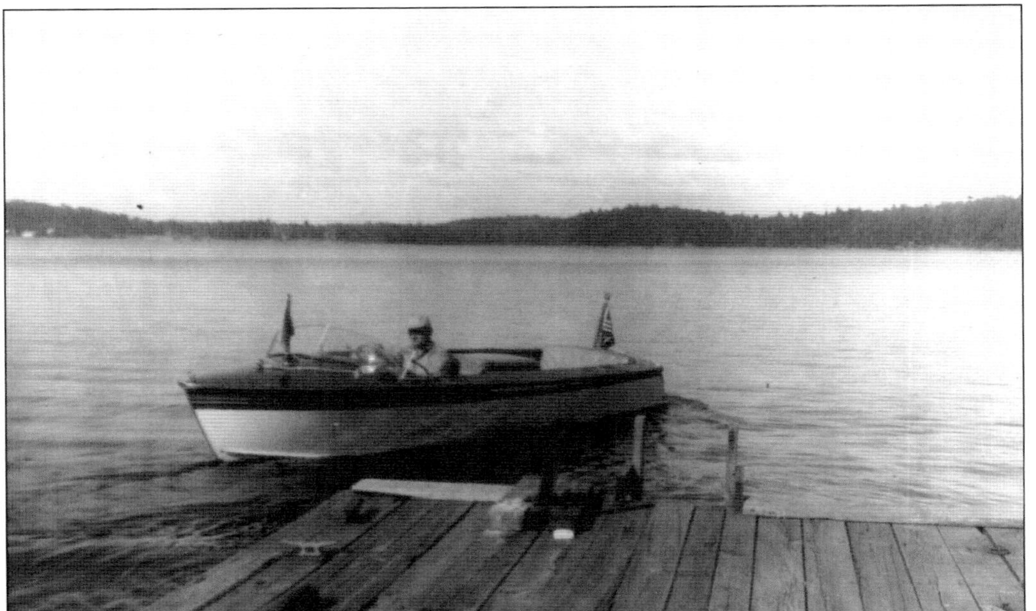

Dr. L. E. Sutton is shown at the wheel of his Higgins inboard in 1946. The boat was made of plywood and painted. Wartime demands restricted the wood types available for boatbuilding during those years. Some of these models have been called "the Volkswagens of motorboats" because of the cheap availability of their materials. (Courtesy of Jeanne Reynolds.)

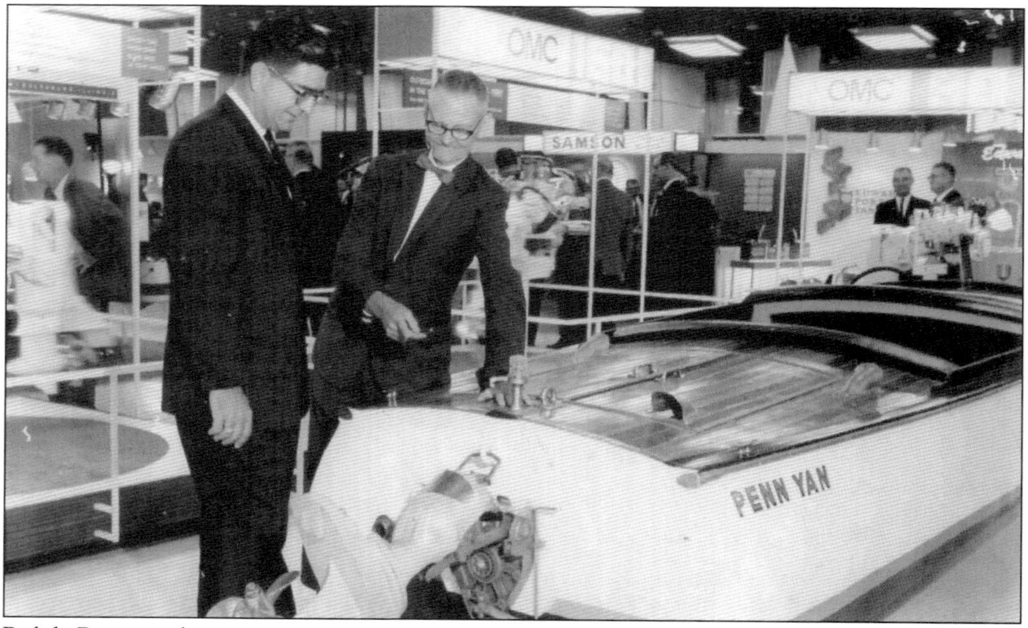

Ralph Brown, who spent many summers in Wanakena, was a man ahead of his time. Brown, a former president of Penn Yan Boats, developed a combination inboard/outboard motorboat in 1930. "We built about seven or eight of them," Brown said later, "but they just didn't catch on. Most boats at that time were either rowed or powered by inboards. Outboard motors struck people as being much easier to handle." He then became among the first to see the potential of the Evinrude outboard motor in the fledgling industry. Brown (above, right) shows a 1932 Penn Yan Boats inboard/outboard motorboat at the 1964 Chicago Boat Show. That boat (below) is now in the Glenn H. Curtiss Museum. (Above, courtesy of the Glenn H. Curtiss Museum; below, photograph by Marilyn Splete.)

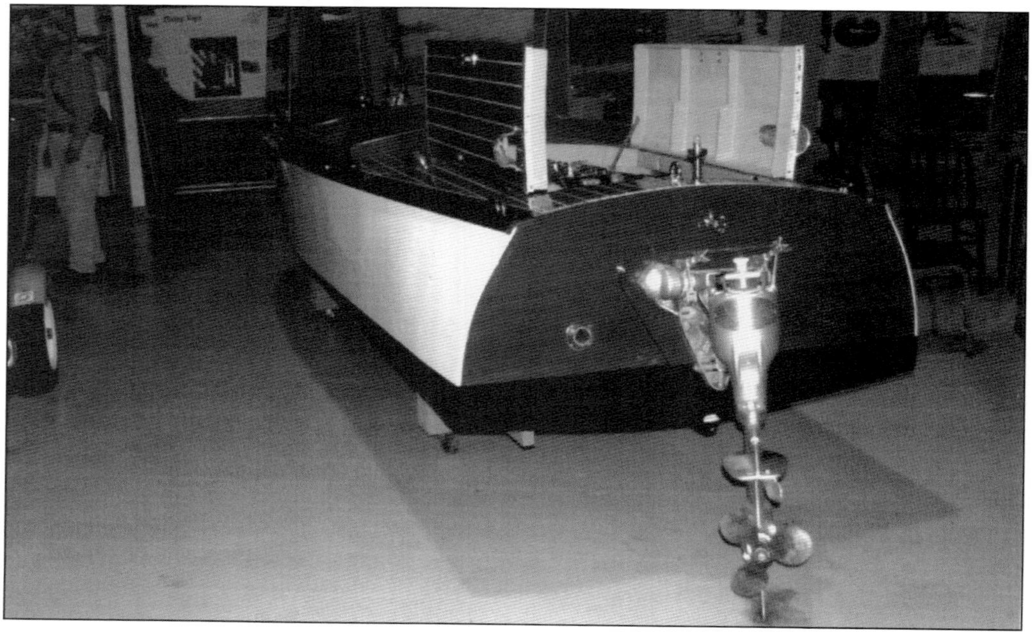

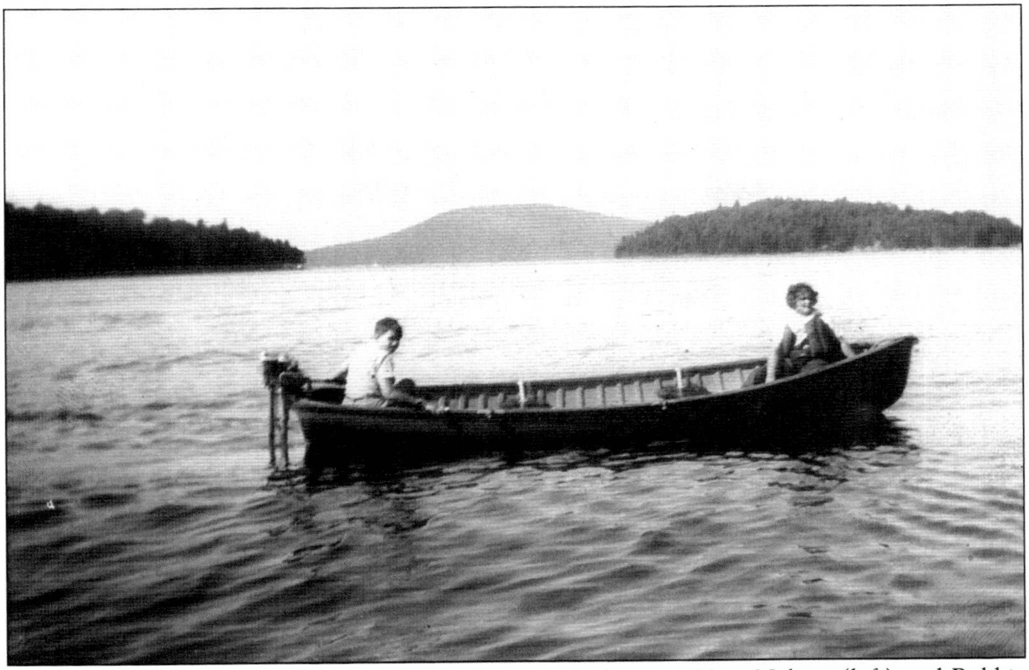

Outboard motorboats caught on with Cranberry Lake boaters. Here Nelson (left) and Bobbie Leavell explore the lake in a wooden skiff with an early outboard motor. The photograph was taken in September 1938, in what appears to be South Bay near Chair Rock. Cole's Point (far left) and Buck Island (far right) are visible. (Courtesy of Anna Fowler.)

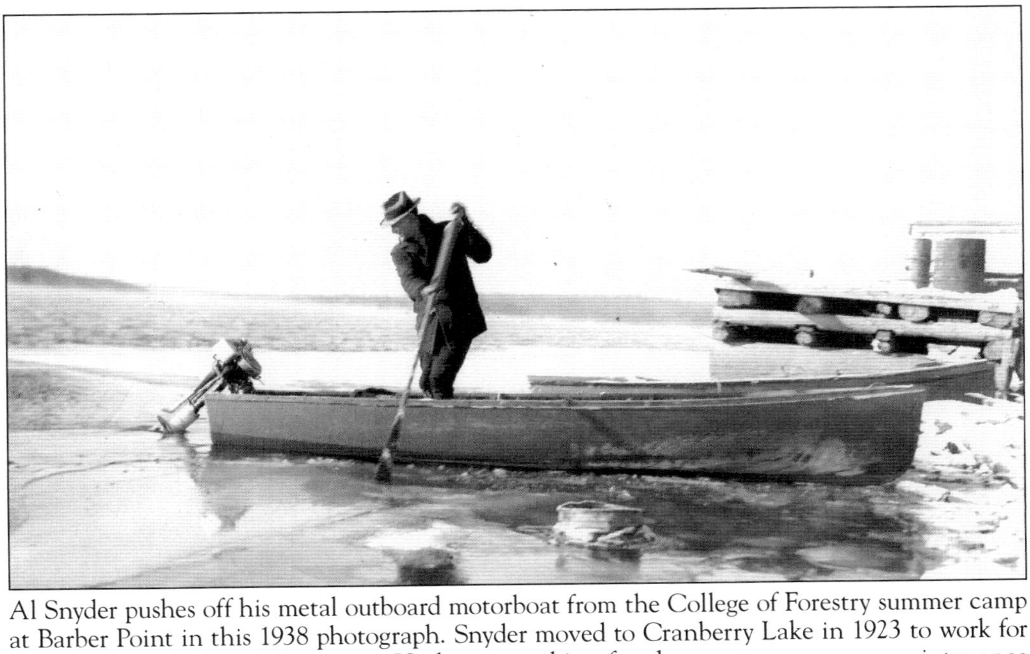

Al Snyder pushes off his metal outboard motorboat from the College of Forestry summer camp at Barber Point in this 1938 photograph. Snyder moved to Cranberry Lake in 1923 to work for the Emporium Forestry Company. He began working for the summer camp as maintenance supervisor in 1938. He retired in 1966. (Courtesy of Jeanne Reynolds.)

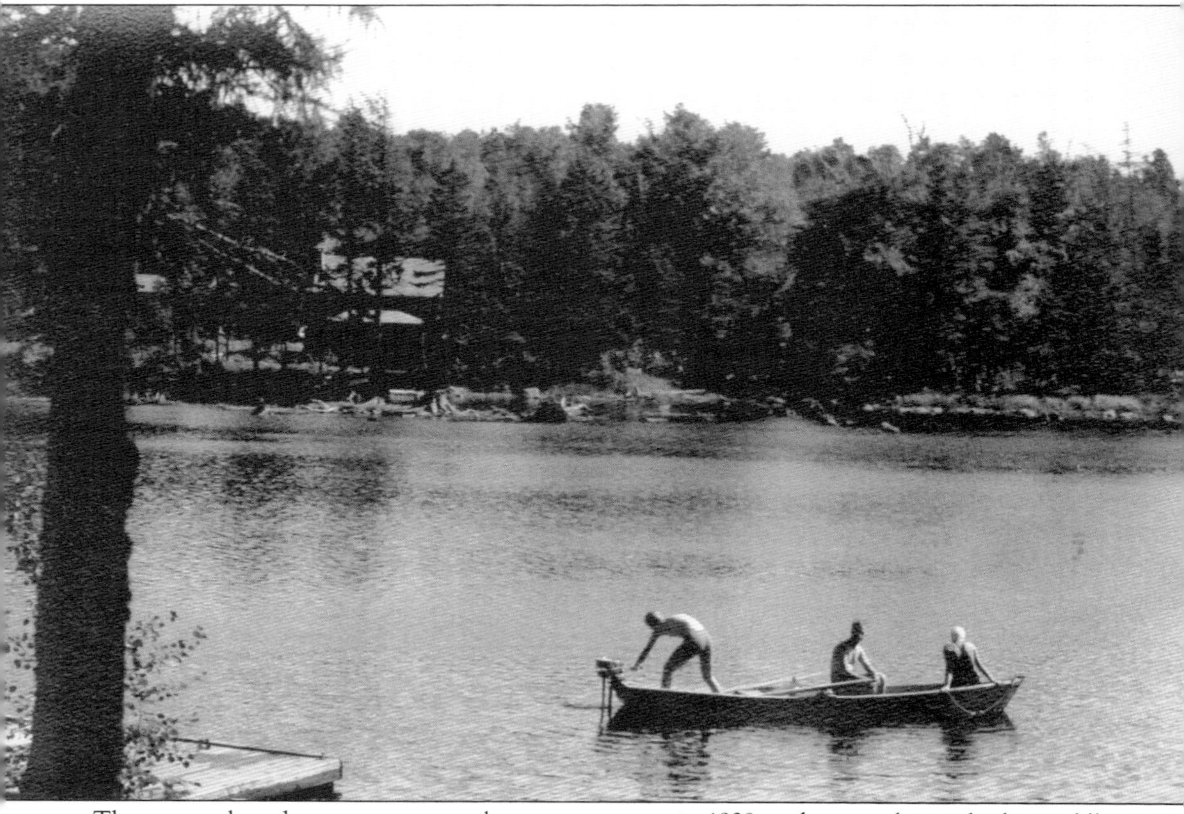

The new outboard motors were not always easy to start in 1939, and many a boater had to paddle in or be towed for repairs when the engine would not turn over. Here an unidentified man is experiencing the time-consuming frustration of the task. His fellow boaters seem content to enjoy the view in Matilda Bay. (Courtesy of Susan Smeby.)

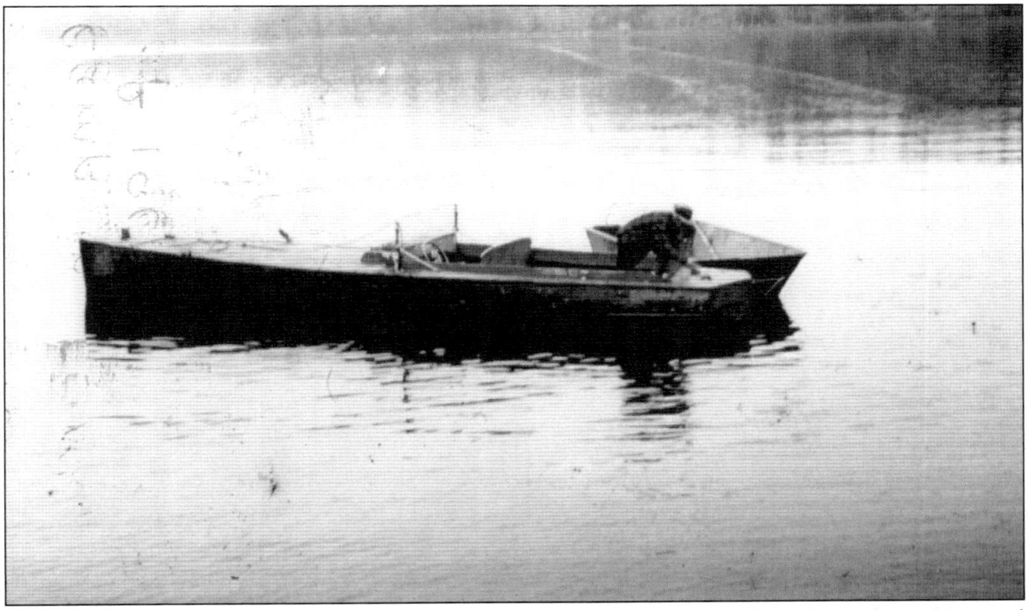

Loyd Davis was a guide who took hunters and fishermen around the lake from the 1930s until the 1960s in his big 30-foot St. Lawrence sports boat, *Lainy*. The front panel wood decking took up half the boat. Passengers sat on two wooden seats, and the small windshield provided little protection from the elements, but it meant extra room for hunting gear in the fall. (Courtesy of Harry K. Sleicher.)

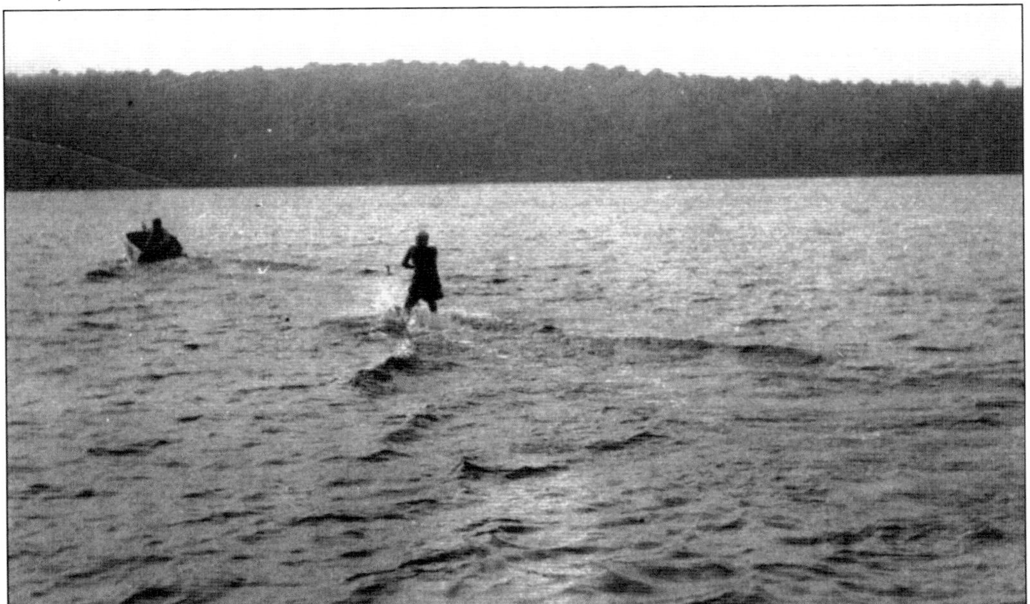

Not only were the boats getting faster, but the thrill of speed and a large lake combined to make the pastime and sport of aquaplaning popular in the 1940s and 1950s. It was the precursor to water-skiing. Pictured here is Grace Smith being towed by Sherm Smith in his outboard motorboat. (Courtesy of Anna Fowler.)

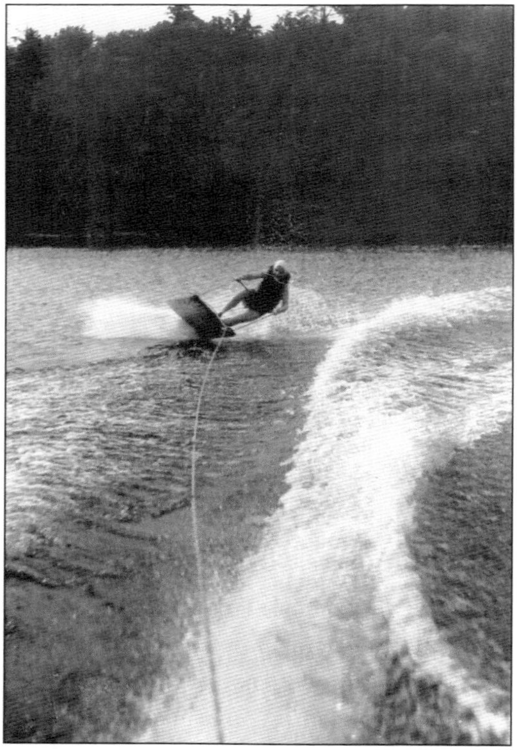

Sally Sleicher is seen aquaplaning in 1948 in front of the Sleichers' camp near Dead Creek Flow. Notice the size of the board on which Sleicher is riding and the handgrips. The boards were wooden. The wake gives an idea of the speed of the boat. (Courtesy of Harry K. Sleicher.)

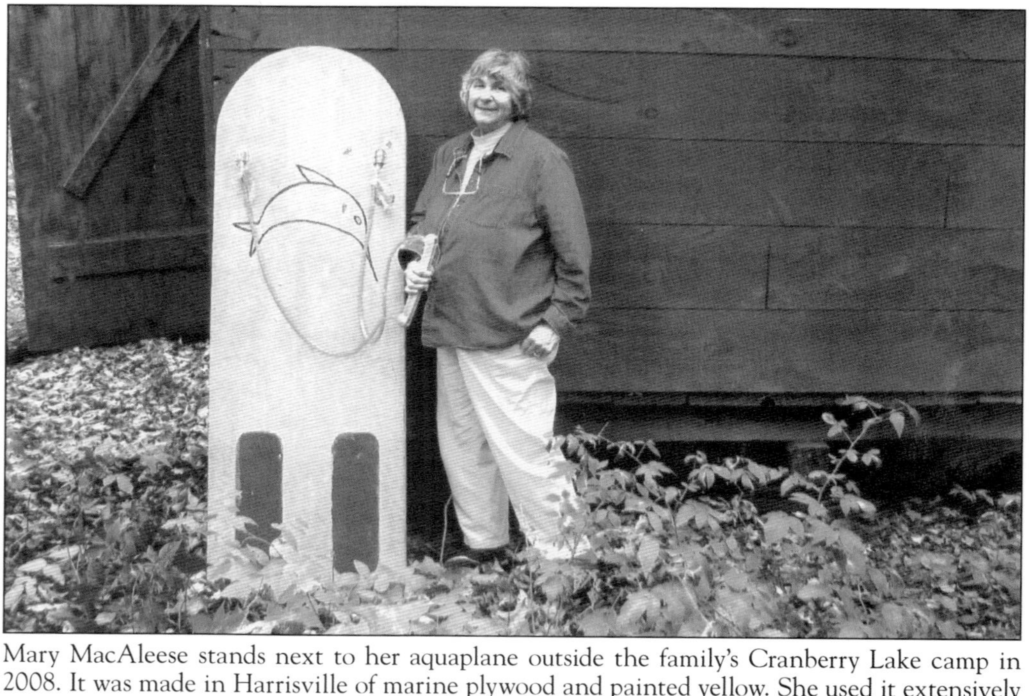

Mary MacAleese stands next to her aquaplane outside the family's Cranberry Lake camp in 2008. It was made in Harrisville of marine plywood and painted yellow. She used it extensively on Lake Bonaparte before bringing it to Cranberry Lake in the early 1950s. The original artwork and rubber treads for the feet remain in good condition. (Courtesy of Mary MacAleese.)

The *Blueberry* was a 1946 Chris-Craft with a six-cylinder Chrysler marine engine. It was built for Mary "Babe" Gillam. Gillam (left) and her friend Helen Whitehead pose in her new boat. The boat was made of cedar and painted blue due to the lack of both mahogany and varnish following World War II. (Courtesy of Eugene Carver.)

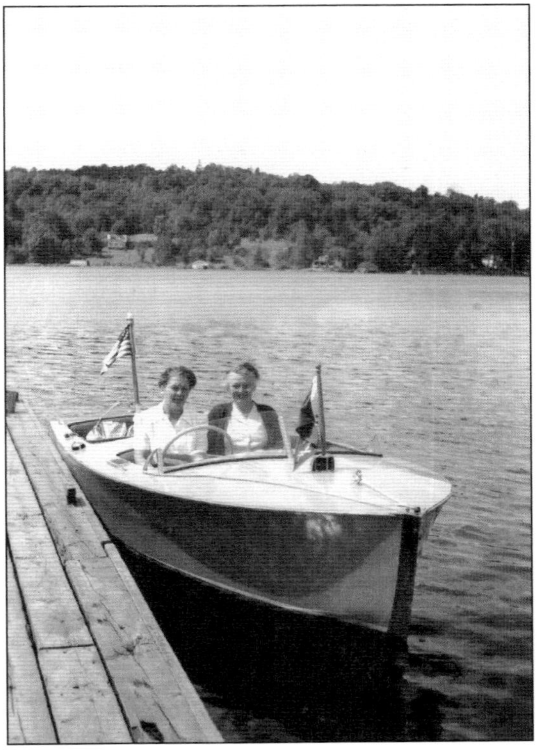

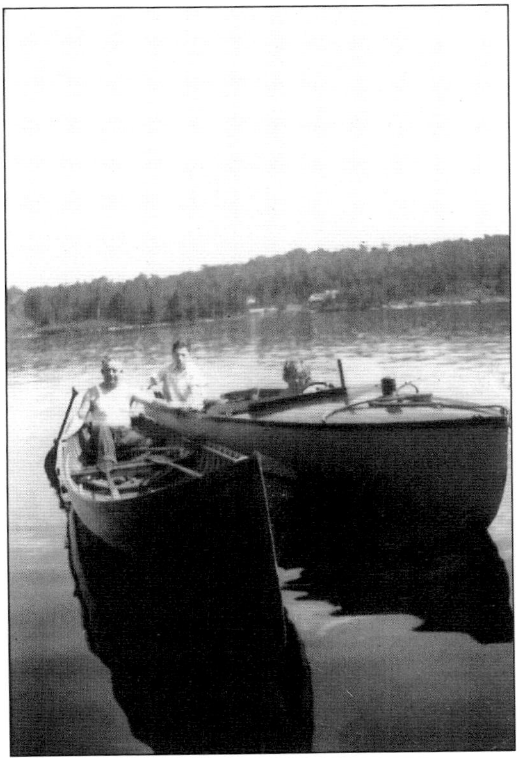

Elmer Hess is seated in the Thompson runabout (right, rear) in 1940, with Barbara Slater. Louis Hess (left) is in the 21-foot McCaffrey guide boat. The guide boat was cut to 18 feet, a motor was added, and Slater recalled later, "I raced the cut-off McCaffrey with a five-horsepower motor in the Cranberry Lake races several times (and won once) in the small outboard class." (Courtesy of Barbara Slater.)

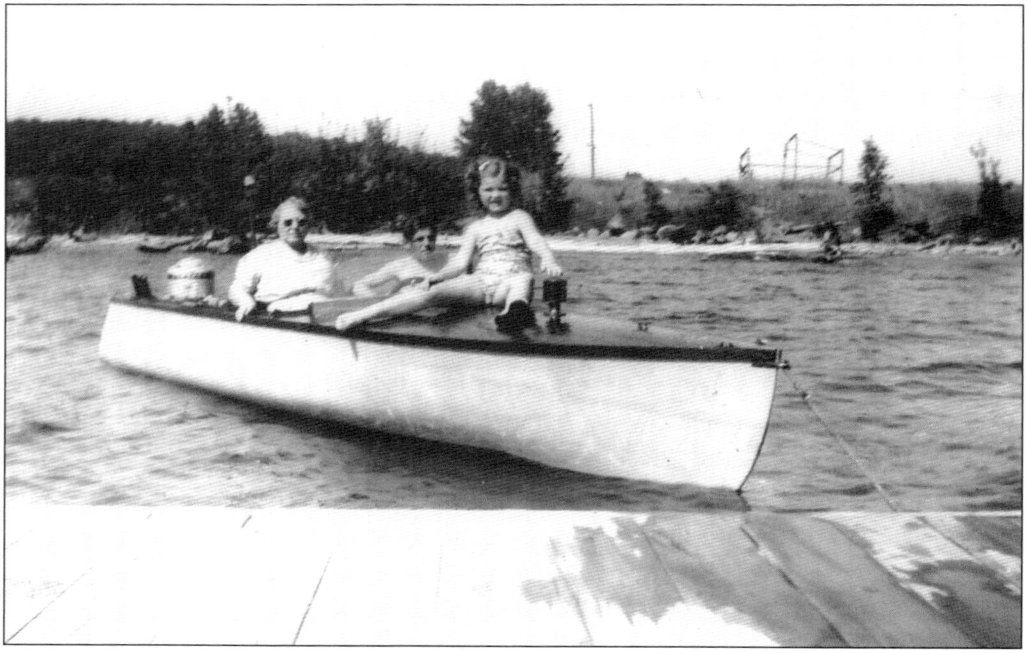

This Thompson runabout belonged to Ruth and George Robinson. Pictured in it are Ruth (left), Elmer Hess (center), and a young Barbara Slater on the bow in July 1940. In 1957, the boat was destroyed in the fire at Rudy Hayes's Boat Shop storage building. (Courtesy of Barbara Slater.)

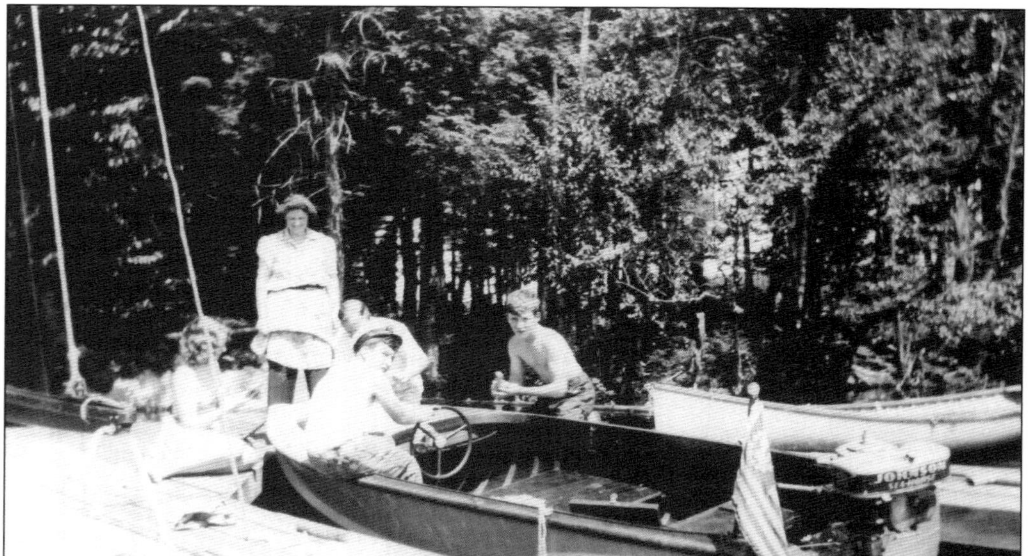

Outings and picnics on the large and small islands dotting Cranberry Lake were popular in the summer of 1941. Pictured here at Chair Rock Island with their Johnson 1941 outboard are Ann Franke Gurley (left, seated), Barbara Leavell Sr. (standing), Carl Franke (partly hidden), Rod Leavell (with hat), and Ted Lynch. (Courtesy of Ann Gurley.)

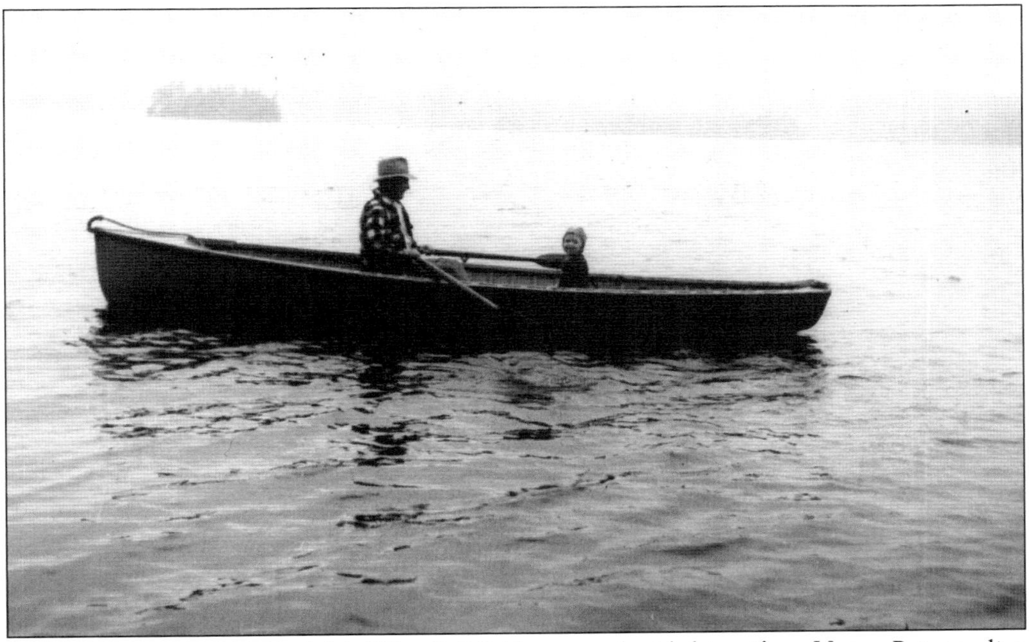

In the summer of 1934, Rudolph "Blondie" Friden moved with his wife to Union Point to live year-round. There is still no road access to Union Point. A rowboat that could also be used as a motorboat was necessary to provide for the trips up and down the lake. Friden is at the oars of his skiff (above), which could accommodate an outboard motor. Grandson Peter J. Ford is along for the ride in 1947. Below, Friden is shown next to the skiff with its Johnson outboard attached. (Courtesy of Mark Friden.)

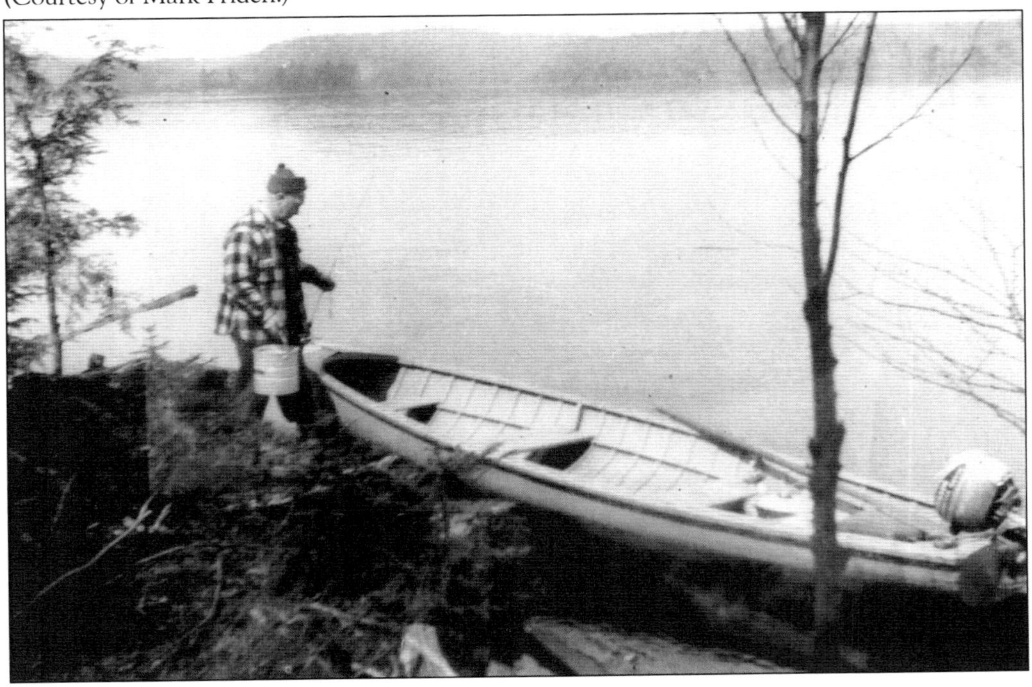

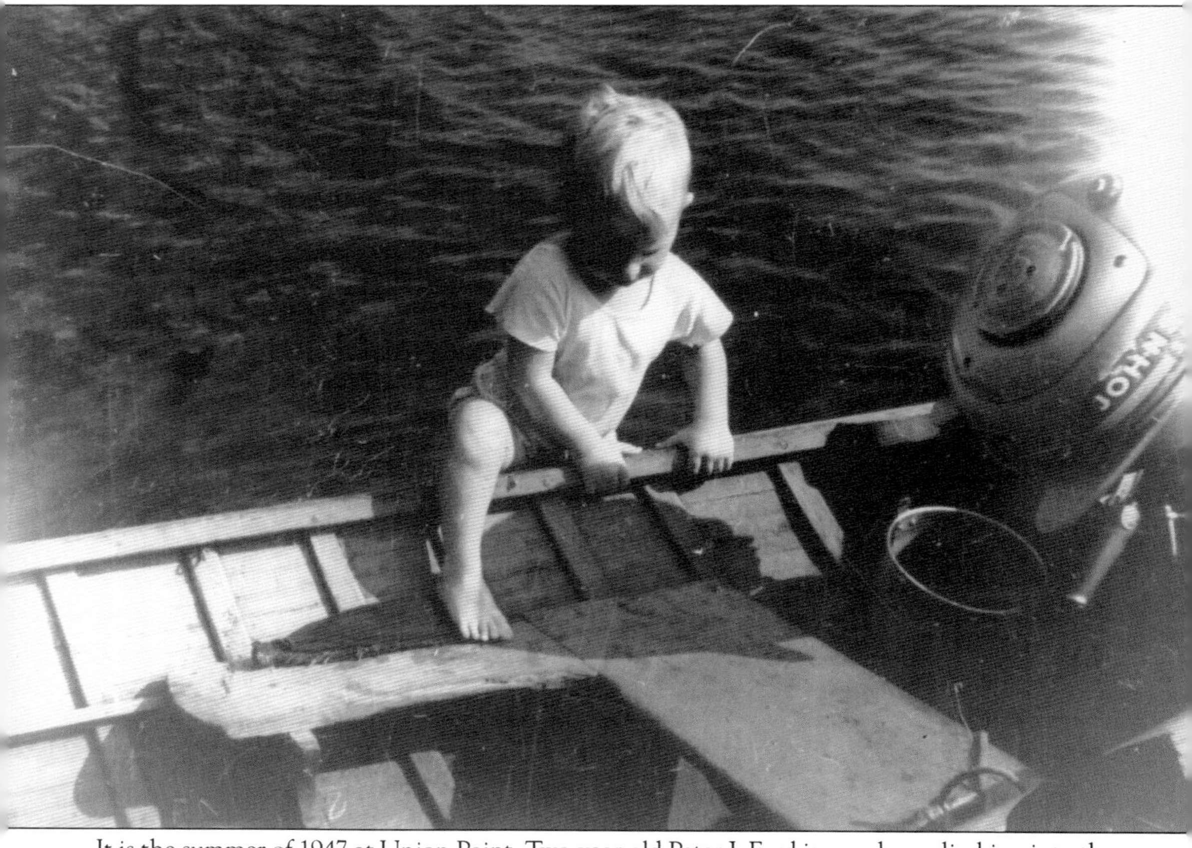

It is the summer of 1947 at Union Point. Two-year-old Peter J. Ford is seen here climbing into the wooden skiff owned by his grandfather Rudolph "Blondie" Friden, intent on reaching the stern seat. The Johnson outboard motor is just visible on the right, set in the up position. (Courtesy of Mark Friden.)

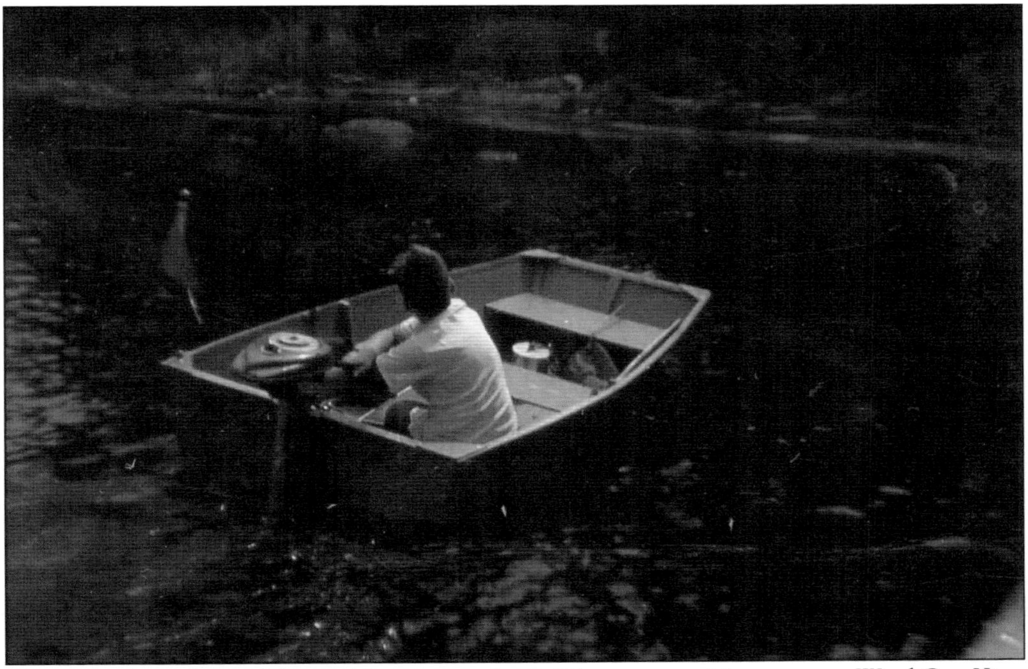

This eight-foot plywood boat with a one-and-a-half-horsepower Montgomery Ward Sea King outboard motor was built from a kit in the cellar of the Barr Pharmacy building in Canton by Robert Barr. David Barr (above) said he and his sister Kathy Barr Raymo (below, in boat) used the boat in the 1960s for exploring the lake near their camp on Columbian Road. He could get it up to a top speed of about seven miles per hour. It leaked all the time. His mother's rule for the boat was that it had to stay within sight of the camp. From time to time, they took it back to Canton and used it on the Grasse River and Little River to go up to Taylor Park. (Courtesy of David Barr.)

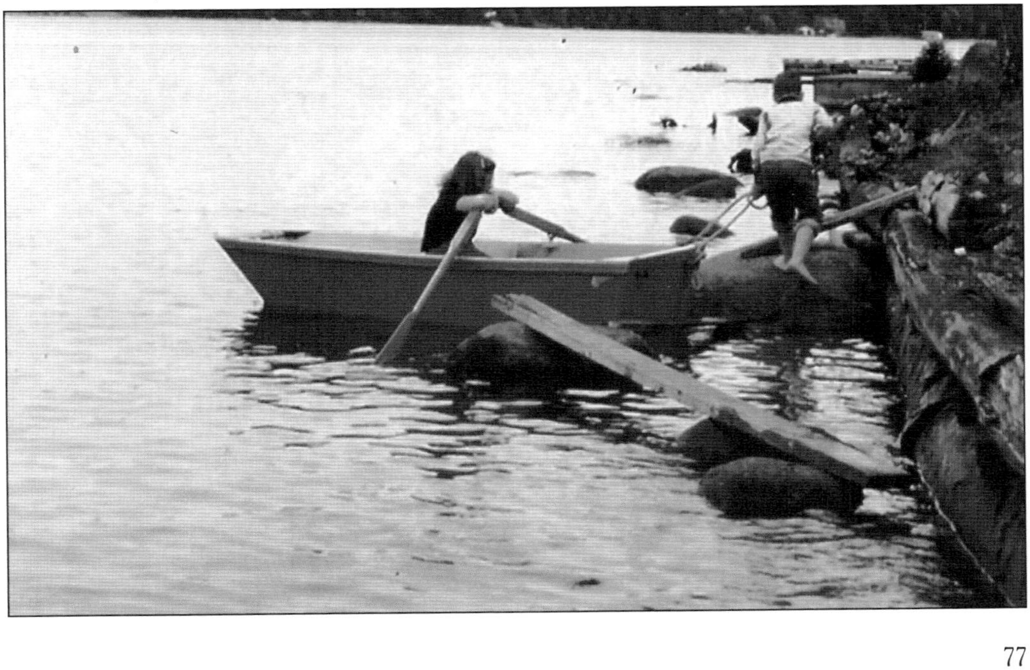

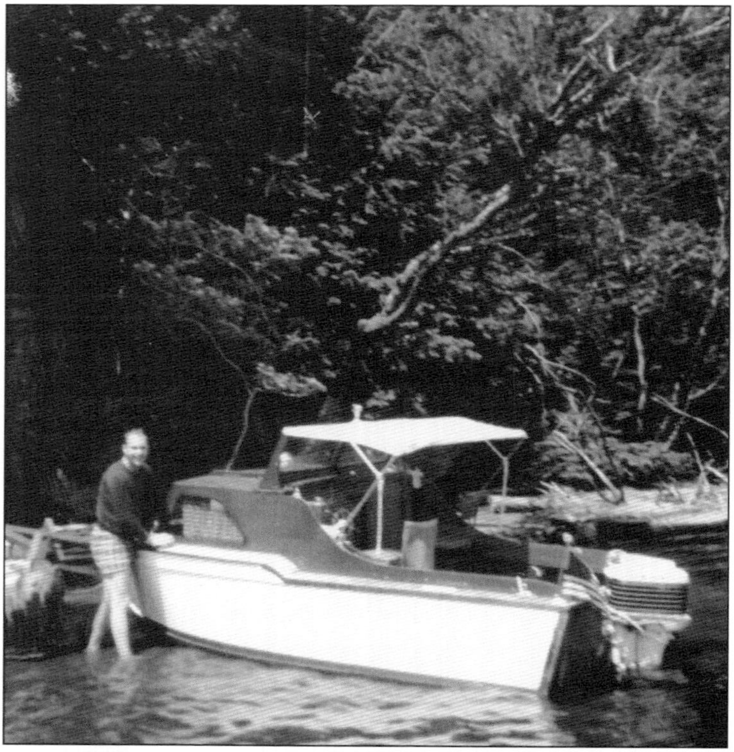

This Chris-Craft cabin cruiser was probably built from a kit between 1954 and 1956. It was owned by Wayne Morrow, former commodore of the Cranberry Lake Boat Club, and used on Cranberry Lake during the 1960s and early 1970s. The photograph was taken in Thompson Bay in 1962. Clint Cook, son-in-law of the owner, stands near the bow. (Courtesy of Phyllis Cook.)

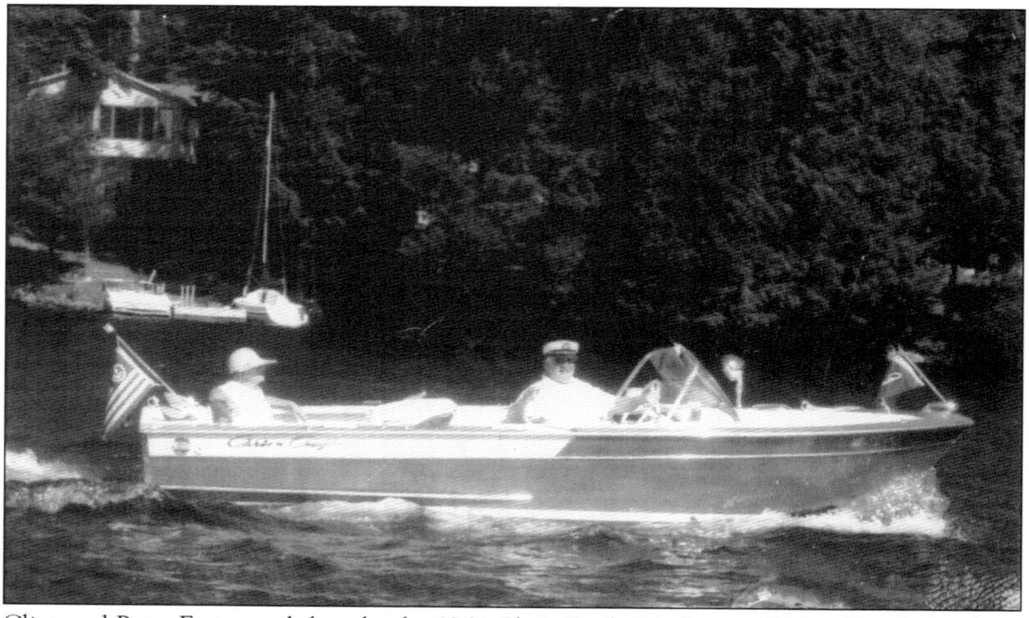

Clint and Patty Farnsworth bought the 1964 Chris-Craft *Pointless* in 2004 in North Carolina. It was built in 1964 but had been completely restored in 2000, down to the original upholstery style and colors. Clint is a former commodore of the Cranberry Lake Boat Club. He and Patty circle the foot of the lake many afternoons on a "cocktail cruise" just before sunset. (Courtesy of Clint Farnsworth.)

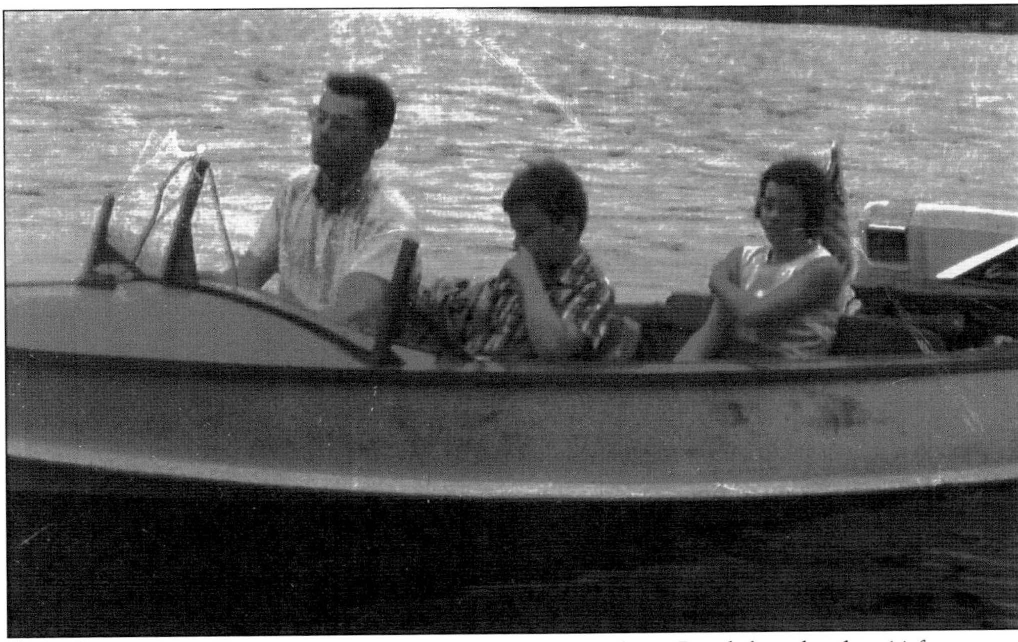

Roy Barr, a Canton pharmacist with a camp on Columbian Road, bought this 14-foot wood Thompson runabout locally around 1950. The original engine was a 25-horsepower Evinrude with a hand-pull start. Riding in it (above) in 1960 are Richard Barr (left, driving), David Barr (center), and Kathy Barr Raymo. Soon after that, the boat was updated. A new, larger windshield replaced the original one; a 40-horsepower Evinrude with an electric start took the place of the old engine. A canvas top was added. Riding in it in 1962 are Robert and Patricia Barr. (Courtesy of David Barr.)

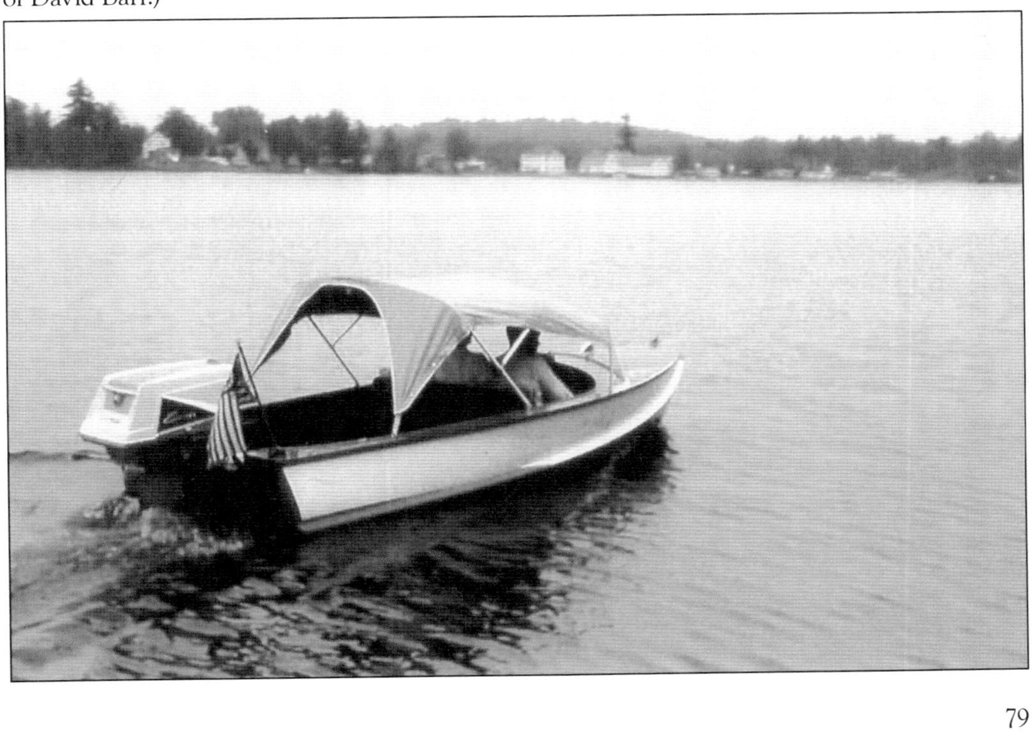

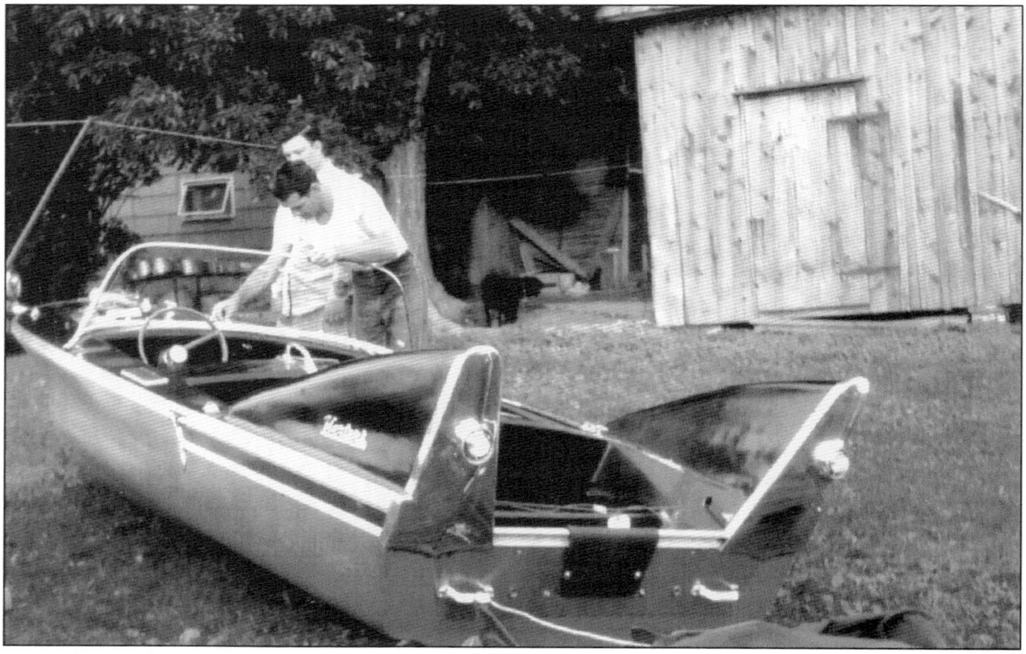

Manufactured in Minnesota by Herter's (a large catalog company, now Cabella's) for Otto Max Giraud, this boat was shipped to Brewerton by railroad. The photograph was taken on a farm there before it ever got to the water. It was made of fiberglass and was bright red with black Cadillac tail fins. Admiring it in 1963 are Donald Giraud (left) and an unidentified friend. (Courtesy of Ernest Giraud.)

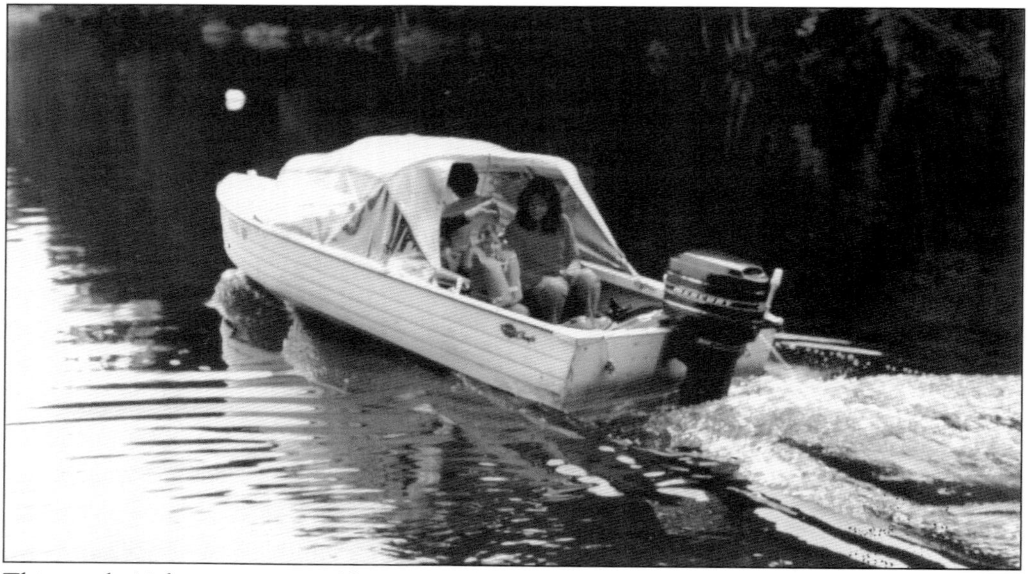

This sturdy 14-foot, nine-year-old Mirrorcraft aluminum runabout served the Lewis family camp at Chair Rock Flow well in all seasons of the year. It was powered by a 40-horsepower outboard motor and owned by the family from 1978 to 1986. It is seen above in August 1981, carrying a group of family visitors on an outing. It also carried many loads of building supplies into the camp over the years. (Courtesy of Charles Lewis.)

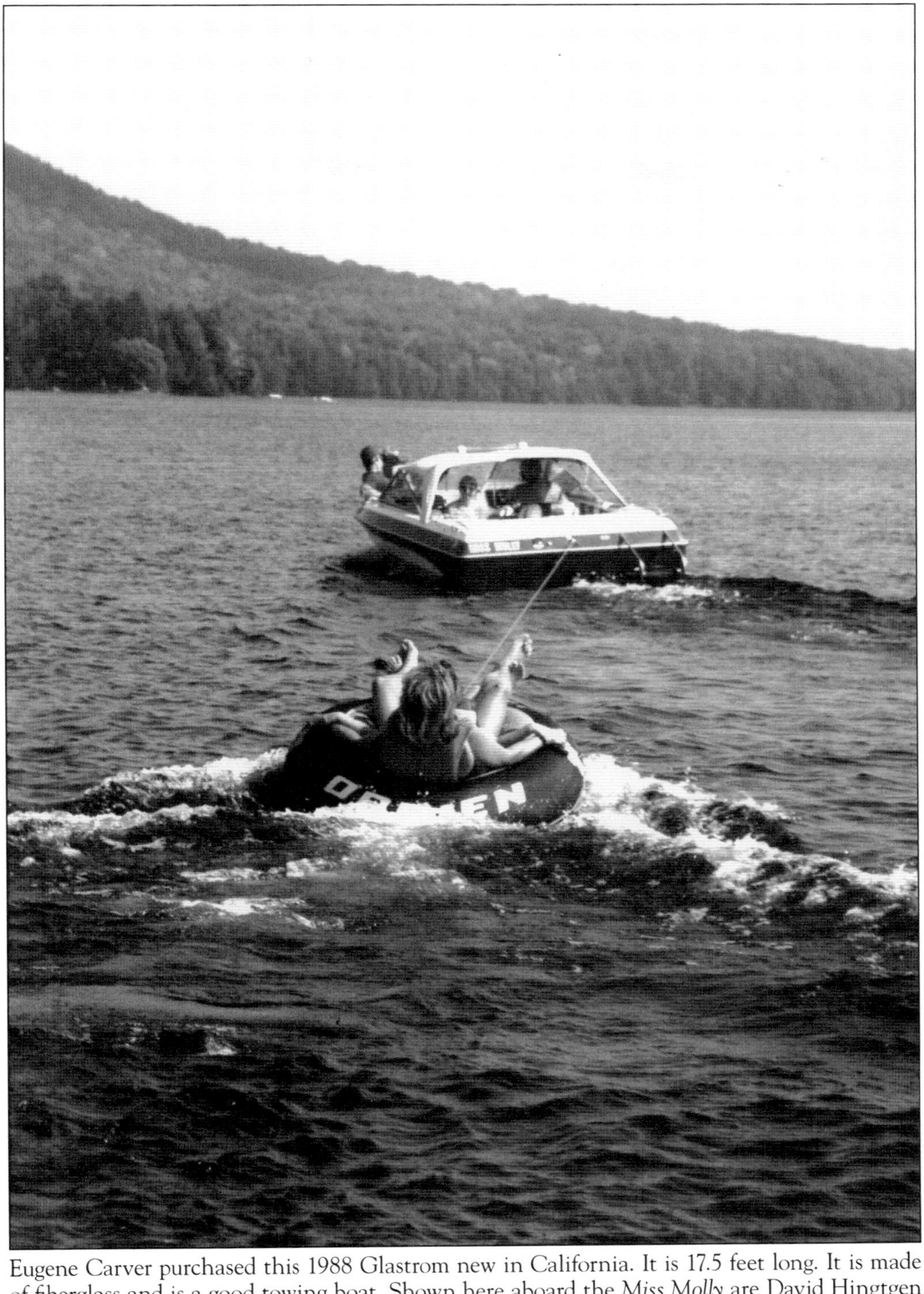

Eugene Carver purchased this 1988 Glastrom new in California. It is 17.5 feet long. It is made of fiberglass and is a good towing boat. Shown here aboard the *Miss Molly* are David Hingtgen (driving), his wife Sara Hingtgen in the tube, and their children and guests. (Courtesy of Eugene Carver.)

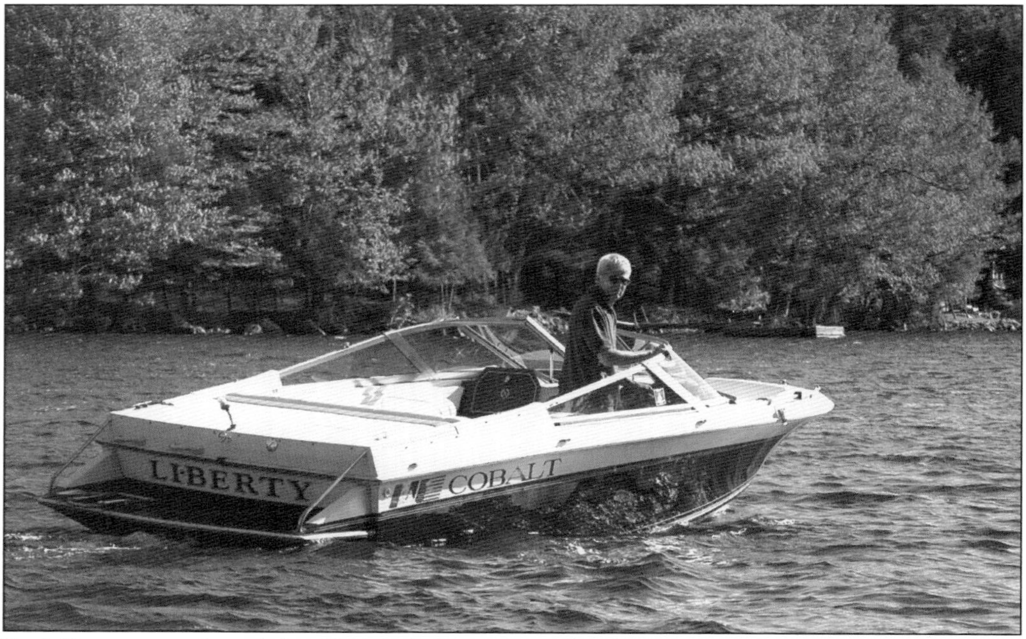

Fred Guevara purchased this 1989 Cobalt in 1999. This boat can reach a top speed of 50 miles per hour but is used primarily for casual cruising. Occasionally it can be seen towing water-skiers or tubers. Guevara (driving) knows of no other Cobalt boats on the lake. (Courtesy of Fred Guevara.)

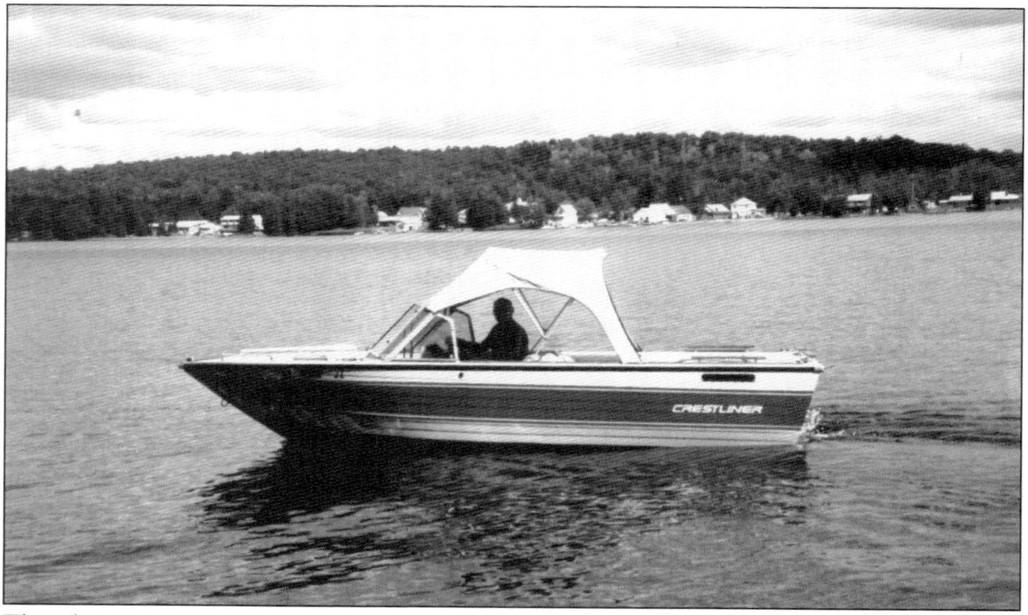

This aluminum Crestliner, purchased in 1999, is typical of family boats. Asked about the boat, Penny Giraud said, "She has seen eagles, loons, deer, sunrises, sunsets, and storms. She has carried cameras, blankets, picnic baskets, bathing suits, fleece jackets, hunters, fishermen, photographers, hikers, and dogs. She has taken canoes and kayaks to low-water bays and children to watch for shooting stars and is still in regular use in 2008." (Courtesy of Ernest Giraud.)

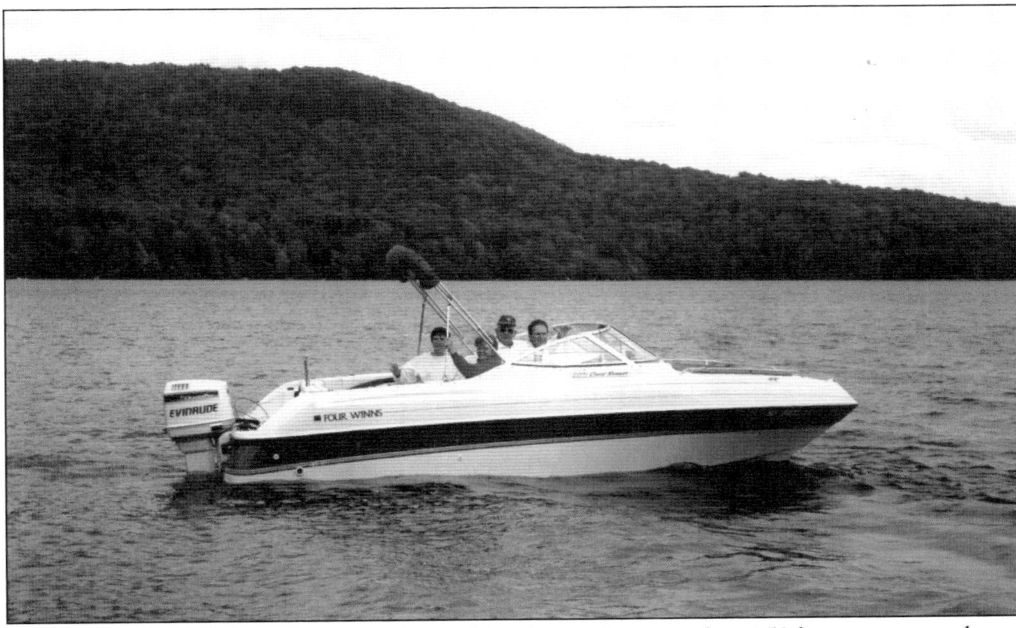

Richard Wilder purchased a new 20-foot 1995 Four Winns with a 150-horsepower outboard motor. Shortly afterward, he saw stress fractures in the bottom of the hull. After he sent a video of the problem to the manufacturer, it replaced it with the 1996 model. It is made of fiberglass and seats nine. Shown are, from left to right, Melissa Wilder, Barbara Wilder, Fred Wilder, and Richard Wilder. (Courtesy of Melissa Wilder.)

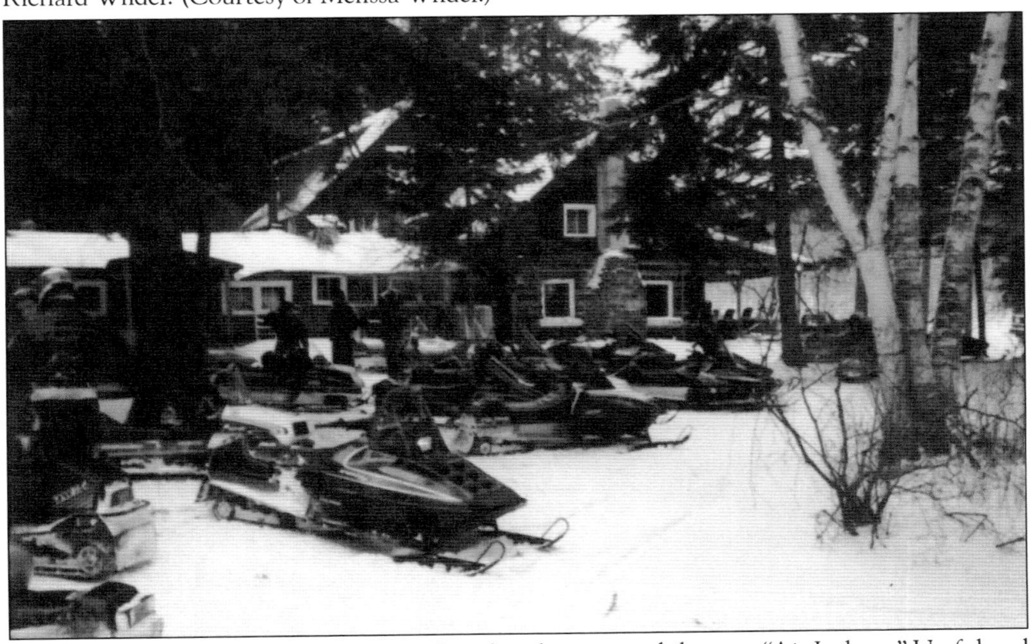

In *What the Hell*, in 1955, Jim Burnett referred to the snowmobile as an "Air Iceboat." Useful and fun, they are now a winter staple. Here a group gathers at the former Wildcliffe Lodge at the head of the lake, where there was a restaurant in the 1950s. The restaurant was also a favorite summer destination. It closed in 2000. (Courtesy of Barbara Slater.)

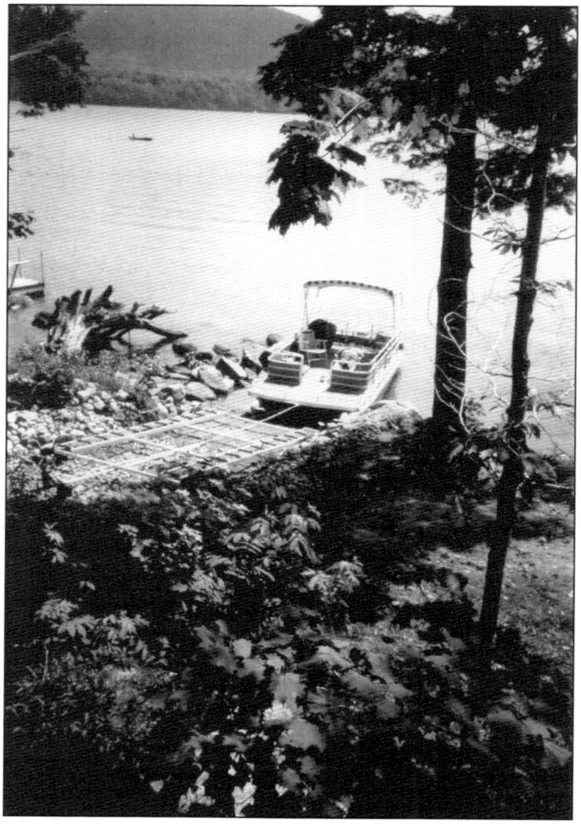

Priscilla Angelo purchased a 24-foot Harris pontoon boat with a 50-horsepower Evinrude outboard engine from H. Clark and Sons in Fisher's Landing in 1982. It is believed to have been the first pontoon boat on the lake. Her father designed the rail system at her camp on Columbian Road with a permanent winch (left) to haul it onto land for the winter. The rails were underwater in the summer. In 1983, she arranged for the St. Lawrence County Chamber of Commerce picnic at the New York State campground and then gave tours of the lake to the attendees from there. Angelo (below, third from right) in the *Bog Boat* is about to take a group of summer school coaches from St. Lawrence University on a lake tour. (Courtesy of Priscilla Angelo.)

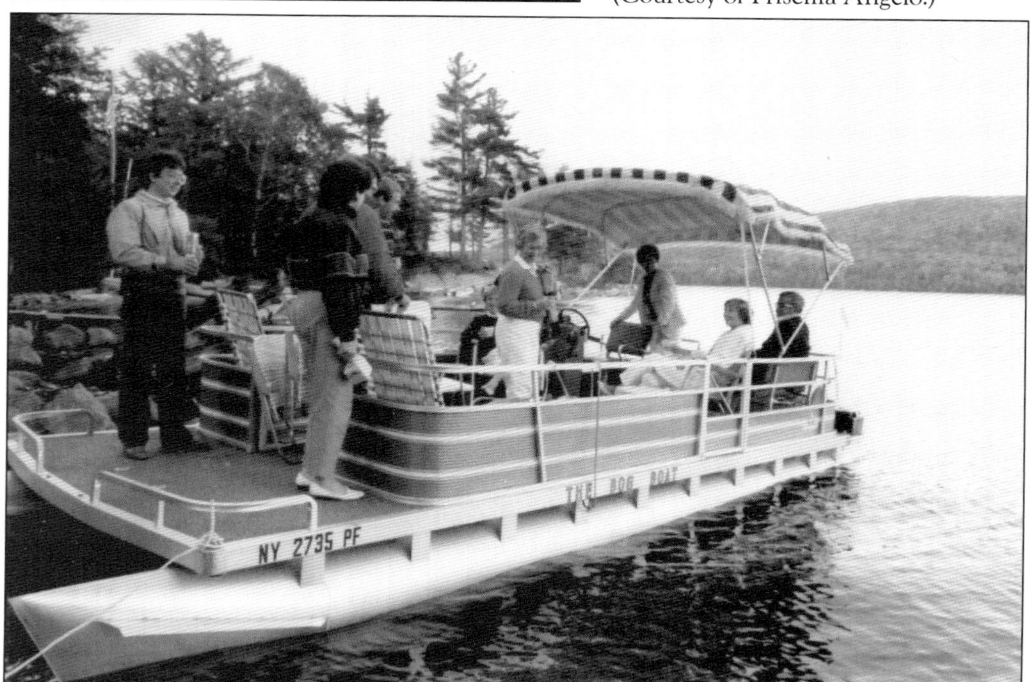

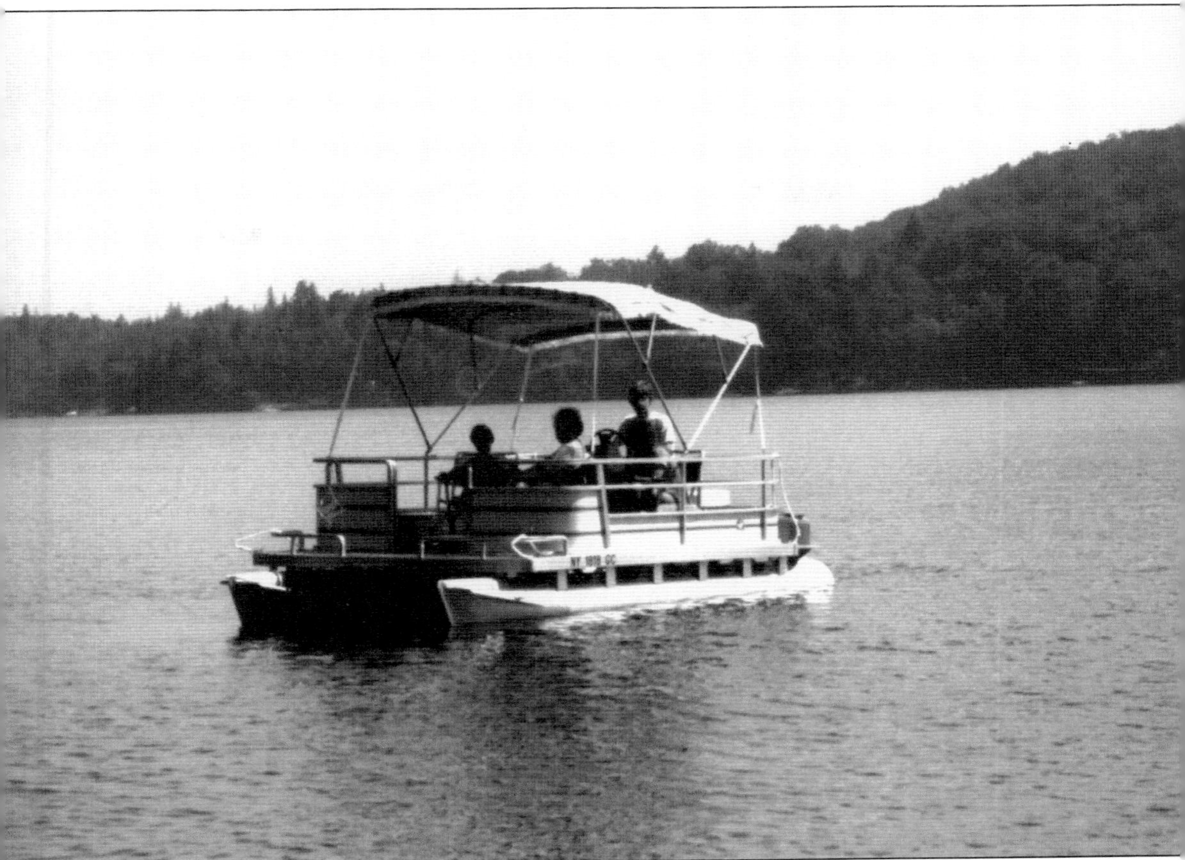

Gladys Kipp purchased the new Sandpiper model of the 1984 Harris float boat. It is 16 feet long including the pontoons; the deck size is 12 feet by 8 feet. It was a very early pontoon boat on the lake and is plain by today's standards, with one seat for the driver and a small console. Passengers step on easily from the dock and sit in folding chairs. (Courtesy of Edward Kipp.)

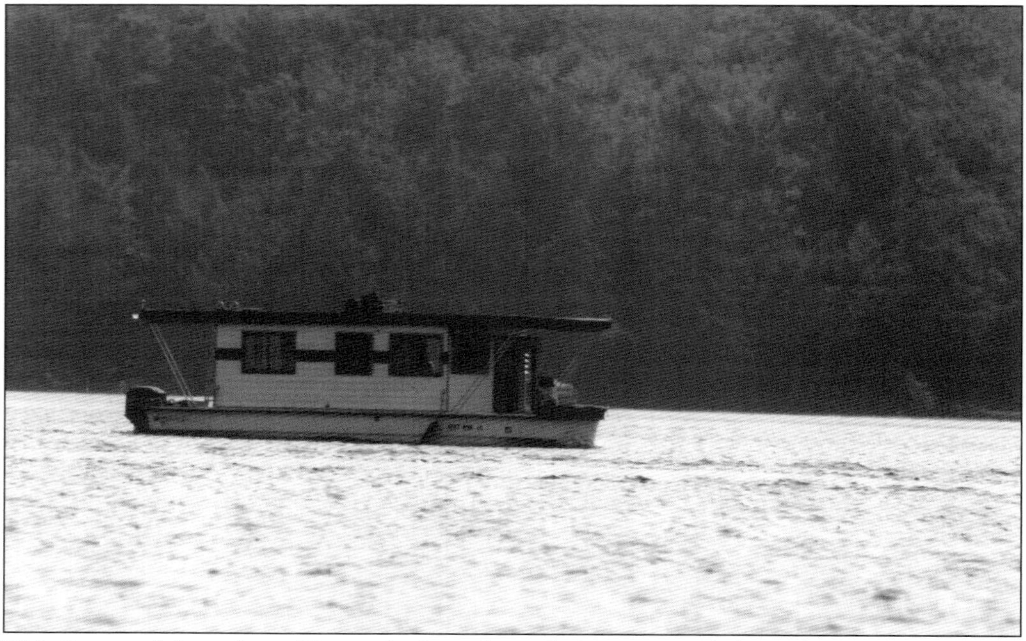

This Sportcraft houseboat, *Flo*, was built in the mid-1960s. It was dedicated in 2006 to Florence Burnett, longtime postmistress of Cranberry Lake. Paul and Marilyn Zimber put the boat in the lake in 2005. The Zimbers say it is "lots of fun, rain or shine, and great for camping up the lake to listen to the loons or watch a thunderstorm." (Courtesy of Paul Zimber.)

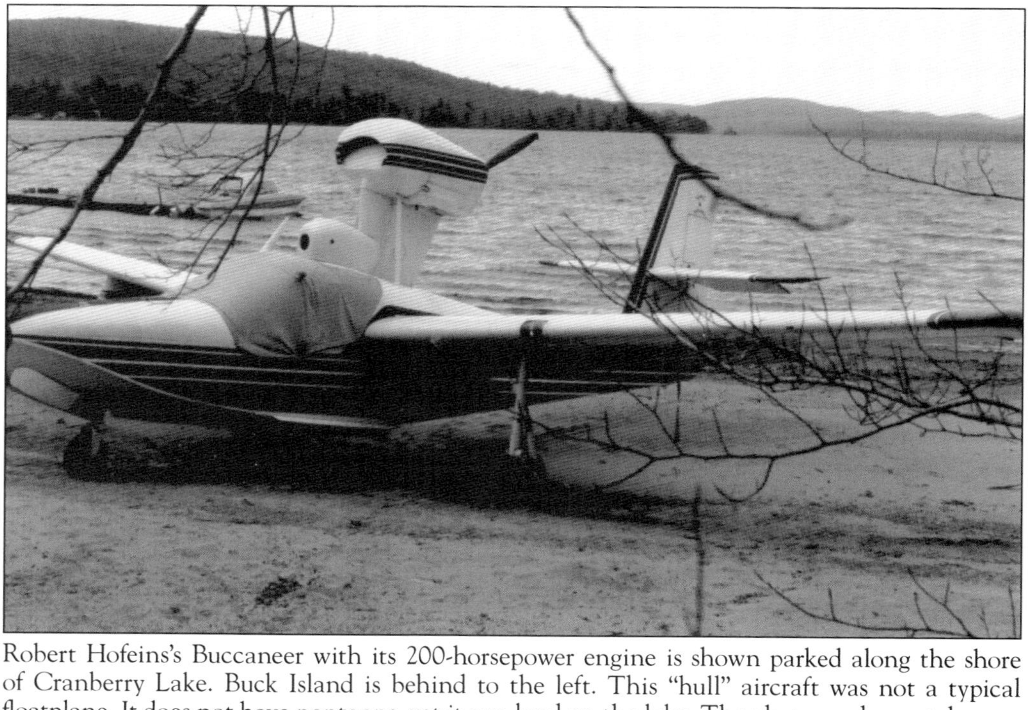

Robert Hofeins's Buccaneer with its 200-horsepower engine is shown parked along the shore of Cranberry Lake. Buck Island is behind to the left. This "hull" aircraft was not a typical floatplane. It does not have pontoons, yet it can land on the lake. The photograph was taken on November 5, 1986. (Courtesy of Charles Lewis.)

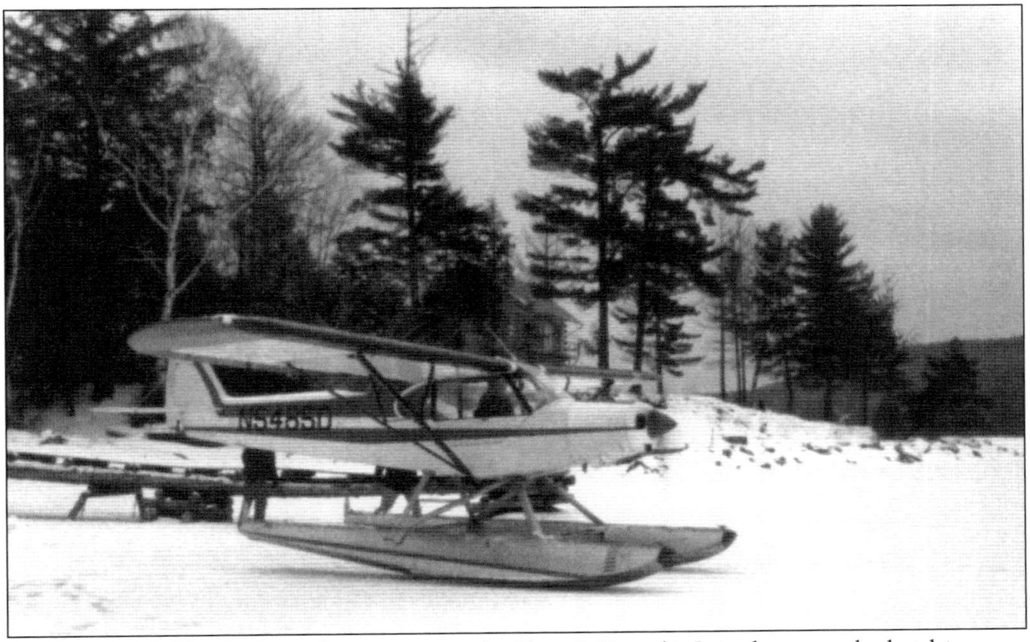

This 1947 J3 Cub was flown for many years by Kermit Remelé. It is shown parked at his camp dock (above) near Lightning Point during the winter of 1986. Local lore has it that a window blew out while flying, and William Barrett, a passenger, said, "Don't worry, I'll get it." He later went out with his snowmobile and retrieved it. While docked at the same spot in the summer of 1988 (below), Remelé stands on one of the floatplane's pontoons. He often gave rides. A floatplane will still occasionally appear over Cranberry Lake, most often at class reunion time at the Ranger School, offering rides to friends and graduates. (Courtesy of Mary Ann Remelé.)

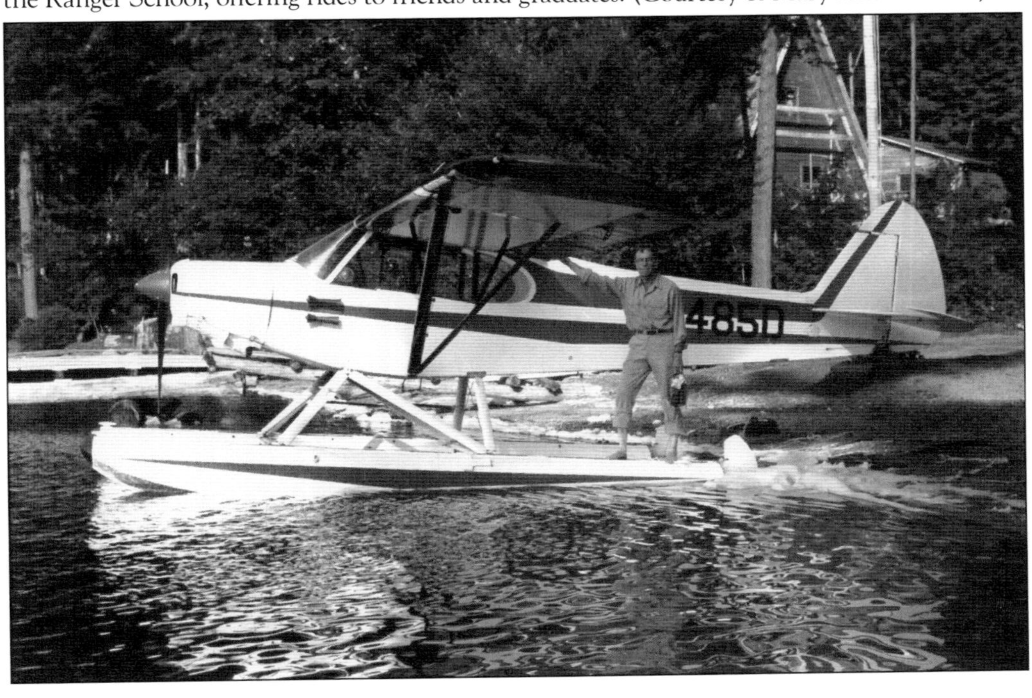

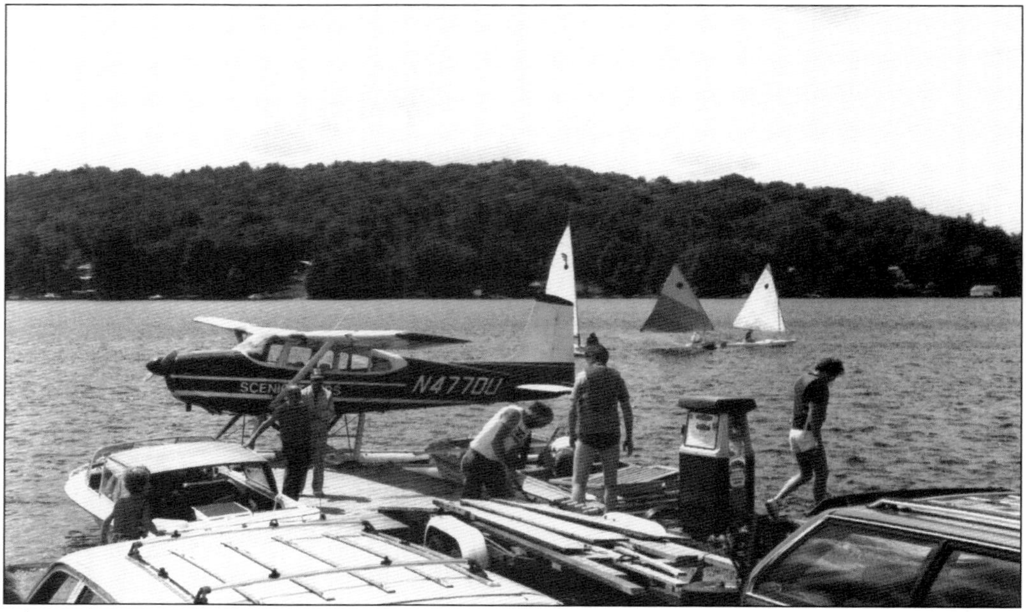

Clarence "Feets" Shelton, a current resident of Star Lake, would take Cranberry Lake residents and their guests for rides over the lake. On a clear, bright Adirondack day, the view was unbelievable. He flew a Cessna 172 floatplane, which had been built in 1966. In this 1987 photograph (above), it is parked at the Emporium Marina boat dock in Cranberry Lake. A 1992 photograph shows Shelton (below) waiting for customers. He is seated in front of Jeanne Reynolds Art Studio in Cranberry Lake. His rides were popular with both residents and tourists. (Courtesy of Jeanne Reynolds.)

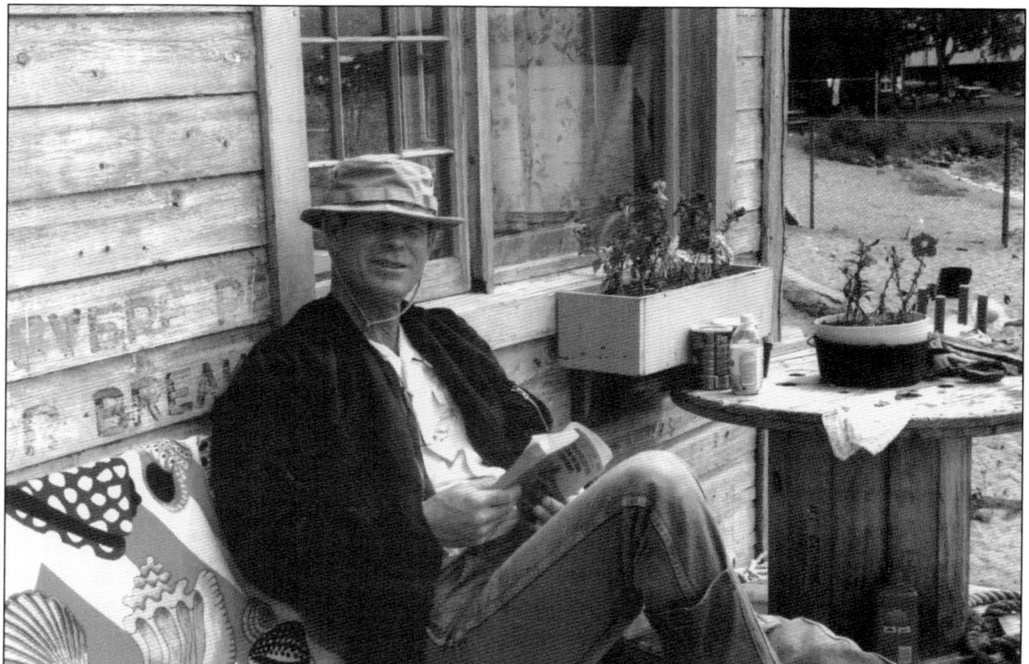

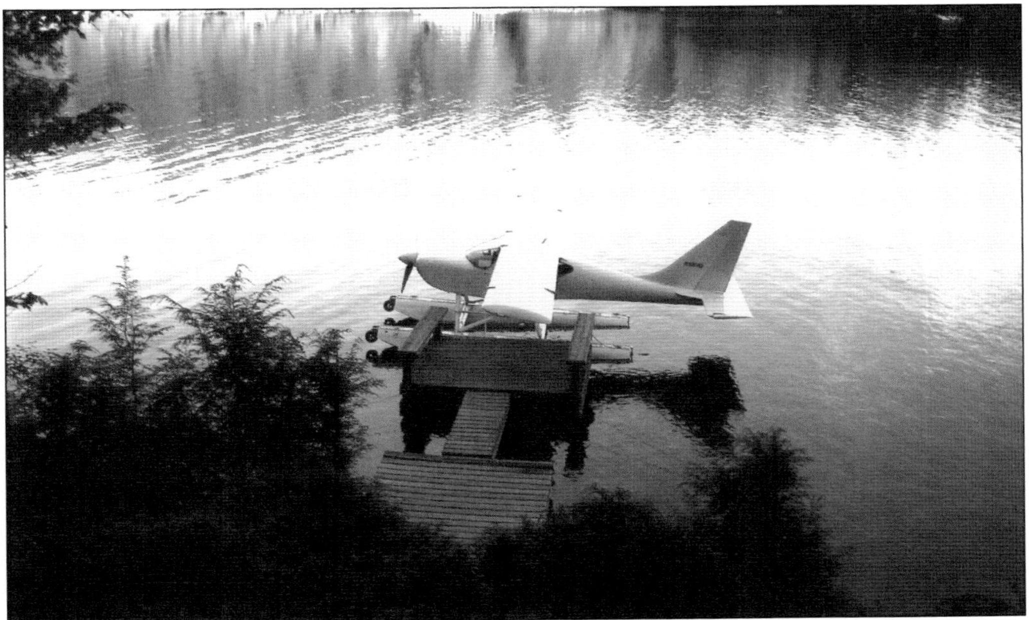

There are a lot of do-it-yourself people in the boat world. Robert Englert finished building this Glastar flying boat at home from a kit in 2004. It has a 200-horsepower engine and cruises at 120 miles per hour. It is seen several times a year parked in front of the Englert camp on Columbian Road. Englert built his first floatplane in 1996. (Courtesy of Robert Englert.)

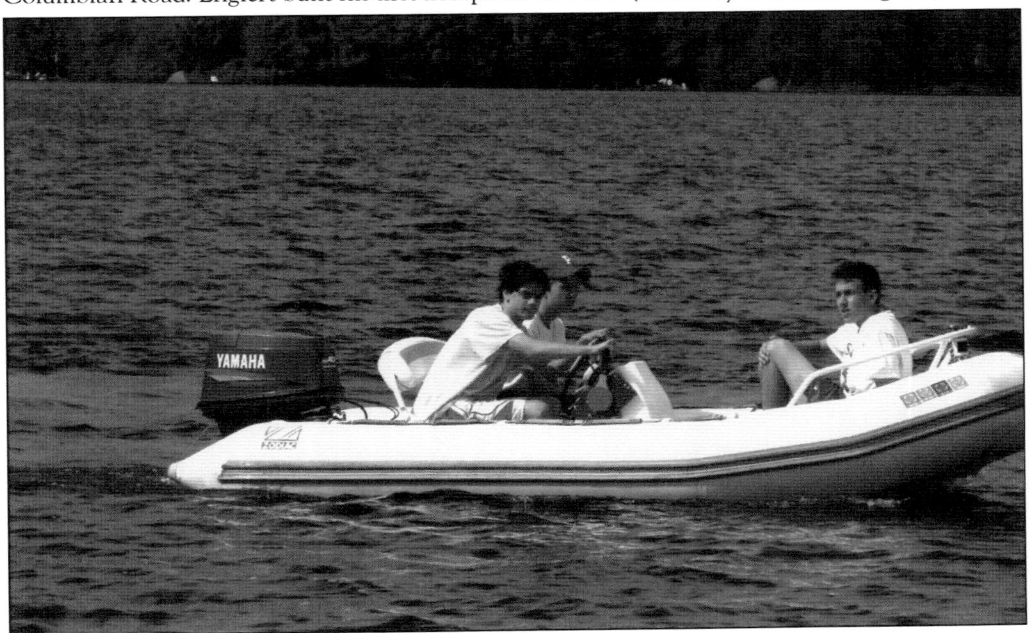

The *Peppermint Patty* is a 13-foot Zodiac. This is a yacht tender usually used with large oceangoing boats and is very safe in rough water. (The U.S. Coast Guard uses them.) Although not seen on lakes very much, the Zodiac is ideal for cruising inlets without worrying about damage to it. Pictured are, from left to right, Evan Betti (driving), Ryan Walters, Dan Lambert (in bow). (Courtesy of Patti Betti.)

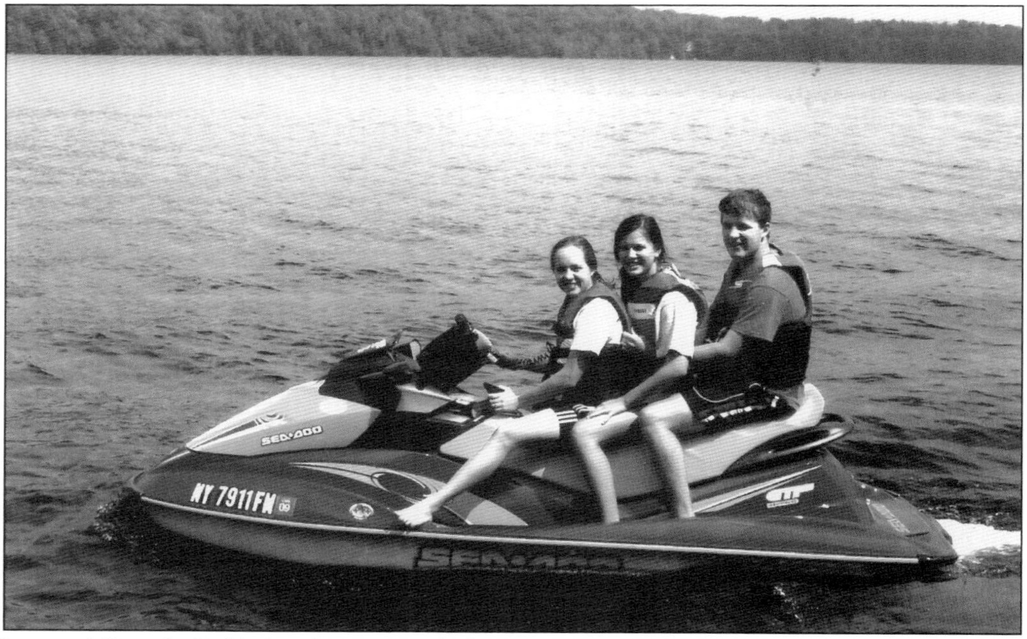

Lee and Beverly Fickbohm have owned their camp on Columbian Road since 1963. Their families spend two to three weeks every summer with them on the lake. Shown here on their 2005 Sea-Doo are grandchildren Katrina Briscoe (left), Dayka Williams (center), and Matthew Briscoe. Their grandmother takes it out on the lake as well. (Courtesy of Beverly Fickbohm.)

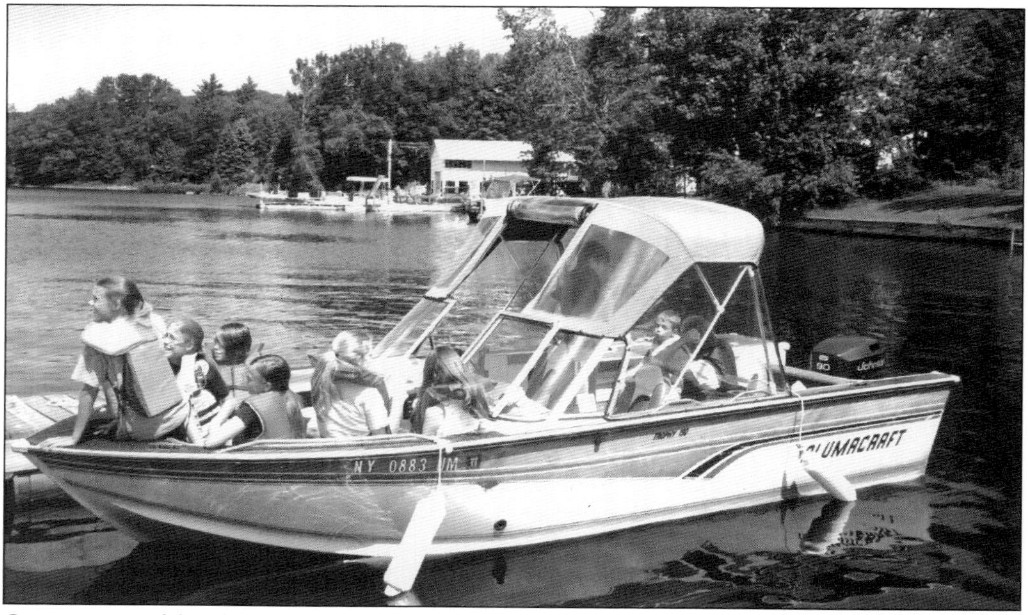

Generations of families have come to love Cranberry Lake. Camps and boats pass along. On South Bay is a camp, Whispering Pines, once owned by David Richardson, former commodore of the Cranberry Lake Boat Club, and his wife, Ann. They left it to their four children, Sara Ricalton, Lori McGrath, Jennifer Richardson, and John Richardson. Shown in their 19-foot Alumacraft are the boaters of the next generation. (Courtesy of Sara Ricalton.)

Four

REGATTAS AND RACES

In the beginning, a regatta meant a rowing, speedboat, or sailing race or a series of such races. Racing competitions began in 1909 with the Cranberry Lake Motor Boat Club's first regatta. That day's events also included a baseball game, swimming and canoe races, a picnic, a boat parade, music, and fireworks. On August 16, 1932, the *Canton Commercial Advertiser* wrote that there were more entrants than usual for the upcoming Cranberry Lake boat races, since other regattas were canceled. Then, on April 5, 1938, Vice Commodore W. A. Terwilliger wrote to Commodore George A. Terry, "I hardly think it is too early for you and I to begin talking about the Regatta. . . . With the recession some of the Mountain resorts are doing away with the speed boat part of their program due to cost." Terry agreed. "Dear Friend," he wrote in the July 1938 newsletter, "having decided that it would be impracticable to attempt a Regatta this year," the boat club committee arranged the following: along with swimming, diving, canoeing, running, and jumping events, it would have "boat racing [only] by Club members and their guests," followed by a buffet supper and dancing. By the 1950s, however, competitive boat racing on the lake was back. On September 14, 1951, the *Gouverneur Tribune-Press* printed the following: "Drivers of outboards from New England, New York, New Jersey and Pennsylvania vied for the championships in the Divisional Championship Outboard races held at Cranberry Lake Saturday afternoon. Winners of the largest racing event ever held in St. Lawrence County will compete in the national event this fall." The races were now sanctioned by the American Power Boat Association and sponsored by the Cranberry Lake Fire Department. In 1962, the Cranberry Lake Fire Department and the St. Lawrence Valley Boating and Racing Association sponsored a "spectacular" outboard regatta. In the 1990s, there were sailboat races with racers following hand-drawn maps. Today the Cranberry Lake Boat Club sponsors a banquet, boat parade, boat show, and picnic. For the centennial celebration in 2009, however, the Rochester Yacht Club was invited to hold sailboat races on Cranberry Lake. The regatta is back.

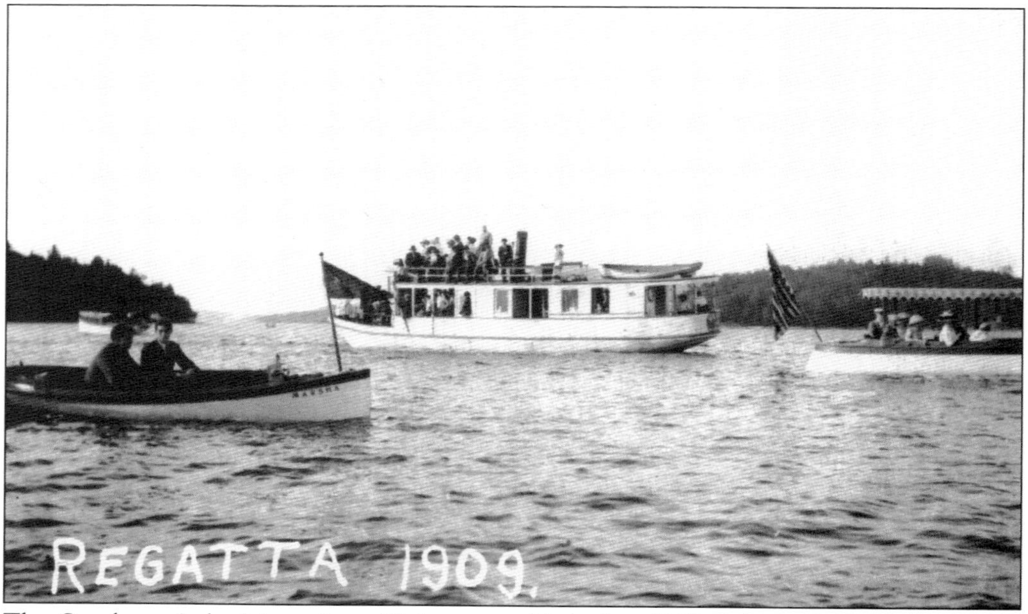

The Cranberry Lake Motor Boat Club was established in 1909. It began holding an annual regatta and field day jointly with the summer colony. Crowds came to enjoy the boat races, ball games, concerts, and fireworks. The workboat *Wanakena* (center), which usually carried mail, freight, and a few passengers, was filled that day with onlookers. The launch on the left is the *Marsha*. (Courtesy of Eugene Carver.)

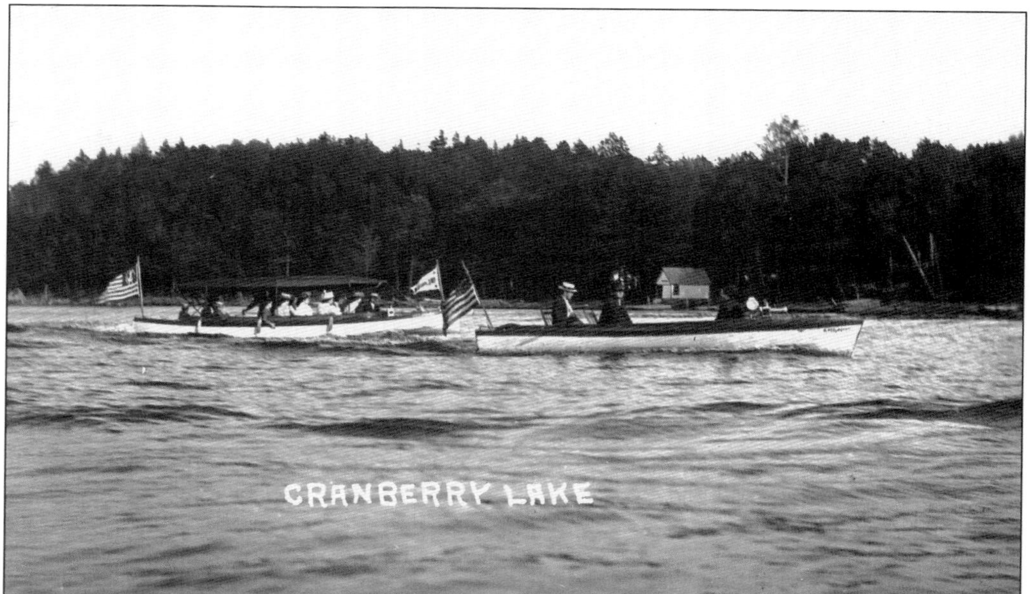

One picture postcard sent from Regatta Day 1909 reads, "Howard, Leland and a cousin of Geo. are in the back of the boat. We were in the act of going past Cash Ford. The boat in the rear is ours. Perhaps you can pick out some of us. Axtells [*sic*] people and Dr. Cramers [*sic*] people were with us besides some others from down the lake." (Courtesy of Susan Smeby.)

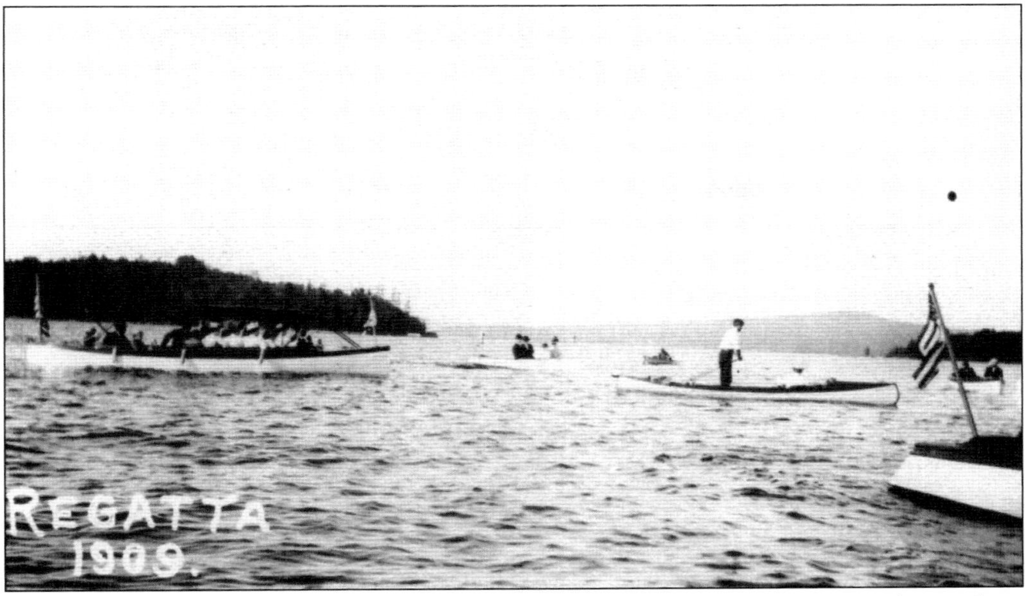

Regatta Day brought together a large company of cottagers, campers, tourists, and motorboat enthusiasts and gave the residents a gala day long to be remembered. Groups of four to a dozen or so filled flag-adorned motor launches. A boat flag was given for the best-decorated boat in the parade. (Courtesy of Eugene Carver.)

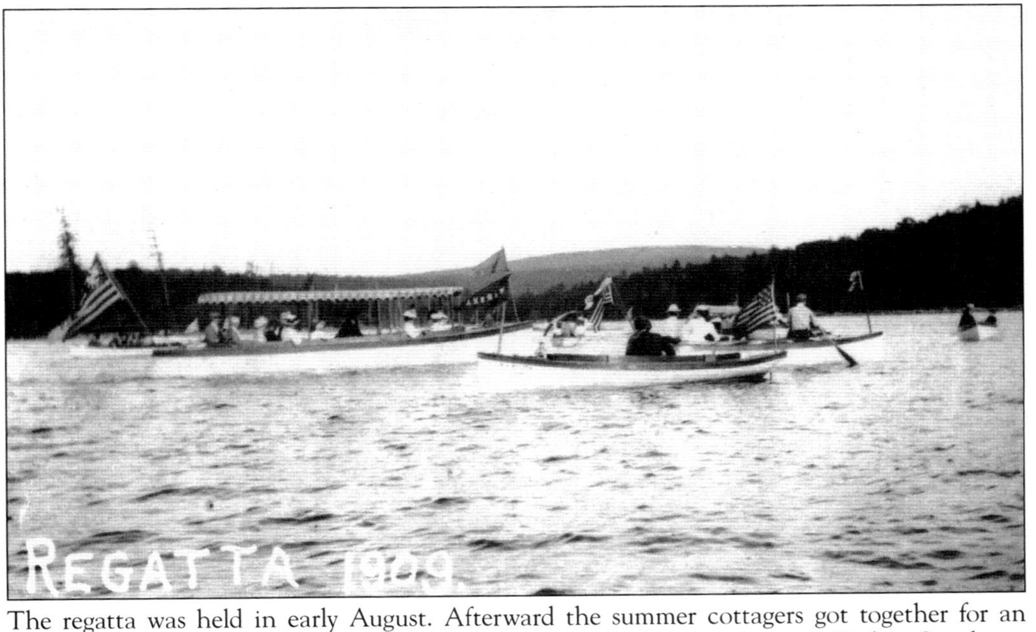

The regatta was held in early August. Afterward the summer cottagers got together for an old-fashioned basket picnic "at some convenient and charming point." Today Cranberry Lake Boat Club members continue the tradition with a picnic at the Pine Cone Restaurant's pavilion on the Oswegatchie River in August, featuring chicken from the grill. (Courtesy of Eugene Carver.)

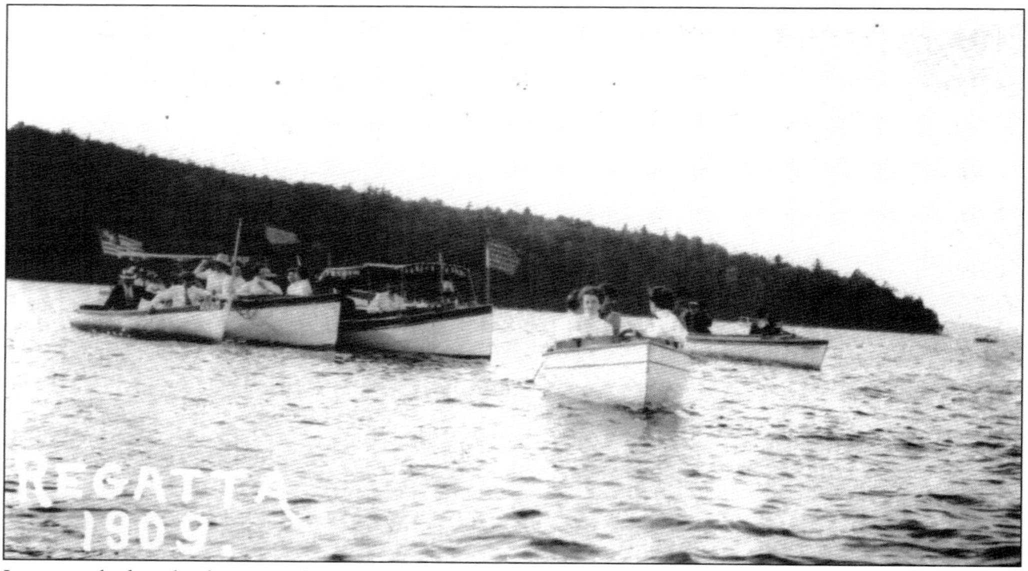

In an early foreshadowing of a 21st-century football tailgate party, five motor launches (one with canopy) are filled with well-dressed partyers on the day of the first Cranberry Lake Motor Boat Club regatta in 1909. Some appear to be tied together. The day gave everyone an opportunity to become better acquainted and promoted good fellowship among members and friends. (Courtesy of Eugene Carver.)

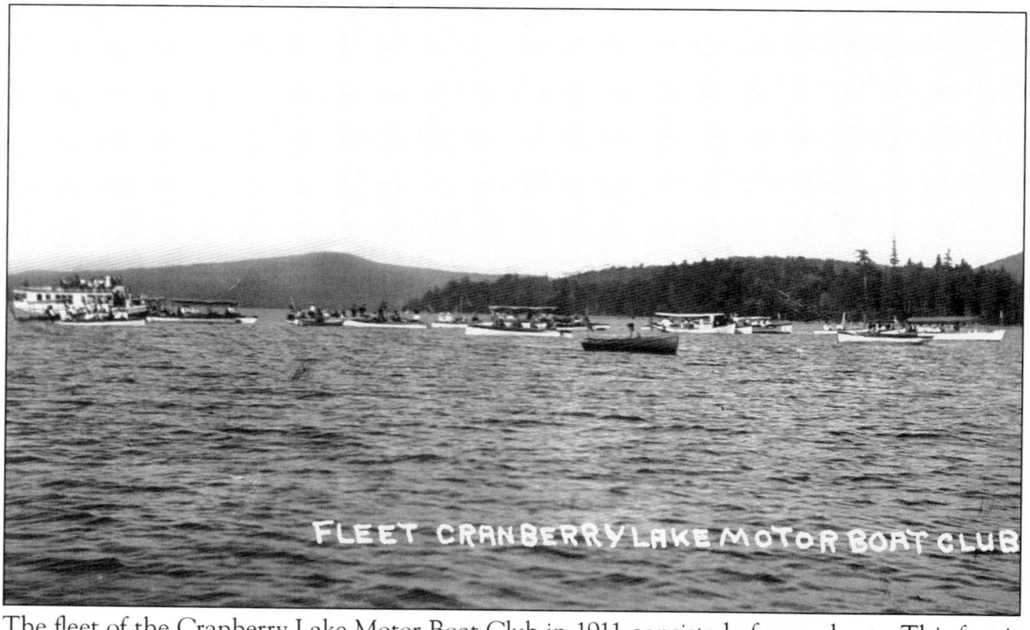

The fleet of the Cranberry Lake Motor Boat Club in 1911 consisted of many boats. This fact is underscored by the writing on the back of this unsent postcard: "Here are only about one-half of the boats that were out that day. See if you can find ours." (Courtesy of Susan Smeby.)

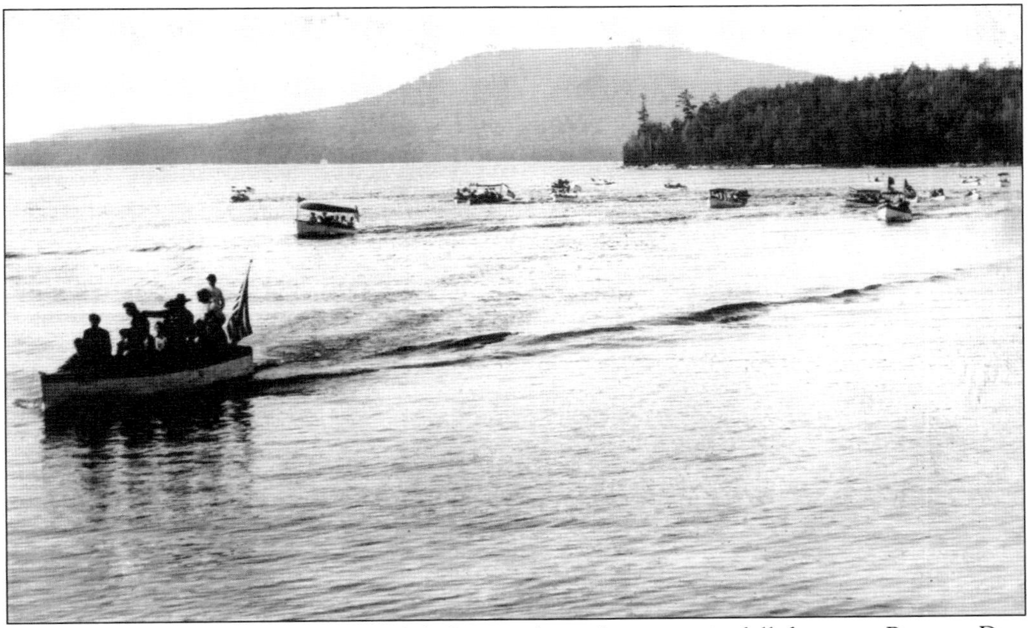

The Cranberry Lake Motor Boat Club fleet took to the water in full force on Regatta Day, August 16, 1911. Charles E. Leach was the fleet captain that year. Motor launches of various sizes, filled with participants (above), leave their wake near Buck Island (right) with Bear Mountain in the far distance. Meanwhile, several persons gather dockside near the Indian Mountain Club. The steamer *Helen*, leaving the dock with a full complement of passengers (below), offered excellent viewing from its top deck. (Above, courtesy of Eugene Carver; below, courtesy of Barbara Slater.)

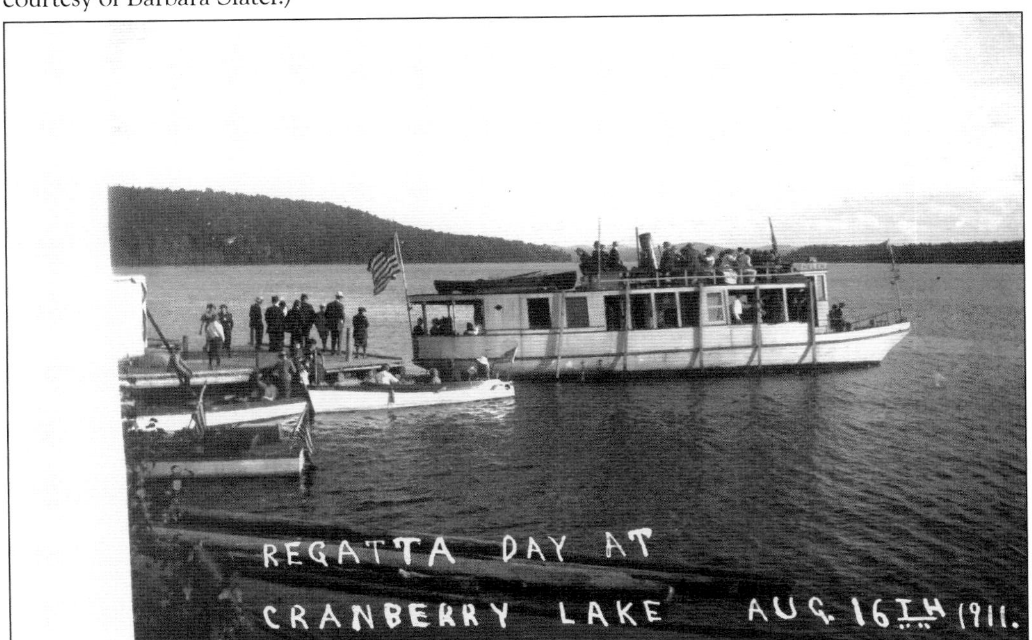

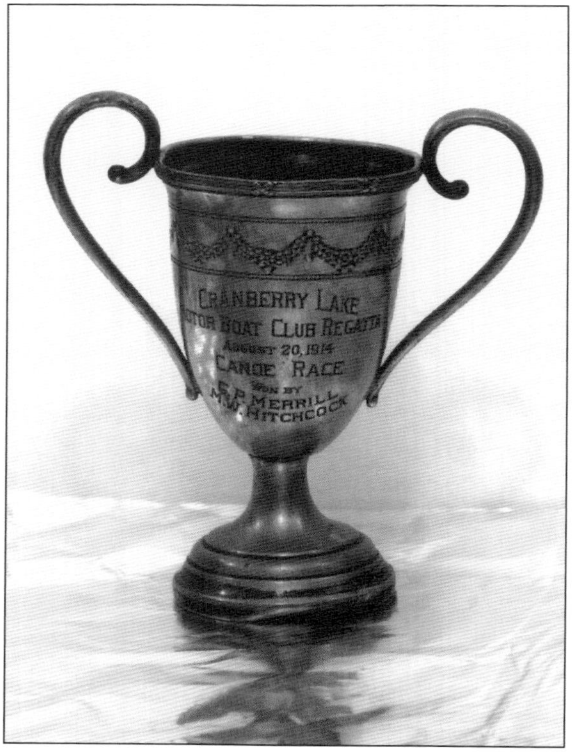

Pewter cups were awarded as prizes during the August 20, 1914, regatta. Two are in the possession of Clifton town historian Jeanne Reynolds. One is for canoe racing (left), won by G. P. Merrill and M. W. Hitchcock. The second is for swimming (below), won by H. Y. Beresford. Prizes of this nature were cherished by the families. (Courtesy of Jeanne Reynolds.)

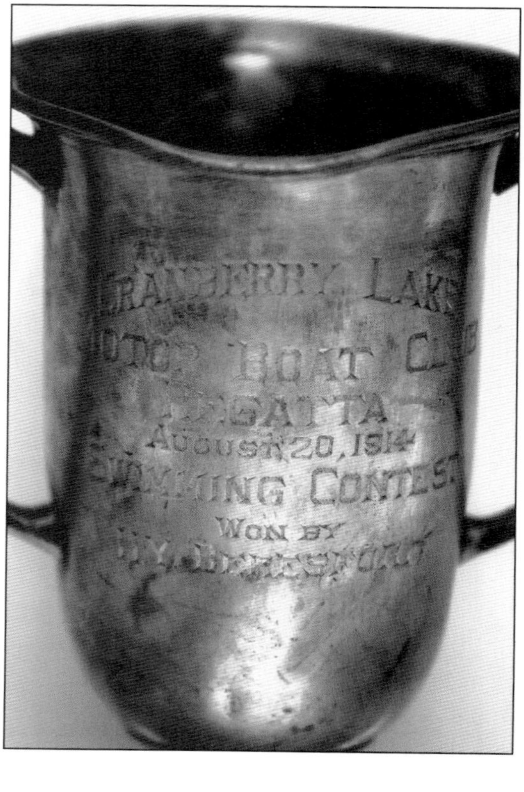

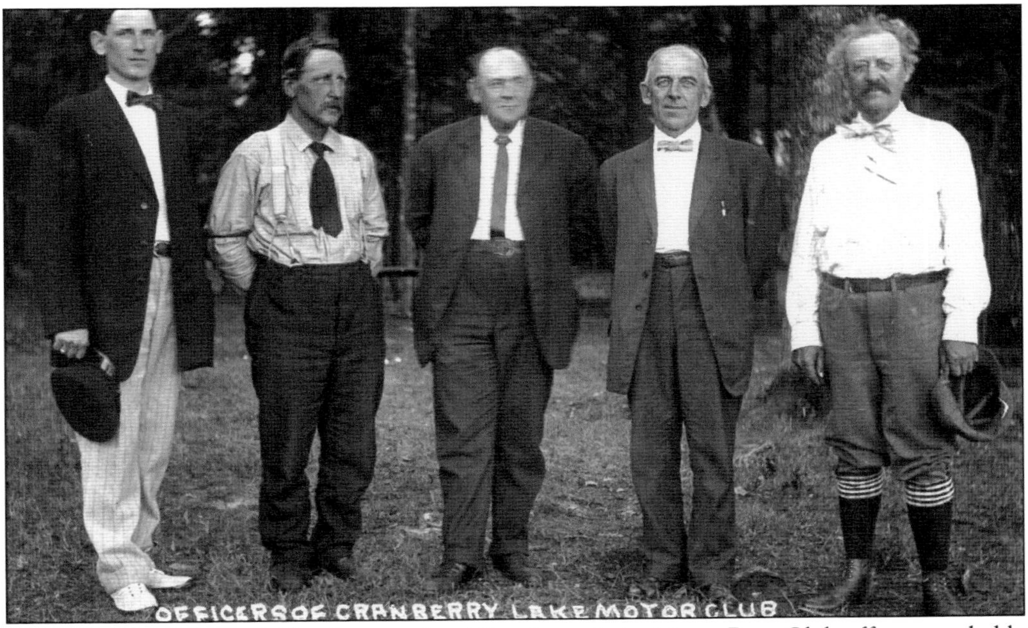

Here is the earliest available photograph of Cranberry Lake Motor Boat Club officers, probably taken in 1911; four are definitively identified. They are, from left to right, either Richard Jesup, owner of the Indian Mountain Club, or Baird Bissell, owner of a sawmill in Cranberry Lake; Charles E. Leach; Rev. J. Foster Wilcox; William F. Andrews, who operated the Rich and Andrews General Store in Wanakena; and Judge Irving G. Vann, first commodore of the boat club. In 1915, Wilcox was presented with a silver loving cup, recognizing his service as commodore and his authorship of *Cranberry Lake, New York, and the Western Adirondack Region*, a booklet published by the Cranberry Lake Motor Boat Club in 1915 for free distribution to promote the Adirondack wilderness. (Above, courtesy of Mark Friden; below, courtesy of Jeanne Reynolds.)

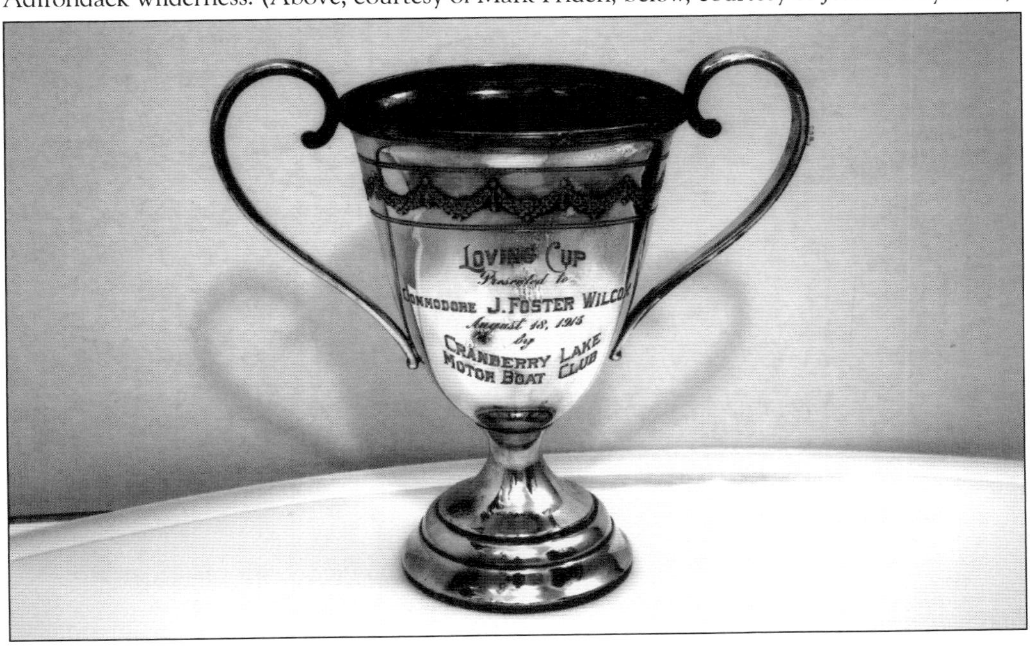

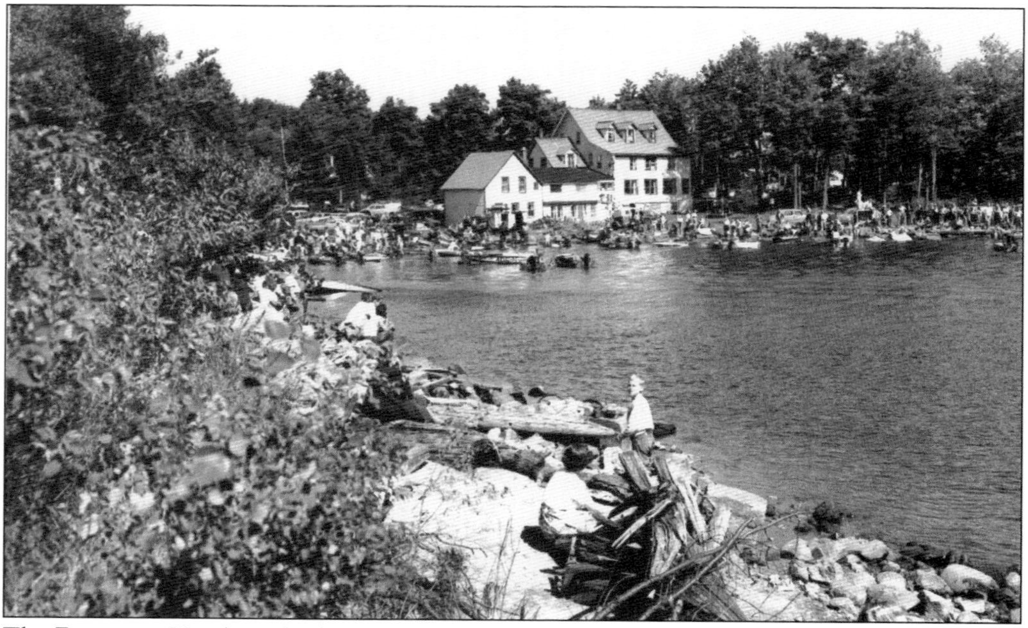

The Evergreen Hotel was built in 1896 and had a panoramic view up the lake from Cranberry Lake village. William MacAleese Jr. was running it in the early 1950s. Boats and spectators gathered in front of the hotel are preparing for divisional outboard races that were run in the years after 1945. The hotel bar was a popular spot for dances during the period. (Courtesy of Barbara Slater.)

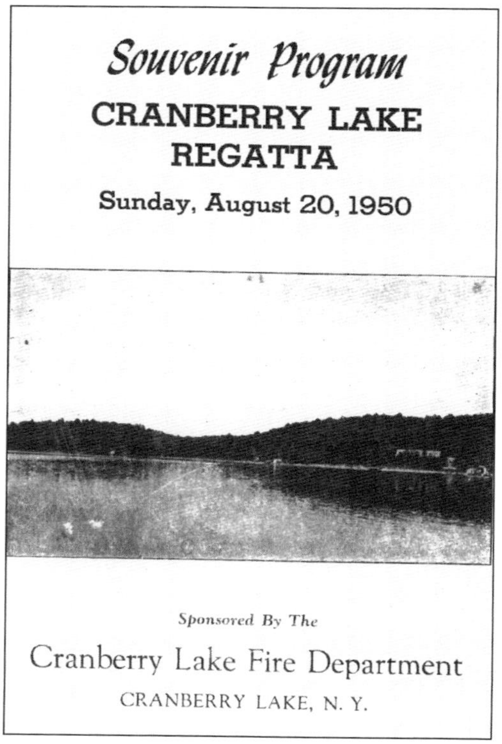

The 1950 regatta was sponsored by the Cranberry Lake Fire Department. Local businesses bought advertisements in this souvenir program. William MacAleese Jr., who owned the Evergreen Hotel, donated the $10 first prize for best-decorated boat. Floyd Davis gave $5 for second place. Others donated cups for swimming races. The fire department donated cups for the boat races that went around Birch Island and back. (Courtesy of Jeanne Reynolds.)

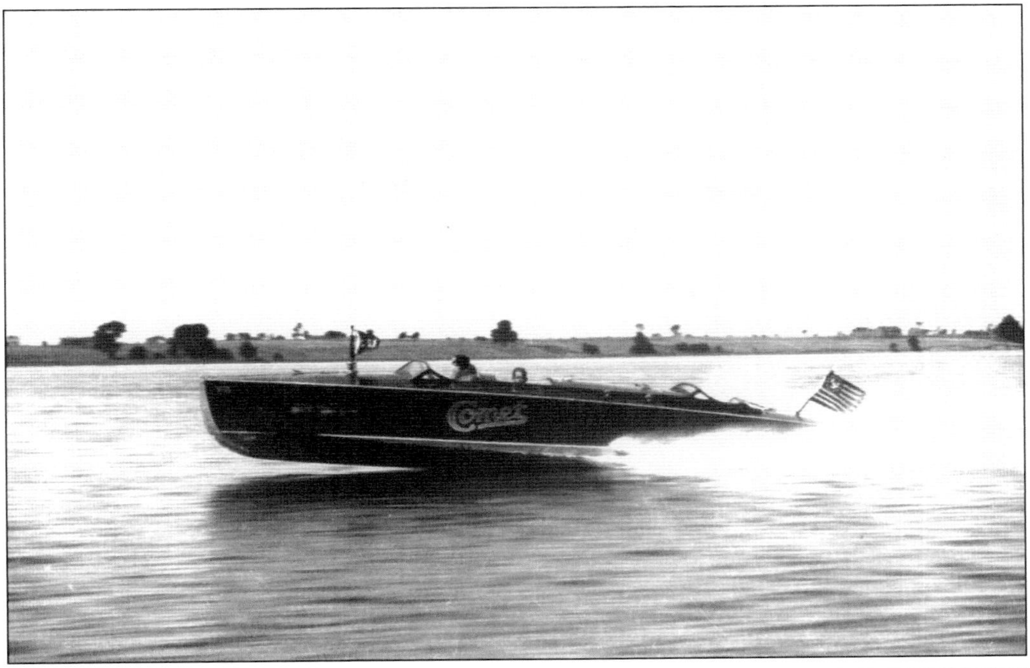

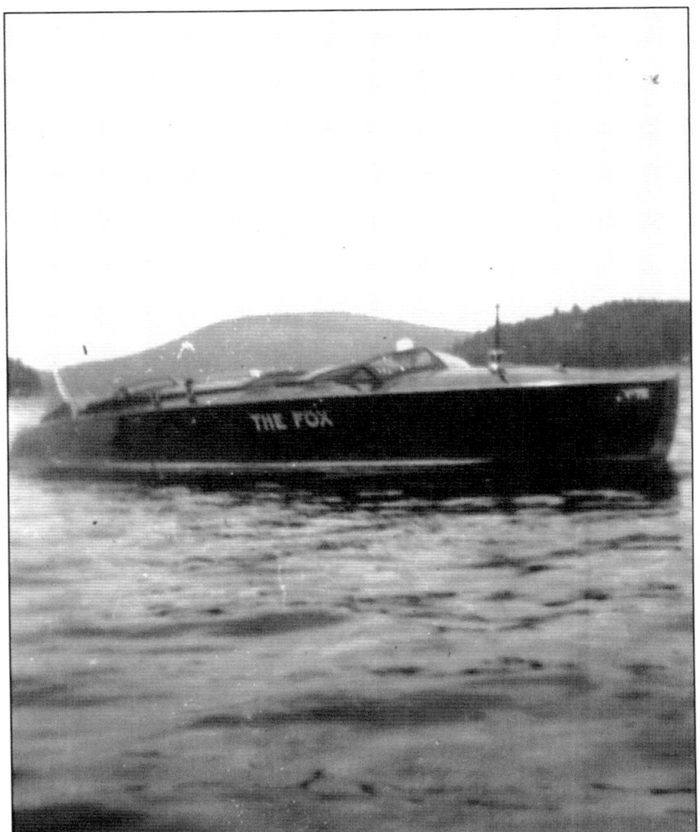

The Fox was a 1926 mahogany inboard runabout called the *Comet* by its first owner on the St. Lawrence River (shown above on the river). Around 1930, Dr. Walter Fox Smith purchased it, brought it to Cranberry Lake, and renamed it *The Fox* (right with Buck Island on the right). It was here that Smith drove the boat in a heyday of regatta races on the lake. The boat was so fast, it is said that natives and guides would bet their houses on it. In one infamous race, a competitor added ether to his gas to gain an advantage. "Dad just put the throttle to the floor and *The Fox* came out the winner by a hair," said granddaughter Grace Smith in a 1984 letter. The boat is being restored. (Courtesy of the Antique Boat Museum.)

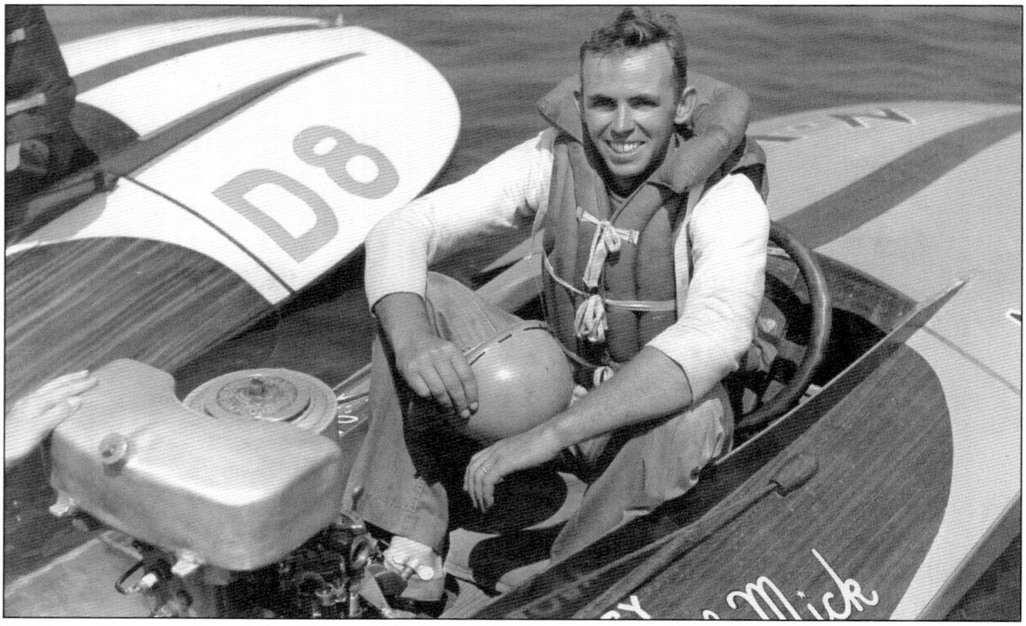

William Barrett piloted this Racing Hydro in the late 1940s. A driver would kneel in his plywood craft. Many of them were powered by Johnson KR engines. Barrett's boat was named *Lil Mick* for his wife, Margaret. Julie Higgins remembers watching from a rock as speedboats such as this one careened around Buck Island and saw two flip over. There were official spotters stationed on Buck Island. (Courtesy of William Barrett.)

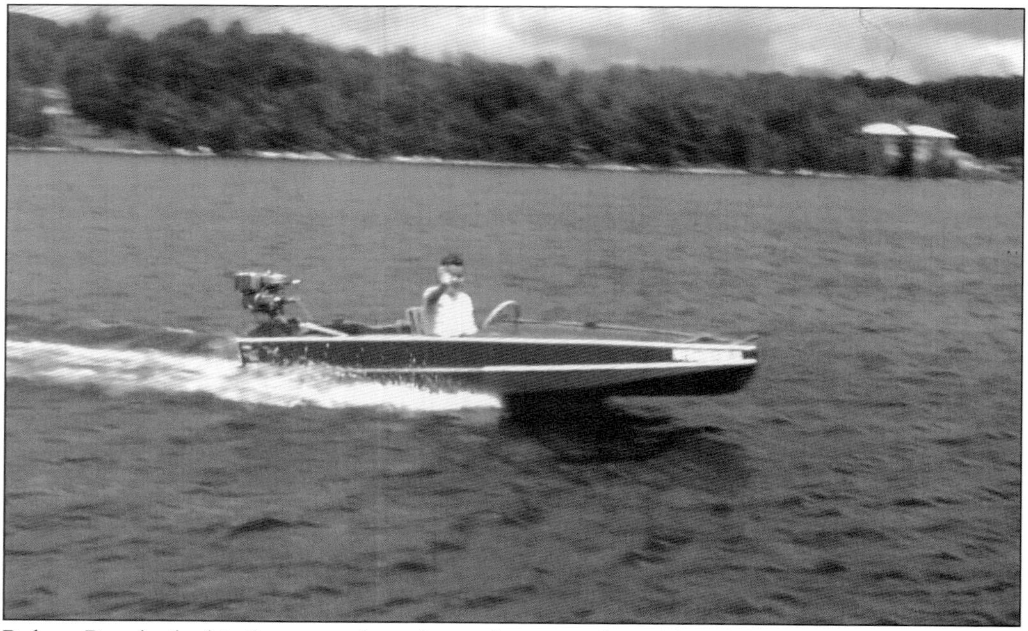

Robert Barr built this flat racing boat from a kit around 1945 but did not race it. It was out of the water in the 1950s but was made seaworthy again for his son David, at age 11, in 1962. David said recently that it was a "cool boat" even though its only gear was " forward," so he had to be careful when starting the engine. (Courtesy of David Barr.)

Nelda Carver Griffith inherited this 1946 Chris-Craft, the *Blueberry*, from her mother, Mary "Babe" Gillam, had it rebuilt, and renamed it *Babe's Blueberry*. Her mother had raced it with great success and was the only woman in the inboard race class at the time. Its size enabled it to make closer and sharper turns than other boats. On August 8, 1951, it won the trophy (right) for the 90- to 110-horsepower class race with T. H. Rautenberg III at the helm. The family kept it on the lake for 60 years until Griffith died in 2006. In this photograph, Allan Jones is at the wheel of the boat. (Right, courtesy of Jeanne Reynolds; below, courtesy of Jay Edel.)

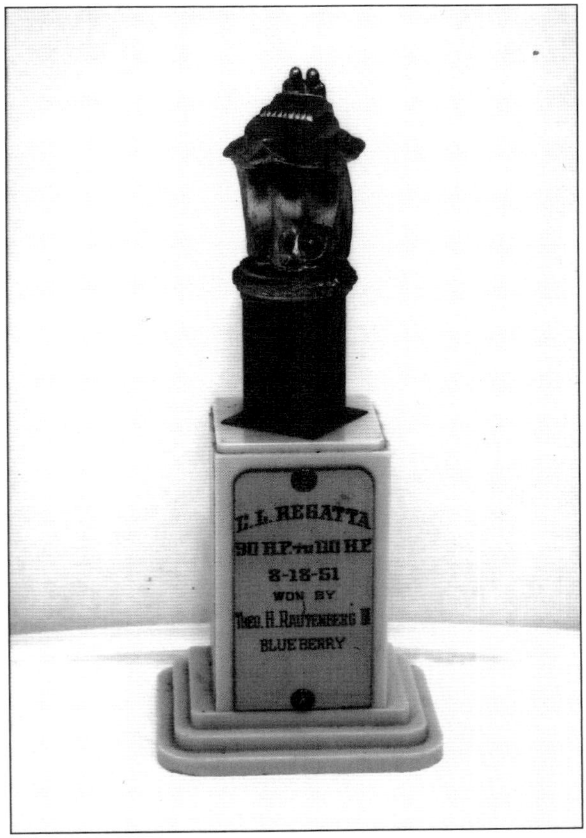

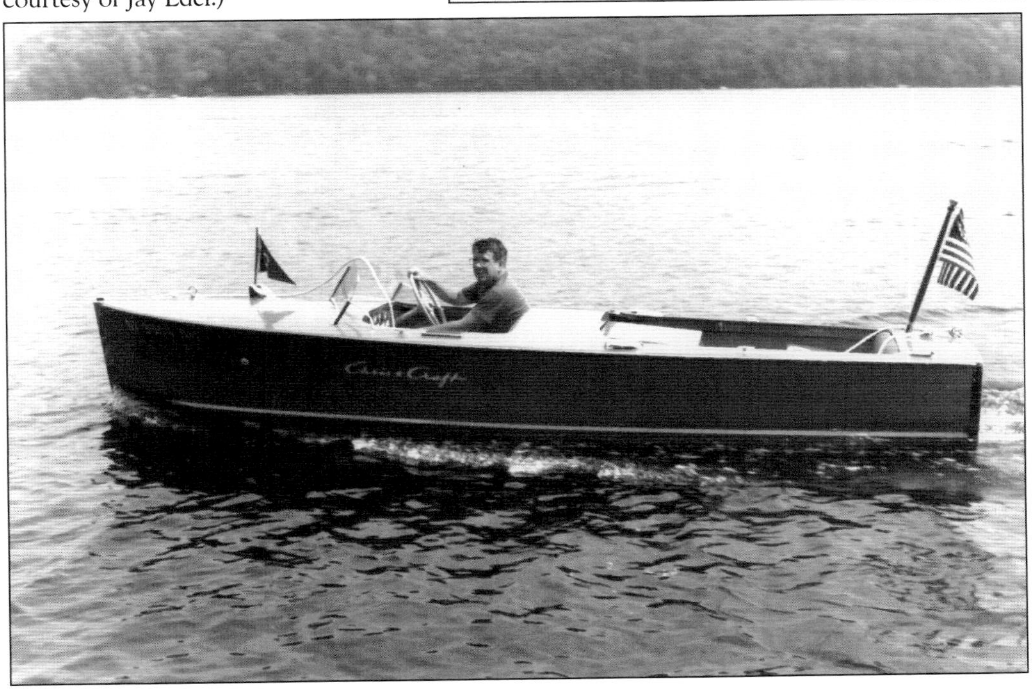

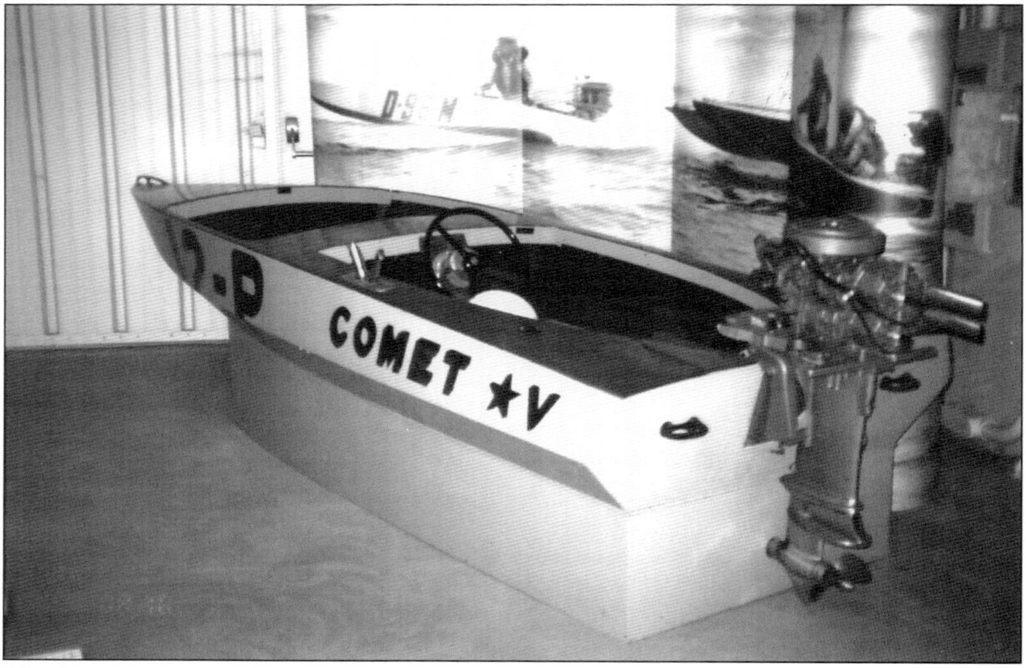

The *Comet V* was a 13-foot wooden outboard runabout built in 1957 by Sid-Craft in Watertown. In 1964 and 1965, driven by Riggs Smith, who had completely restored the boat after he bought it, the *Comet V* won first place in the 36-cubic-inch stock outboard class 90-mile Cranberry Lake Marathon. (Photograph by Charles Lewis, courtesy of the Antique Boat Museum.)

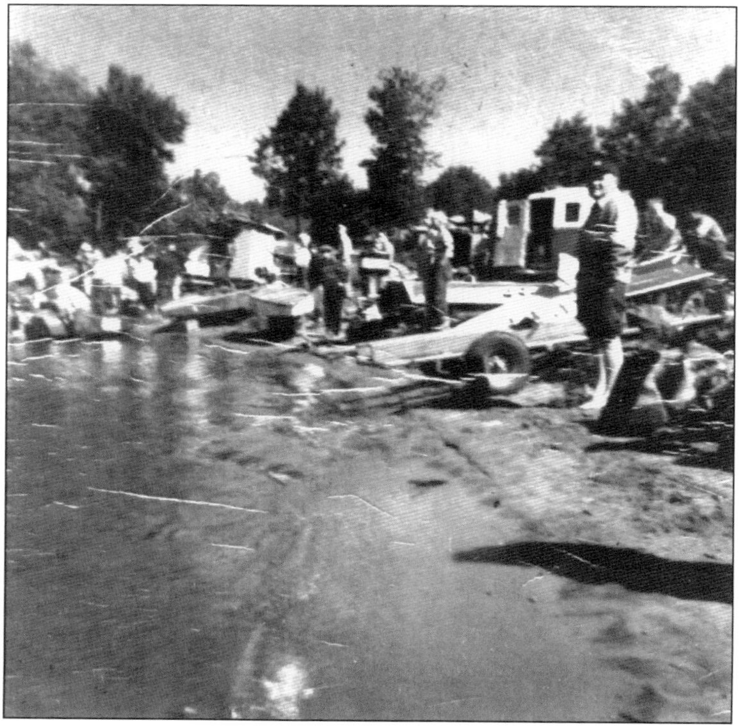

Outboard racing and the boats that participated captivated local audiences. The arrival of these boats in 1951 for races on Cranberry Lake drew interested spectators. Popular drivers enjoyed a fan base, particularly those who lived in the immediate region, and families and friends came to watch. (Courtesy of Jeanne Reynolds.)

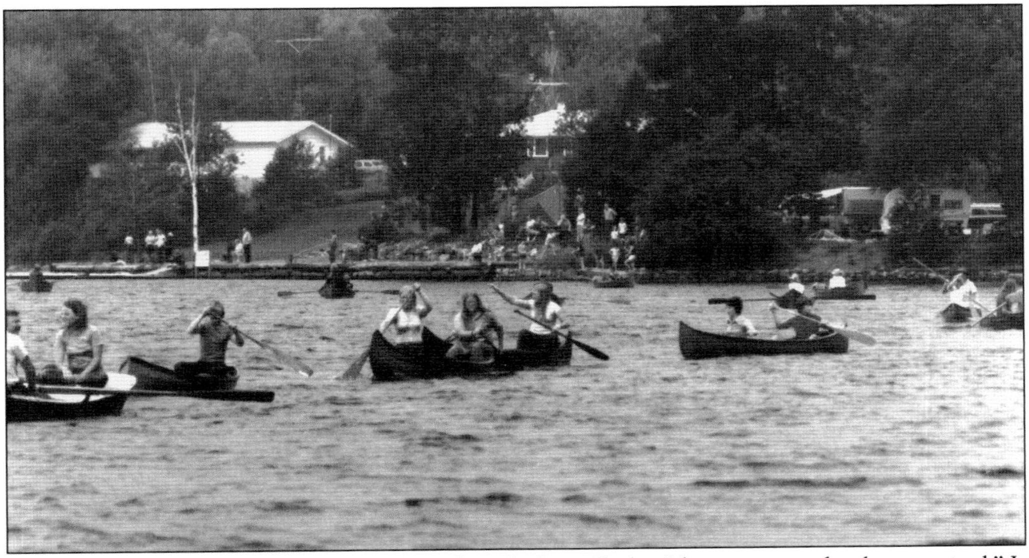

Hallie Bond, in *Boats and Boating in the Adirondacks*, called it "the great wooden boat revival." It grew out of a 1960s reaction against mass production but was not a rejection of modern materials. Boatbuilders simply began to build lighter, sturdier, and faster models of traditional canoes, guide boats, skiffs, and rowboats, and the public loved them. The public also kept the old family boats around, and the next generation used them too. A group of entrants leaves shore in a 1970s regatta (above). Below, Dottie Heffner (with hat) and Nelda Carver Griffith (in front boat) participate in another 1970s regatta. (Courtesy of Beverly Fickbohm.)

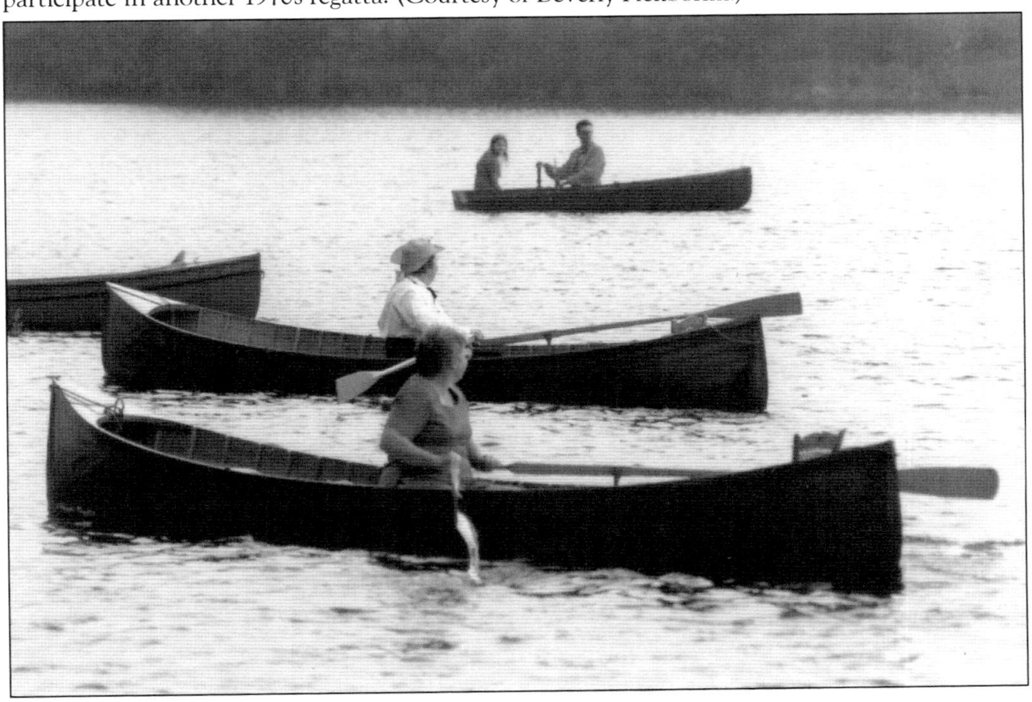

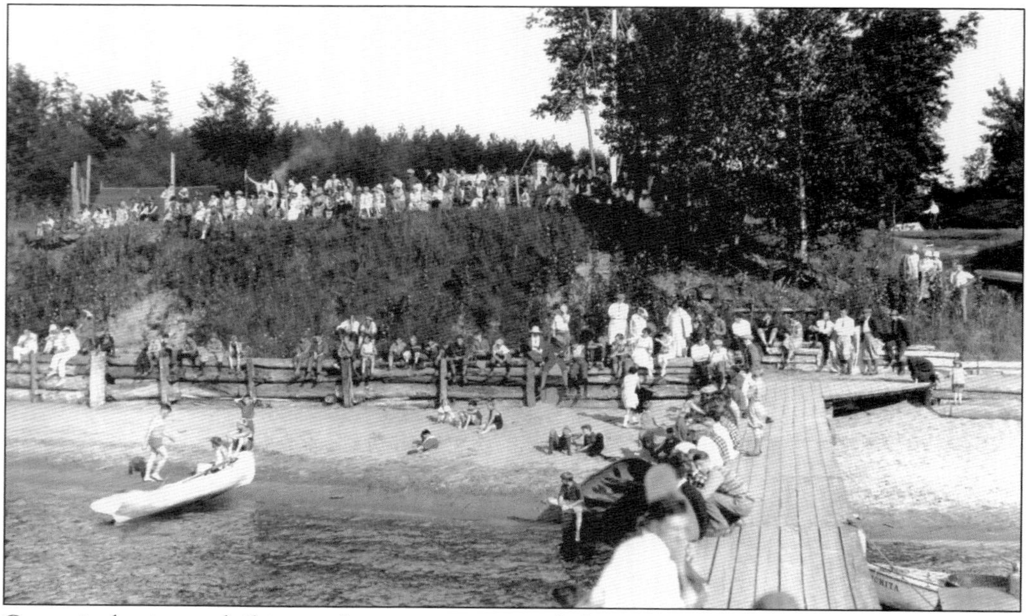

Canoe jockeying and tilting and canoe racing provided excitement at the annual field day of the College of Forestry's sophomore summer camp in the 1920s and 1930s. The *Camp Log*, an official publication of the school, includes many student anecdotes about happenings on those days. Often summer camp students raced in competition with their counterparts at the Ranger School, with great rivalries developing. (Courtesy of the F. Franklin Moon Library, SUNY ESF.)

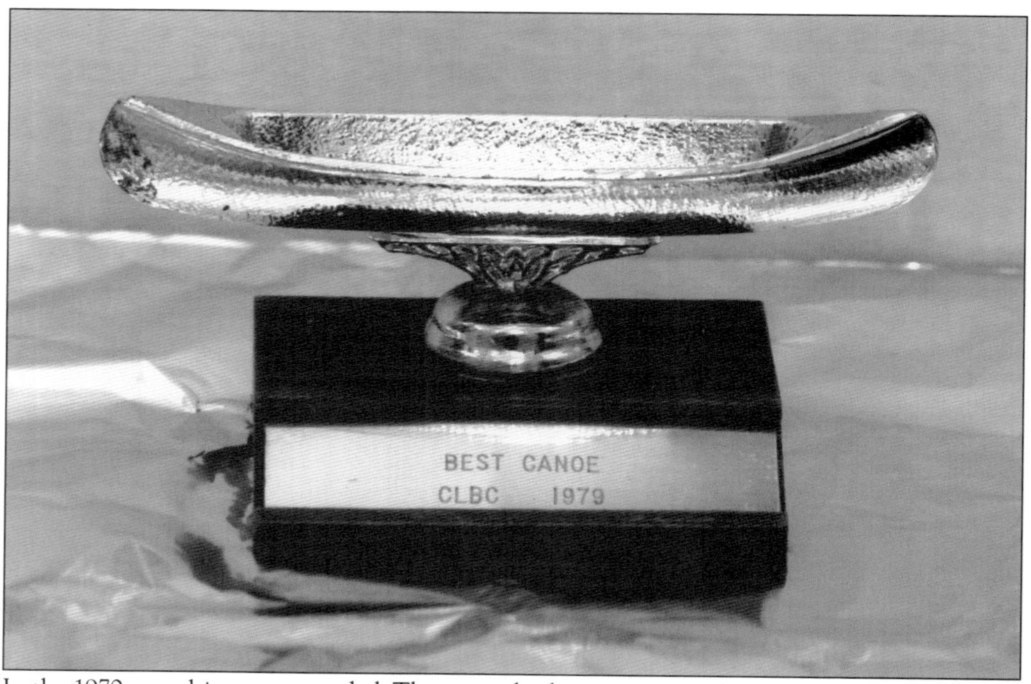

In the 1970s, trophies were awarded. The example above is engraved "Best Canoe, CLBC, 1979." There is no award winner identified. (Courtesy of Jeanne Reynolds.)

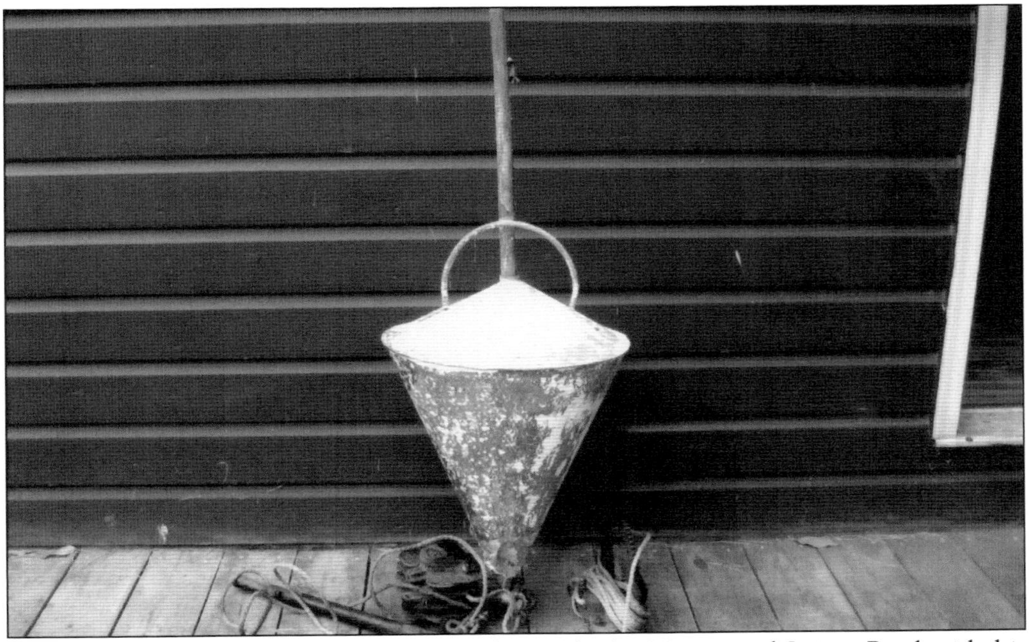

Former Cranberry Lake Boat Club commodores Charles Martin and Leiper Read said this race buoy (above) dates to the 1940s, when impromptu sailboat races (below) were common. Several buoys were used to mark the course. The races took place at least once a week, most often on Saturday afternoons. Cole's Point (left) was the usual starting area. These races were not associated with the Cranberry Lake Boat Club but were rather informal affairs. Regular participants included Bob Hofheins, Dick and Polly Herzer, Rod Leavell, the Coles, the Sleichers, the Arnolds, and the Vickers. (Above, courtesy of William Gleason; below, courtesy of Anna Fowler.)

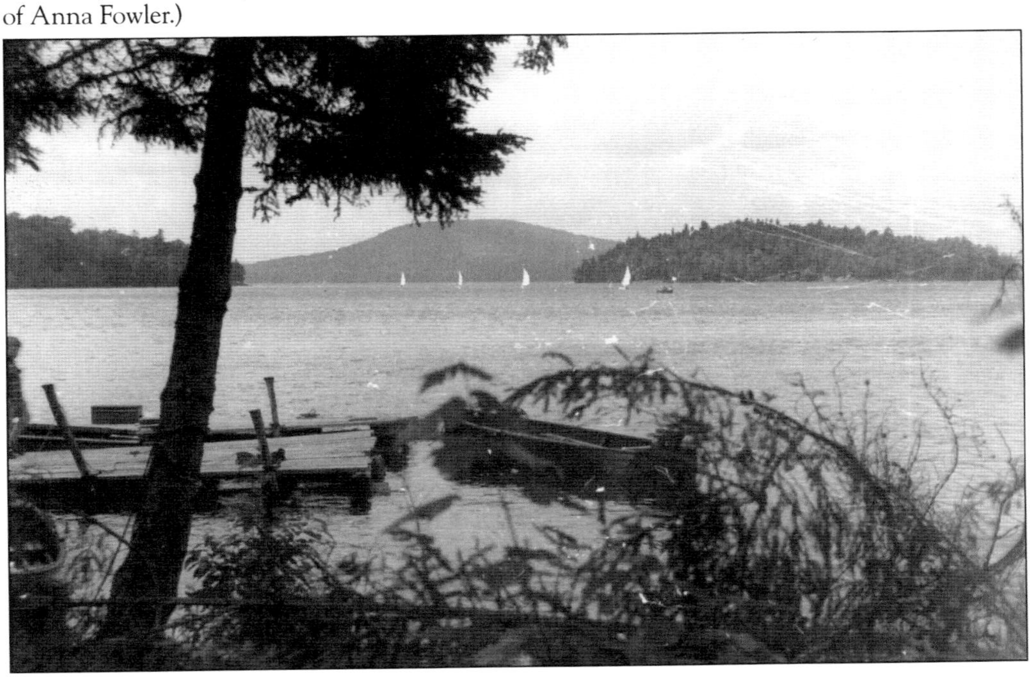

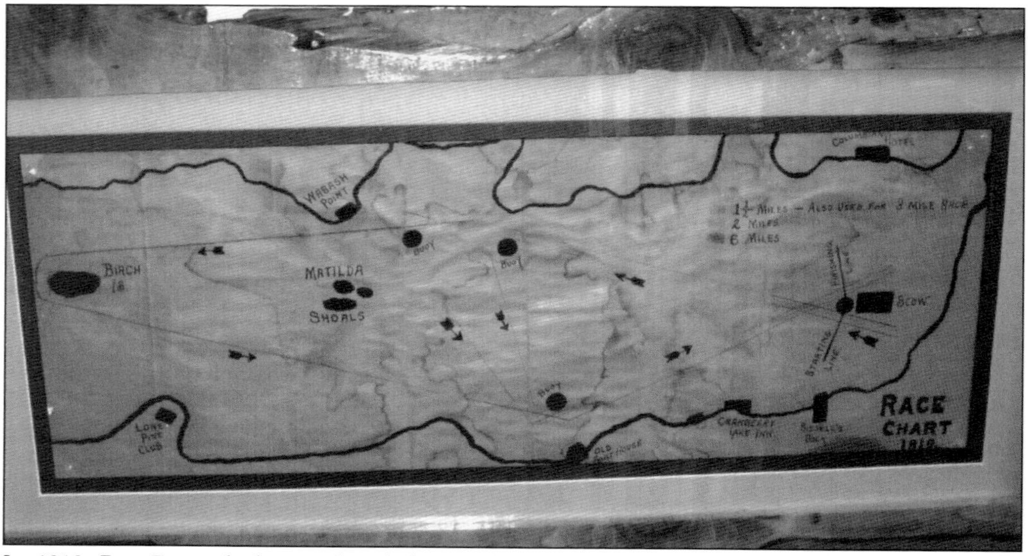

In 1912, Roy Peacock drew a detailed race chart map for the regatta on the back of a folded paper grocery sack. It survived, was rediscovered in 2007, and was framed. Peacock was an early graduate of the Ranger School in Wanakena. His son Paul Peacock was there when it was presented to the boat club at its boat show on July 5, 2008. (Photograph by William Gleason, courtesy of Jeanne Reynolds.)

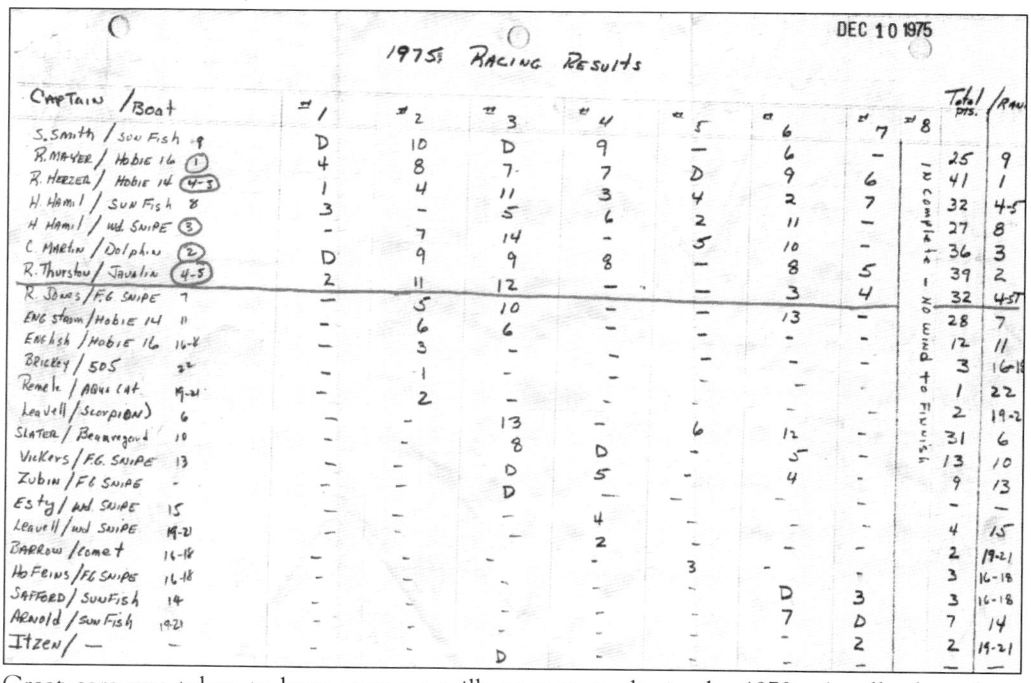

DEC 10 1975

1975 Racing Results

Captain / Boat		#1	#2	#3	#4	#5	#6	#7	#8	Total pts.	Rank
S. Smith / Sun Fish	9	D	10	D	9	—	6	—	Incomplete – No wind to finish	25	9
R. Mayer / Hobie 16	(1)	4	8	7	7	D	9	6		41	1
R. Herzer / Hobie 14	(4-5)	1	4	11	3	4	2	7		32	4-5
H. Hamil / Sun Fish	8	3	–	5	6	2	11	–		27	8
H. Hamil / wd. Snipe	(3)	–	7	14	–	5	10	–		36	3
C. Martin / Dolphin	(2)	D	9	9	8	–	8	5		39	2
R. Thurston / Javelin	(4-5)	2	11	12	–	–	3	4		32	4-5T
R. Jones / F.G. Snipe	7	–	5	10	–	–	13	–		28	7
Engstrom / Hobie 14	11	–	6	6	–	–	–	–		12	11
English / Hobie 16	16-18	–	3	–	–	–	–	–		3	16-18
Brickey / 505	22	–	1	–	–	–	–	–		1	22
Remele / Aqua Cat	19-21	–	2	–	–	–	–	–		2	19-21
Leavell / Scorpion)	6	–	–	13	–	6	12	–		31	6
Slater / Beauregard	10	–	–	8	D	–	5	–		13	10
Vickers / F.G. Snipe	13	–	–	D	5	–	4	–		9	13
Zubin / FG Snipe	-	–	–	D	–	–	–	–		–	–
Esty / wd. Snipe	15	–	–	–	4	–	–	–		4	15
Leavell / wd Snipe	19-21	–	–	–	2	–	–	–		2	19-21
Barrow / Comet	16-18	–	–	–	–	3	–	–		3	16-18
HoFeins / FG Snipe	16-18	–	–	–	–	–	D	3		3	16-18
Safford / SunFish	14	–	–	–	–	–	7	D		7	14
Arnold / Sun Fish	19-21	–	–	–	–	–	–	2		2	19-21
Itzen / —	–	–	–	D	–	–	–	–		–	–

Great care was taken to keep accurate sailboat race results in the 1970s. A tally sheet from 1975 shows that 23 sailboats entered at least one race that year. The finishing positions are listed for seven races. (The eighth did not finish due to lack of wind.) The final ranking for the year is in the far right column. R. Mayer, with a Hobie 16, was in first place. (Courtesy of Robert Thurston.)

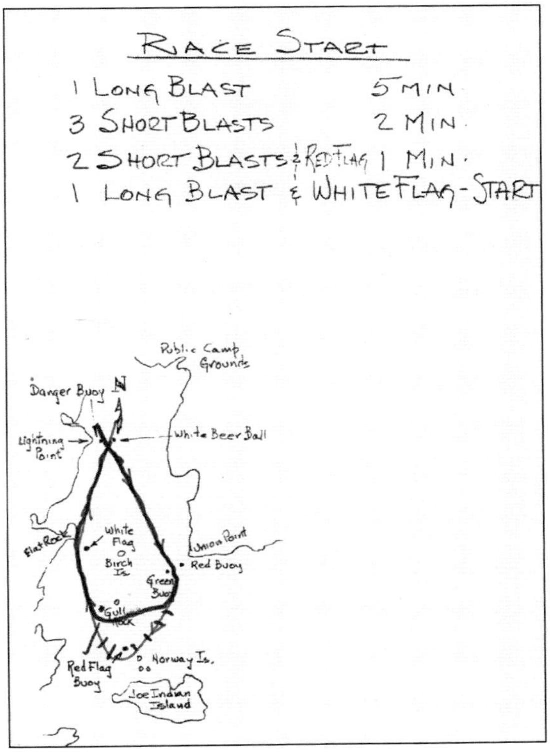

A pair of white beer balls east of Lightning Point marked the start and finish of sailboat races in the 1970s. Leiper Read, who organized these events for many years, used a hand-drawn map to show the route and direction for the sailors. They would leave Lightning Point, sail past Union Point, around Gull Rock, and back between Flat Rock and Birch Island to Lightning Point. (Courtesy of Leiper Read.)

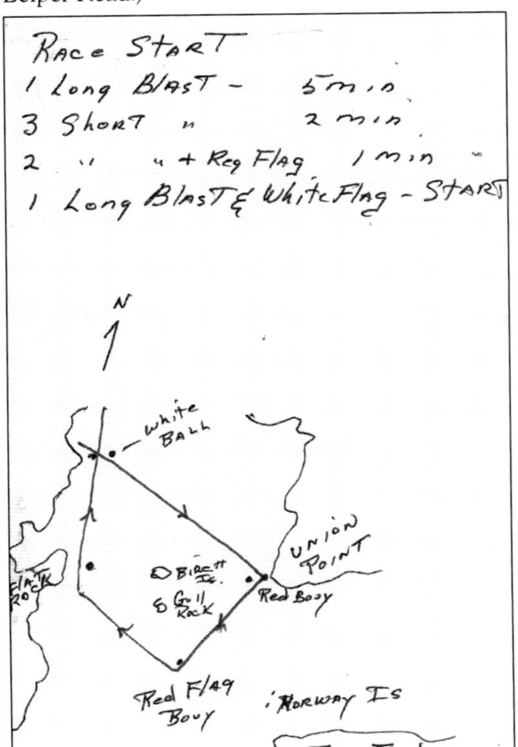

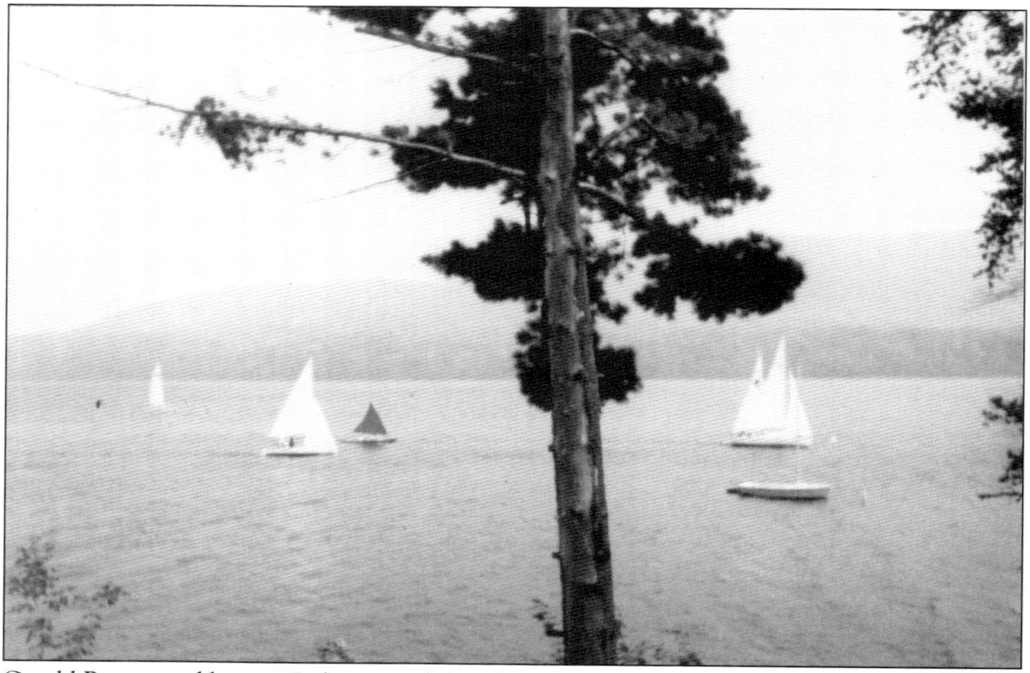

Gerald Bogart and his son Robert raced their homemade sailboat (described on page 35) in the Cranberry Lake regatta in September 1990. It was built from a kit by Frank Bogart. They are in the third boat from the left, with a red sail. (Courtesy of Gerald Bogart.)

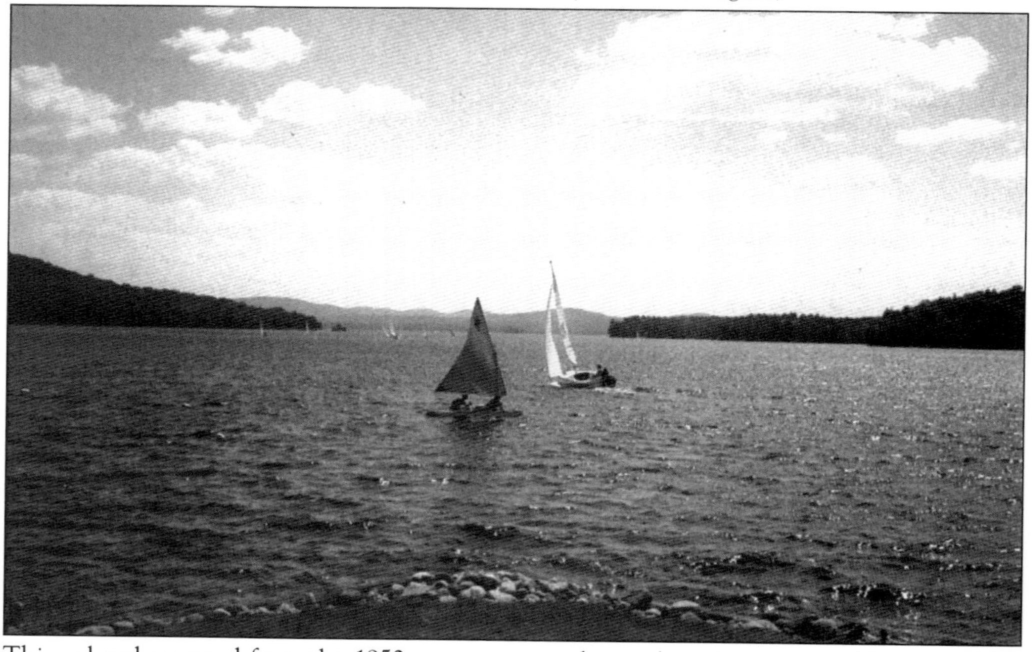

This colored postcard from the 1950s was very popular, and copies are owned by many from around the lake. The sailboats are at the foot of the lake by Cranberry Lake village. A Sunfish is the closest boat, but it appears that some race might be in progress as at least three other boats are pictured. The wind is clearly up with waves aplenty. (Courtesy of Peter VandeWater.)

Five

Comings and Goings

In the beginning, there were trains, and visitors came mostly to hunt and fish. By 1883, Riley Bishop was running Bishop's Hotel at the foot of the lake. He had a dock for his guests. In 1911, the Emporium Forestry Company added docks and built the Grasse River Railroad from the village to Childwold, which brought more visitors. To the south, at Wanakena, where the Oswegatchie River emerges from the hills and flows into Cranberry Lake, the Rich Lumber Company built a hotel across the street from the town dock. It also built a railroad line to Benson Mines. More visitors came.

Soon hotels on the lake had their own boats to transport guests. Other boats carried passengers, mail, and freight from one dock to another. Boat races began and ended at docks, watched by people on other docks. Family cottages had docks.

George Given's general store in Cranberry Lake had a dock. When George and Jeanne Reynolds owned the store from 1965 to 1975, they built the present pier out from the marina. Their son, Dick, built another dock later and charged the boat club for its use. After 1980 and 1981, the Cranberry Lake Boat Club leased a dock from the Emporium Marina.

The only places to get work done on boats in the 1930–1950 period were at Rudy Hayes's Boat Shop or Streeter's, owned by Bill Streeter from 1940 to 1945, and by Loyd Davis after that. Both were on Columbian Road. Davis sold his property to Sherm Smith in 1957, who sold it to Paul VerSteeg in 1964, who sold it to the State of New York in 1973. The marina there now serves as the land base for the SUNY ESF summer camp at Barber Point. The Cranberry Lake Boat Club still leases a dock from the Emporium Marina. Today visitors come to the two public docks by car. One is the town dock in Wanakena; the other is the New York State public access ramp on Columbian Road. Both can be reached from State Route 3. There are no trains anymore.

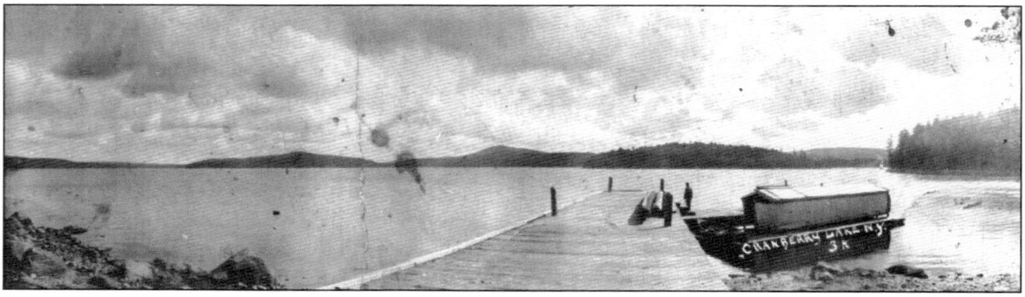

This rare double-size postcard from around 1890 shows how far out docks could extend. This allowed boats to arrive safely during all water levels. A dock this large could accommodate several boats. This view is believed to be from near Deremo Point with Buck Island in the distance straight off the end of the dock. The large barge probably carried construction materials. (Courtesy of Barbara Slater.)

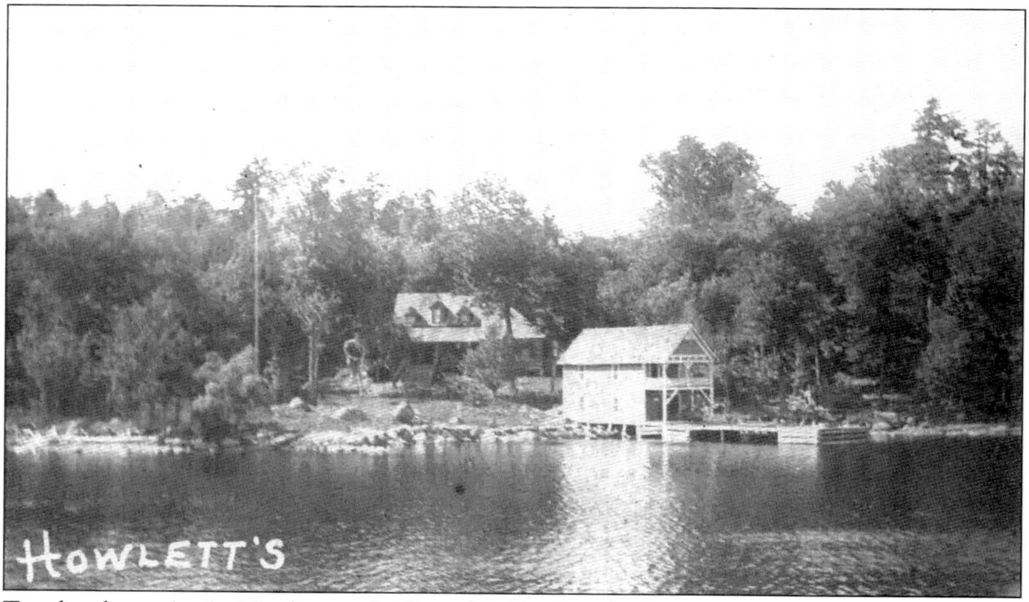

Two brothers, A. A. Howlett and Albert H. Howlett, built a large log cabin called Tramps Retreat on the west side of Dead Creek Flow in 1886. The Howletts' dock became a landmark. It was more of a clubhouse than a hotel and many prominent figures came ashore. Frederic Remington (artist), Chester Lord (editor of the *New York Sun*), and Irving Bacheller (author), all stayed here. (Courtesy of Eugene Carver.)

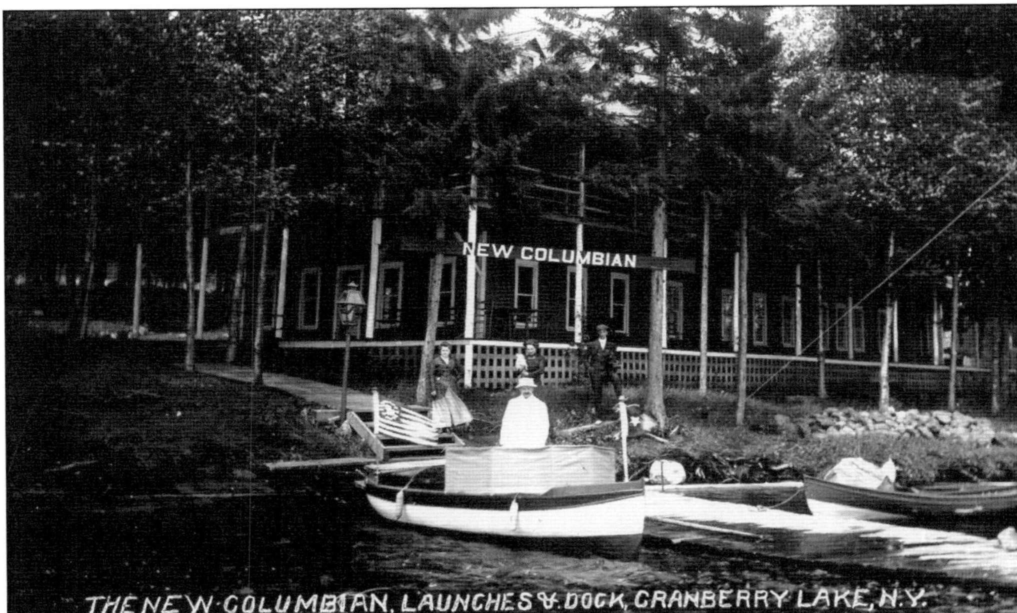

The New Columbian Park Hotel (above), also called the Columbian Inn and the New Columbian Inn Park Hotel, was built in 1897 by Charles Dewey on the west shore of Cranberry Lake. Boats met the train at Wanakena and brought guests down the lake to the hotel. The rooms were well furnished, large, and airy. Its long porch faced the easily accessible dock where four well-dressed ladies (below) are considering a paddling excursion. There were rowboats, canoes, and launches available for guests to use. It was torn down in 1935. Columbian Road is named after the hotel. (Courtesy of Peter VandeWater.)

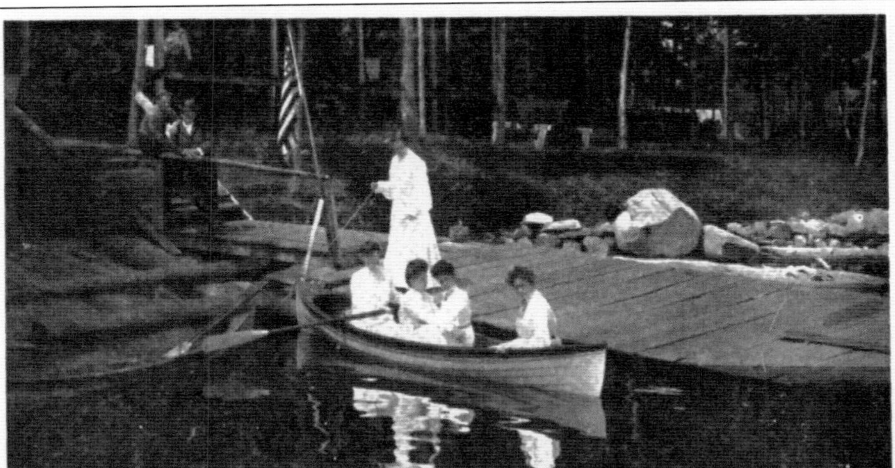

At the Columbia Landing, Cranberry Lake in the Adirondacks

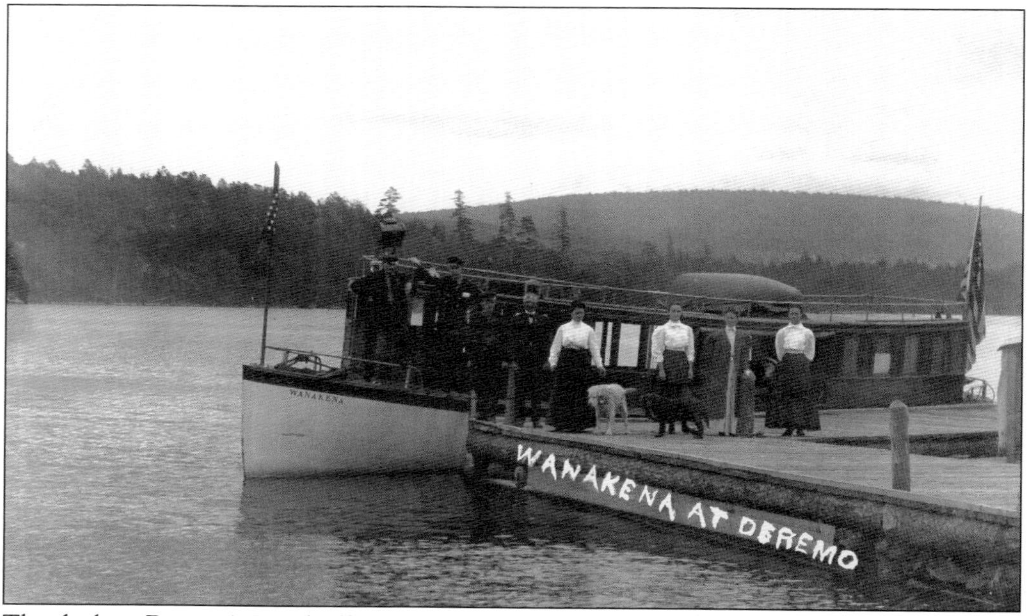

The dock at Deremo's Hotel offered a sweeping view of Cranberry Lake looking north. In its day, the hotel was popular with summer tourists. They came by the boatloads in steamers such as the *Wanakena* to an expansive dock with space for many smaller boats too. The hotel was built in 1903 between Witch Bay and Cole's Point. It burned to the ground in 1907. (Courtesy of Peter VandeWater.)

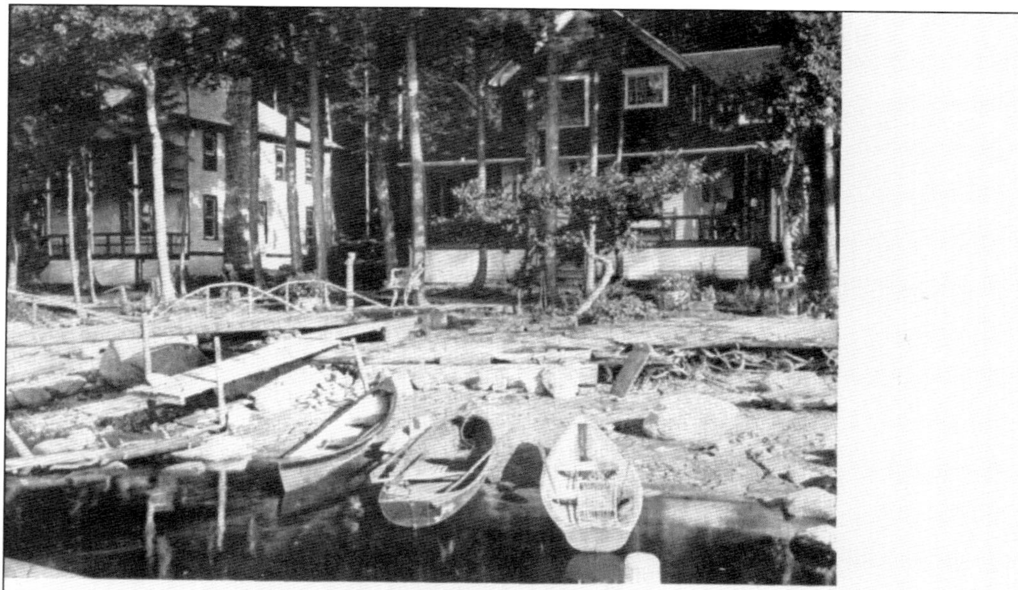

The Bear Mountain Camp, also called Baldersons, was built by John Balderson and his wife, Anna, in 1905. The property on which the original farmhouse building (right) and the annex (left) stood grew through acquisitions to over 14 acres on the south side of Bear Mountain. This area just north of Eagle Island was prone to heavy winds, affecting the use of any dock. (Courtesy of Mark Friden.)

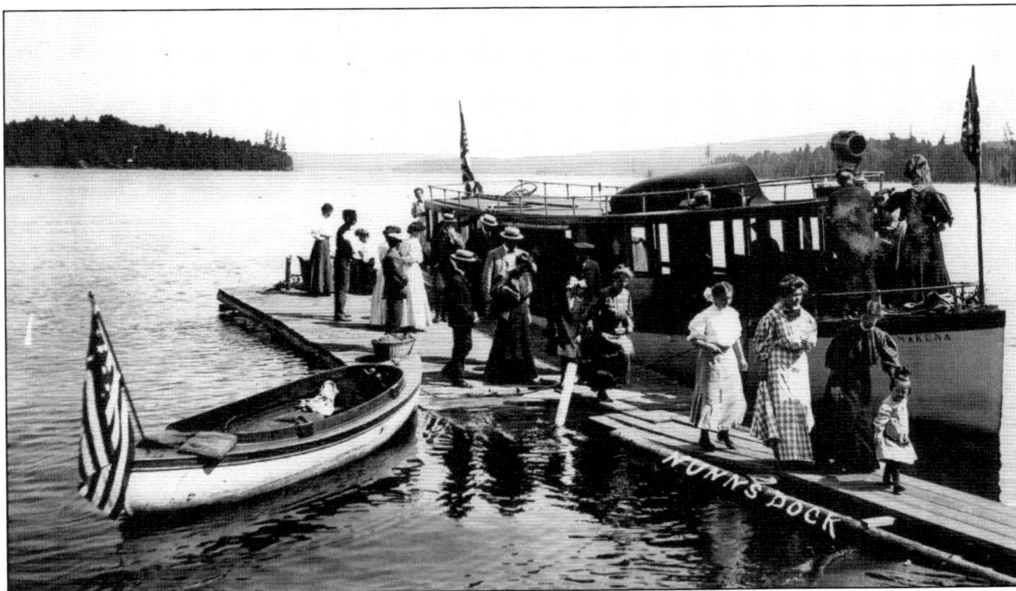

Passengers departing the *Wanakena* (above) around 1905 walk single file from the dock up the ramp leading to Nunn's Inn, women and children going first. No luggage is visible, so they may be returning from an outing or arriving for dinner at Nunn's Inn. Buck Island is behind (left). The inn conducted excursions to Olmstead Pond and Sliding Falls that would depart from this dock. The ramp they would follow (below) was exceptionally long, extending 80 feet toward the wide veranda of the hotel. This accommodated the changing levels of water in the lake. It also provided protection for walkers from the mud along the shore. (Courtesy of Susan Smeby.)

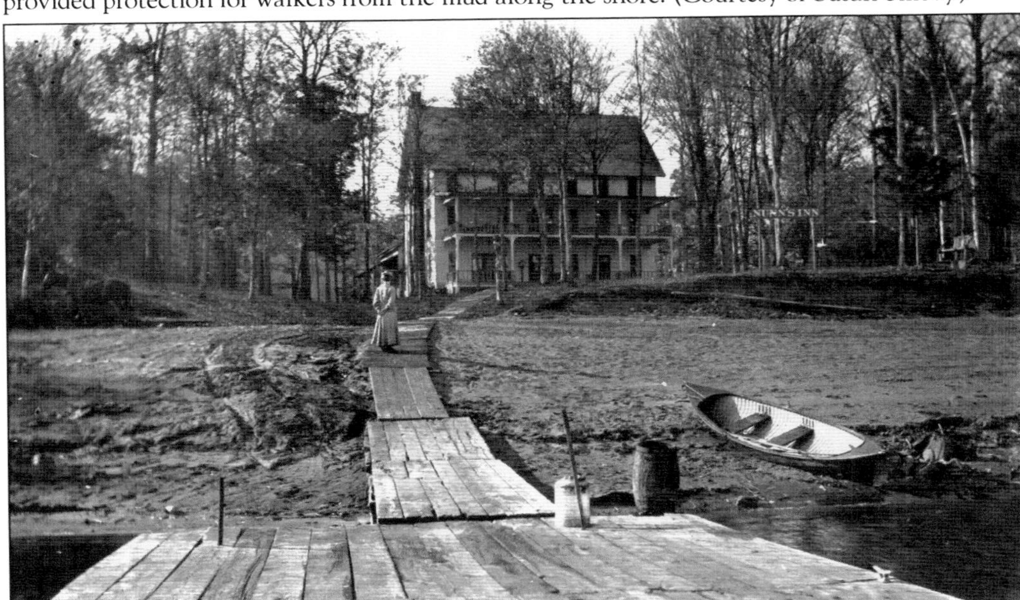

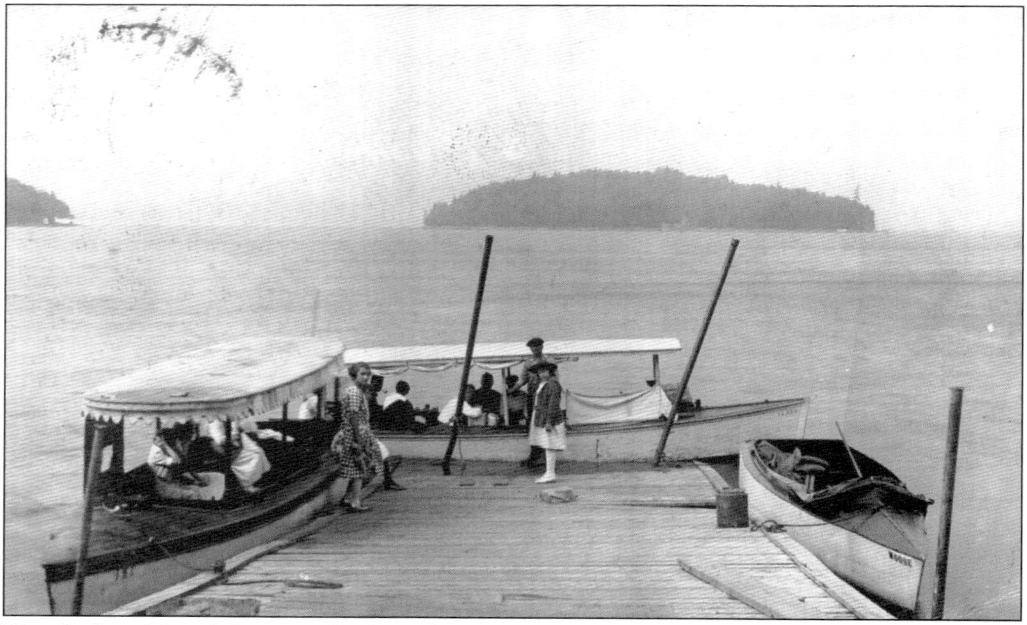

The dock at Nunn's Inn was built at this prime location at the head of the lake in 1898. It became the clubhouse of the Indian Mountain Club in 1911. Its motor launch *IMC* is on the left. The back of the postcard reads, "Dear Ma and Pa—This is where we landed, it is a very fine place to stay. Wish you could see it." (Courtesy of Peter VandeWater.)

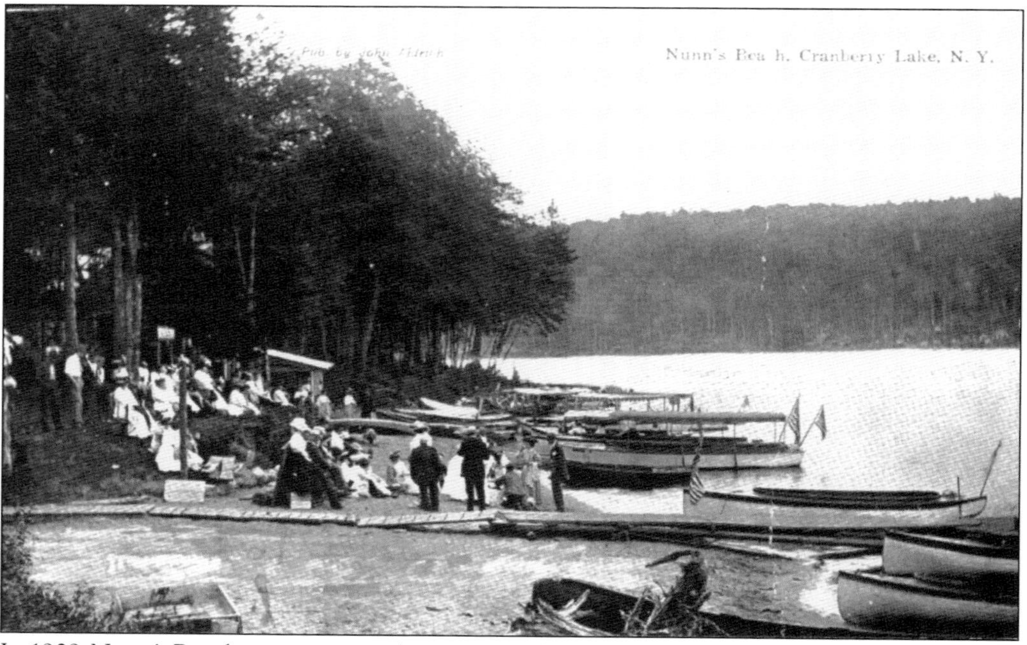

In 1909, Nunn's Beach was enjoying the same popularity as Nunn's Inn. The long ramp from the dock to the inn is visible in the foreground. Few places could accommodate as large a number of launches as are tied up here. The photographer, John Aldrich, is looking west toward the land behind Cole's Point. (Courtesy of Peter VandeWater)

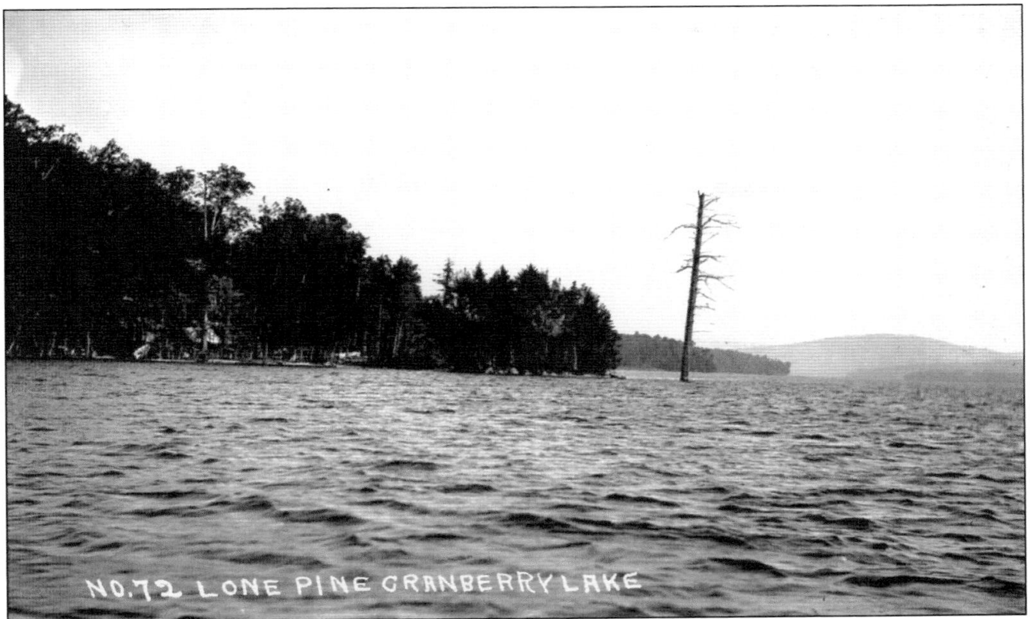

Lone Pine Inn was first a clubhouse built by men from Syracuse in 1906. It had a fine small dock, but the lone pine nearby evoked awe. It stood sentinel on the most prominent point on Cranberry Lake. Docks are points of reference, so are trees. From the north, the clubhouse is left of the pine, which no longer stands. Lone Pine Road bears the name. (Courtesy of Peter VandeWater.)

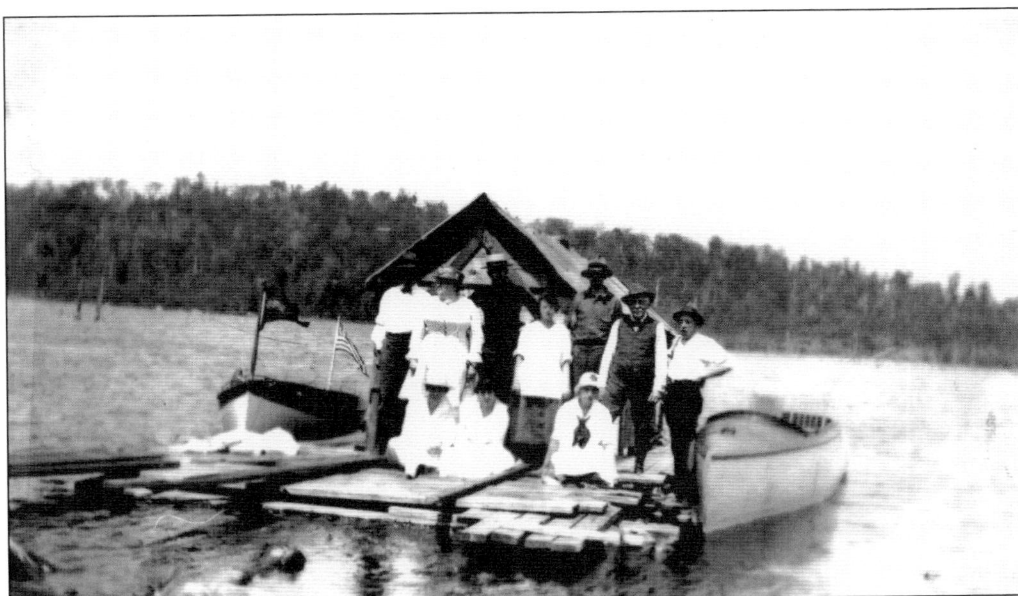

This photograph from around 1910–1920 shows what appears to be a floating boathouse tied to the end of a dock. It may have been built to protect one of the fast racing boats on the lake inside while other launches are tied up on either side. There is no consensus on its location. Some think it was at Janack's Landing on Dead Creek Flow. (Courtesy of the Wanakena Historical Association.)

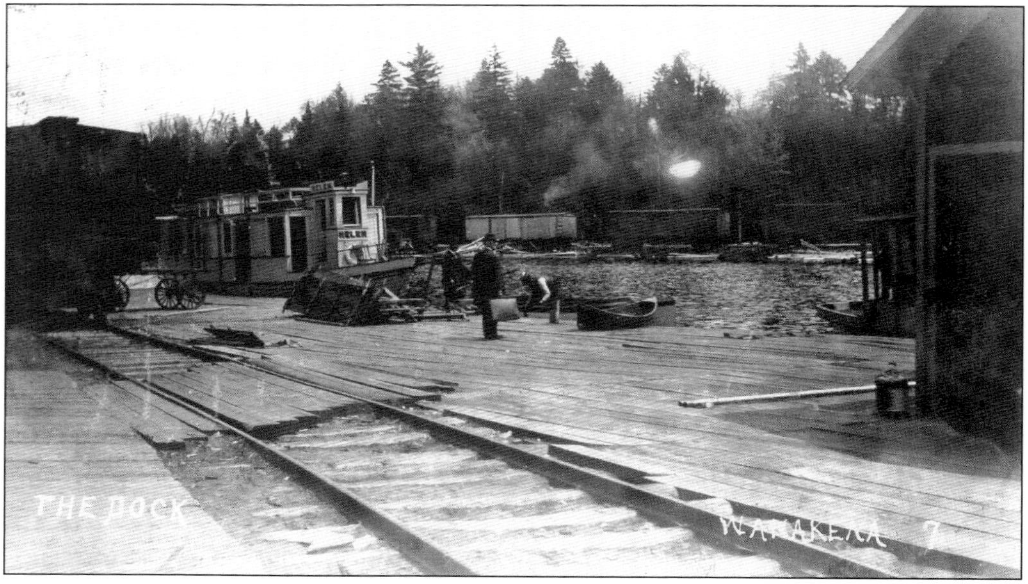

The town dock at Wanakena was a working dock for the Rich Lumber Company. It put in the railroad tracks right next to the dock on the Oswegatchie River to facilitate loading. On the left, from around 1905–1907, is the *Helen*, which carried freight as well as passengers. Across the river is Bissell's dock with lumber waiting to be put on the train. (Courtesy of Susan Smeby.)

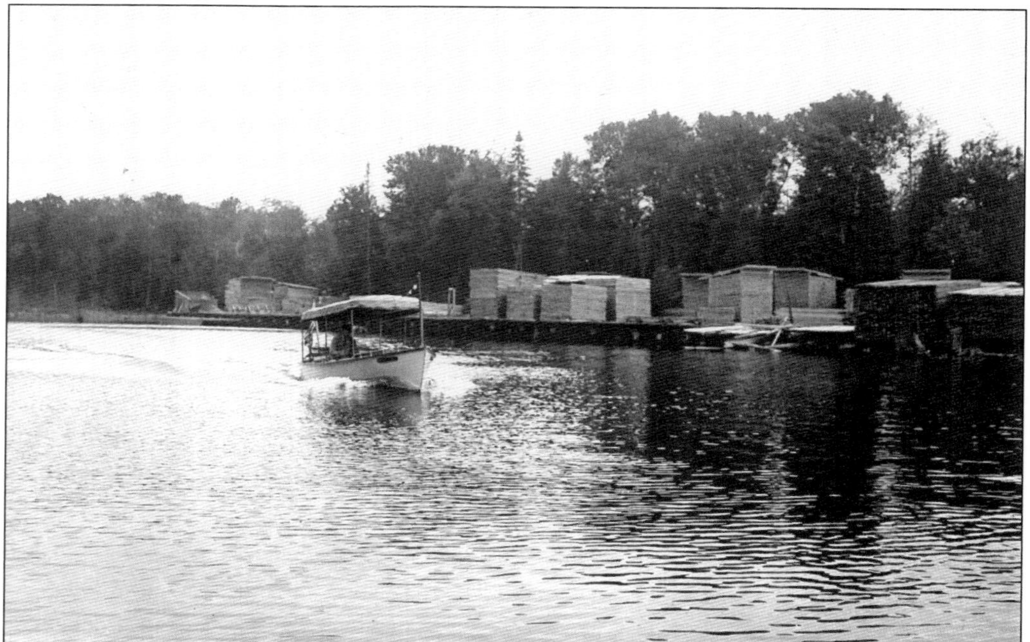

The gas-powered launch *Mohican*, owned by Charles Bates and available for charter, passes Bissell's dock on the south shore of the Oswegatchie River across from the village dock in Wanakena. Bissell owned a sawmill in Cranberry Lake and would tow his lumber by barge to Wanakena, so it could be shipped to market on the Rich Lumber Company's railroad. (Courtesy of Peter VandeWater.)

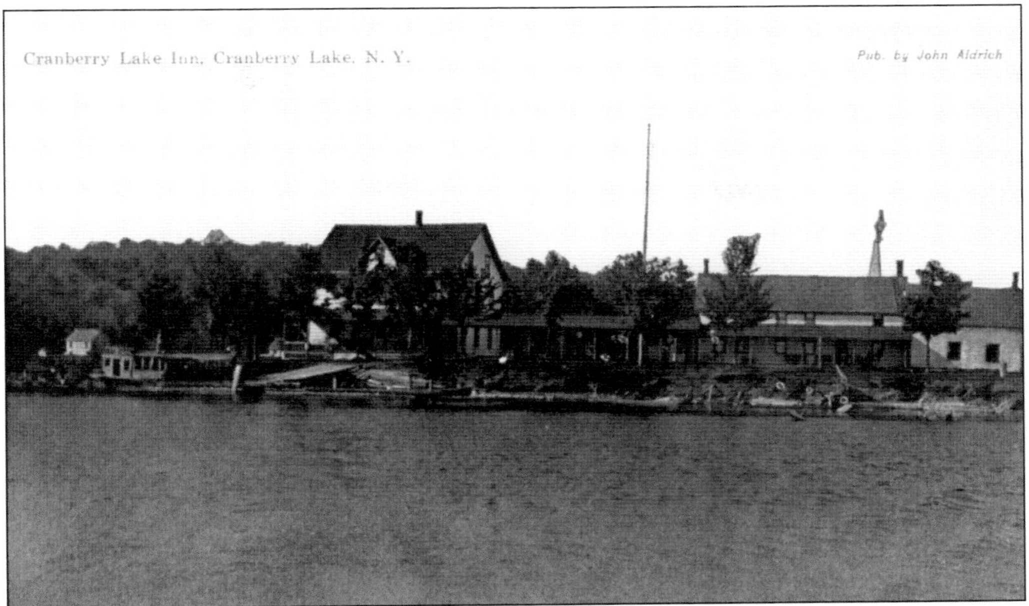

Since 1871, with the exception of 1926 to 1945, there has been an establishment at the foot of the lake where the present Cranberry Lake Lodge stands. The first place, Bishop's Hotel, catered to hunters and fishermen. In 1910, the Emporium Forestry Company bought the inn and dock. The *Helen* (above, left) regularly stopped there, and later boaters used the dock as a race start and finish line. Below is a later view of the hotel and dock as seen through the pine trees from the east. There were popular trails through the woods in that area. (Courtesy of Peter VandeWater.)

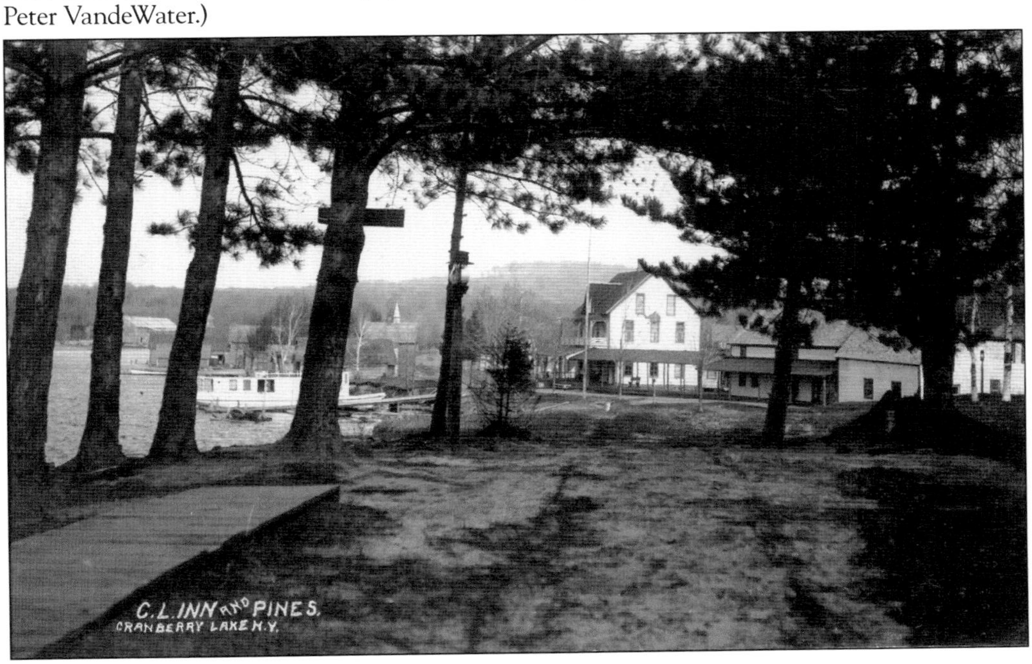

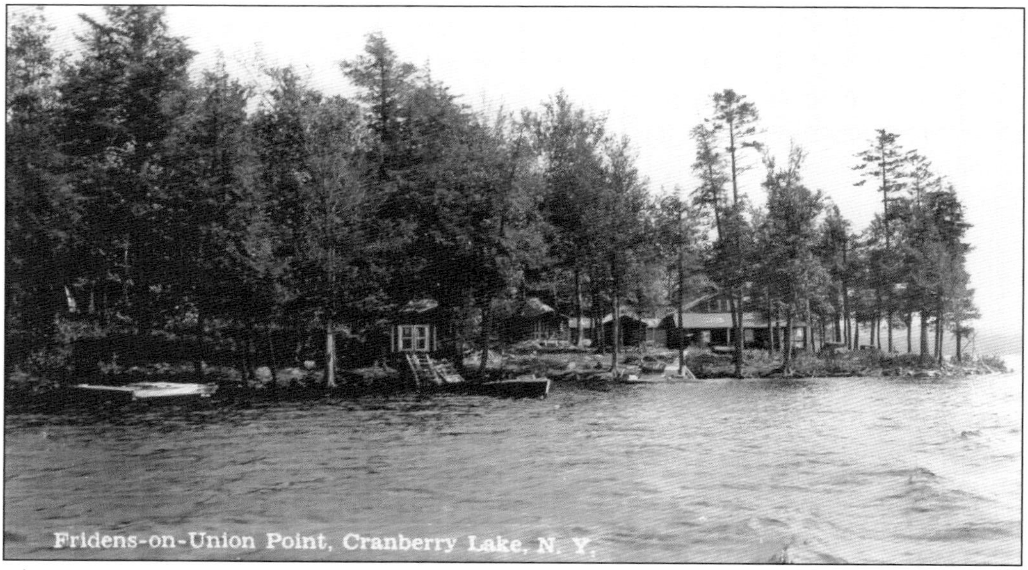

There are several cottages at Union Point, each with a dock and at least one boat. There are no roads. Rudolph "Blondie" Friden bought the original 1907 camp on the point in 1934 as a year-round residence. In the winter he drove his Ford Model A over the ice and stored it behind the camp. Or he would walk the three miles to town. (Courtesy of Mark Friden.)

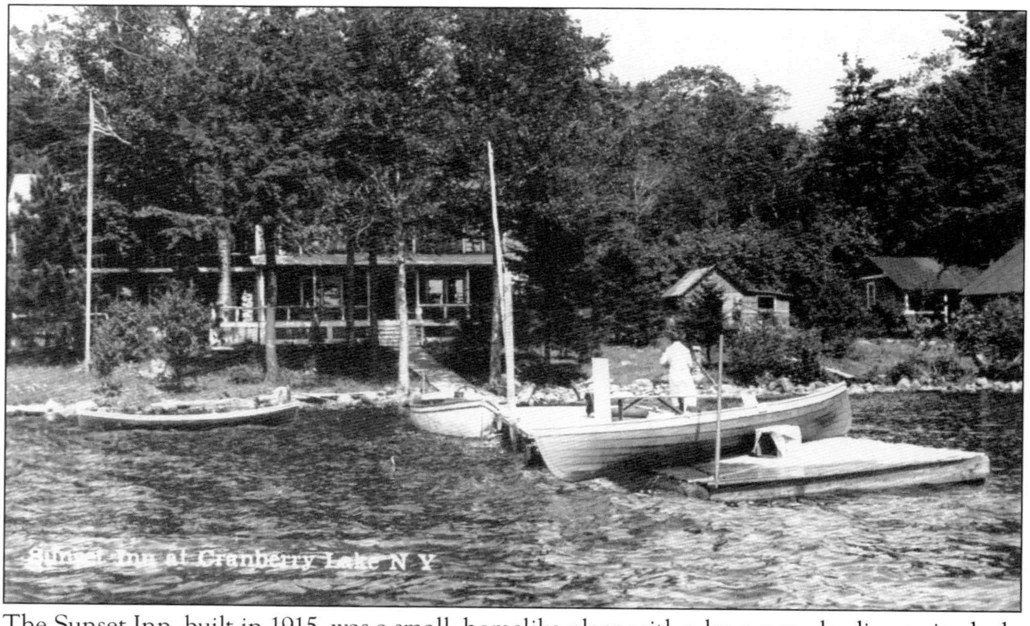

The Sunset Inn, built in 1915, was a small, homelike place with a long ramp leading to its dock. It was on the east shore of the lake and had commanding views of spectacular Adirondack sunsets. The property was called Morning Glory Lodge when it was owned by Arthur Kleps in the mid-1960s. Kleps's friend Timothy Leary, a well-known advocate of LSD, the hallucinogenic drug, is believed to have spent time here. (Courtesy of Peter VandeWater.)

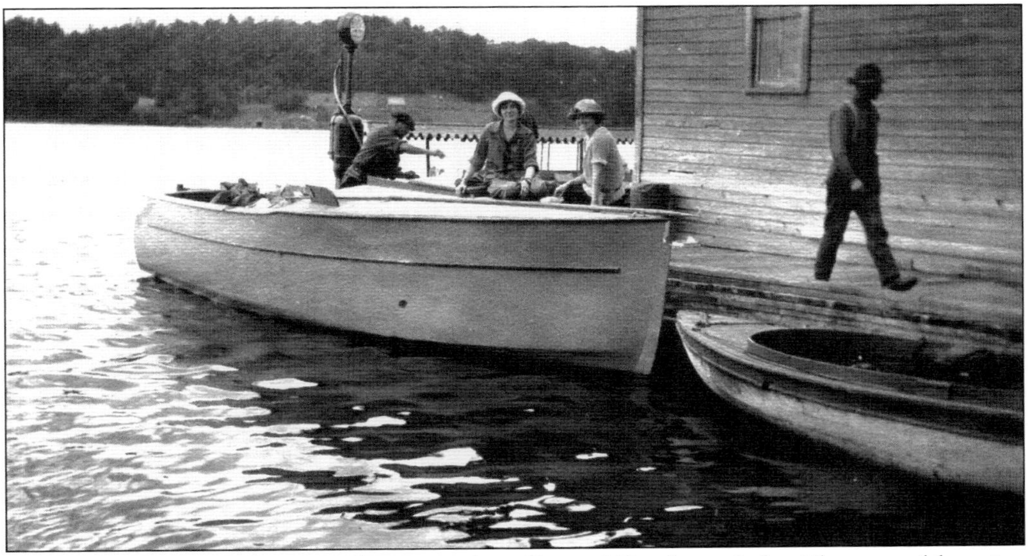

George Given operated a general store in the village of Cranberry Lake. The central location of the store and its wide walkway to the dock, as shown in this 1930s photograph, made it easy for customers to dock their boats and pick up orders from the store. (Courtesy of Mary Ann Remelé.)

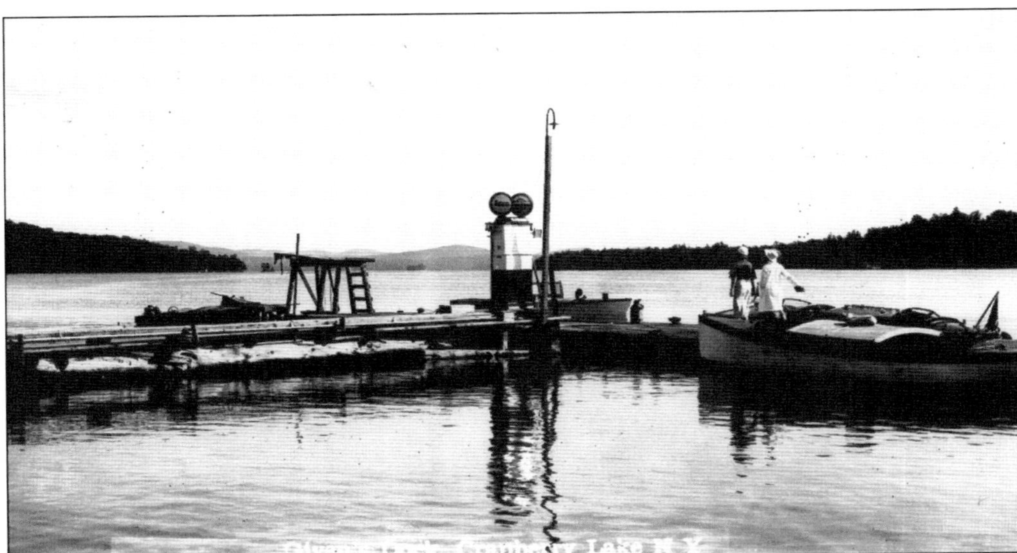

Later Given and his sons ran the general store. By the 1940s, Given's Dock had added more services. There were now two gasoline pumps and an expanded dock space. It was one of the busiest spots on the lake, with most of the refueling for boats taking place here. (Courtesy of Jeanne Reynolds.)

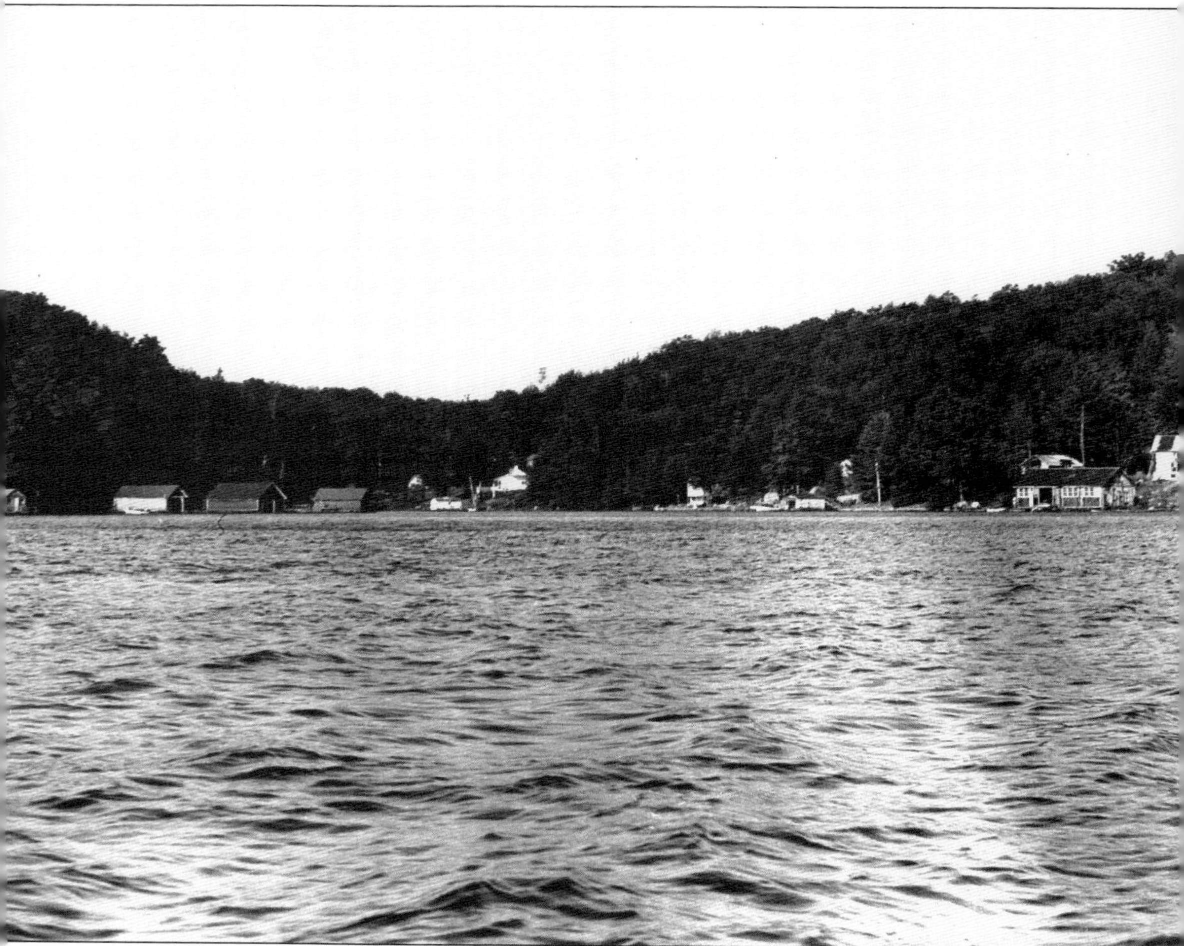

To a boater, the most important dock is the dock at the repair shop. Rudy Hayes bought an old barnlike building around 1915. He towed it down the lake to establish Rudy Hayes's Boat Shop in Chipmunk Bay (second building from the right), photographed in 1945. He built steel rails into the lake with a heavy steel cable to haul large boats into his shop. He could cram in two 30-foot boats at once, plus several canoes and small boats. He was an excellent mechanic and made a living for years working on Cranberry Lake boats and selling gas and oil. He also offered boat storage. In 1957, when he was 74 years old, his boathouse caught fire, taking his home with it. He survived. (Courtesy of Eugene Carver.)

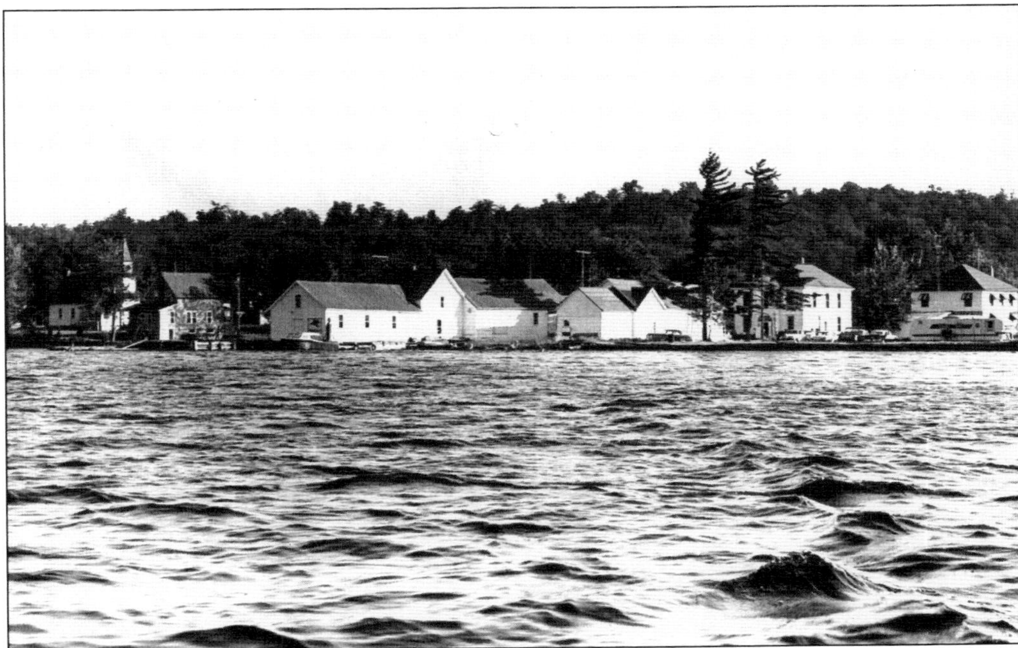

This photograph of the Cranberry Lake waterfront was taken in the 1940s. To the right of the second building from the left is the dock area. A Mobil "Flying Red Horse" gasoline advertising sign can be seen on the third building from the left. That building is above water. The space was filled in, and the Emporium Marina sits there today. (Courtesy of Eugene Carver.)

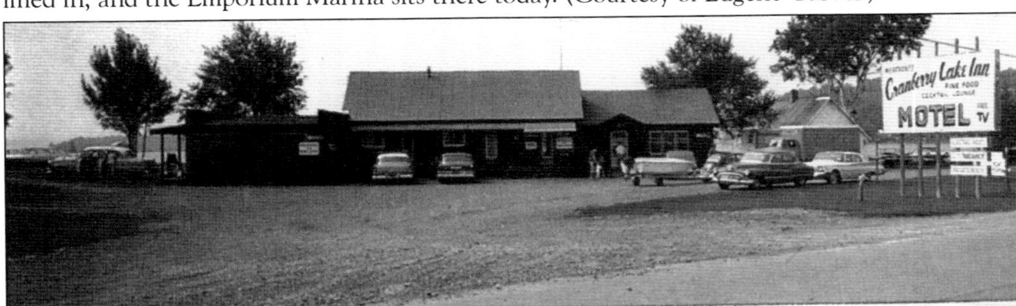

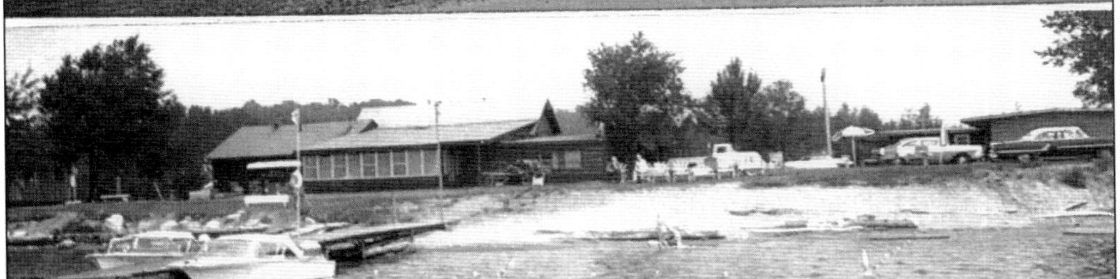

The Cranberry Lake Inn and Motel as seen here in the 1950s provided docking space for its dinner and overnight guests. Charles Merchant was the proprietor at this time. It was widely known for fine meals and excellent hospitality. The Merchant family ran the inn until 1986. (Courtesy of Peter VandeWater.)

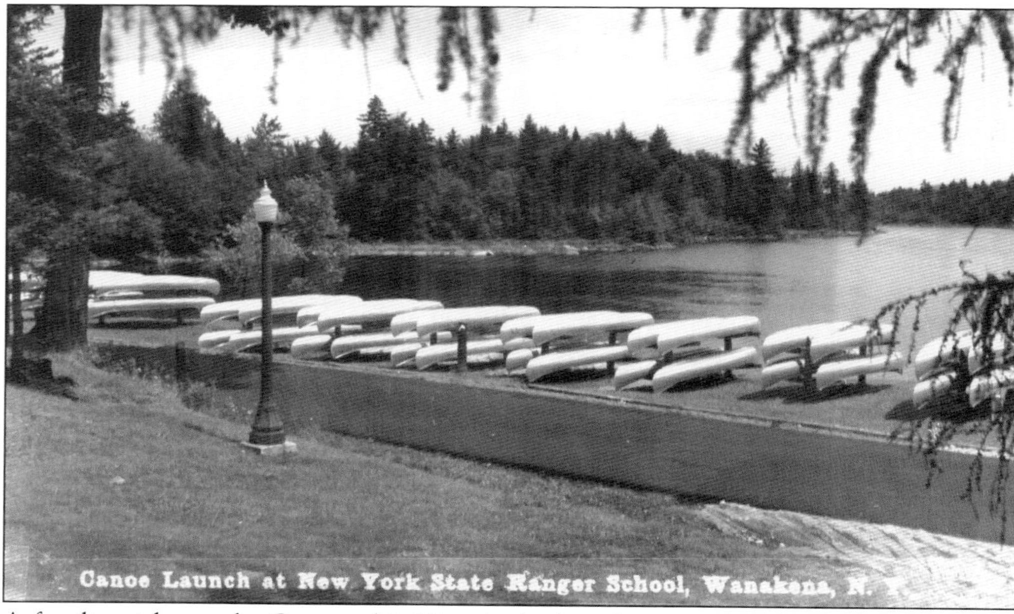

A familiar sight on the Oswegatchie River is the launch site at the New York State Ranger School, now the SUNY ESF Ranger School. It was completed in 1912 and graduated its first class in 1914. James F. Dubar, the superintendent, also served as a director of the Cranberry Lake Motor Boat Club. A large section of nearby forest preserve bears his name. Students make good use of the canoes. (Courtesy of Peter VandeWater.)

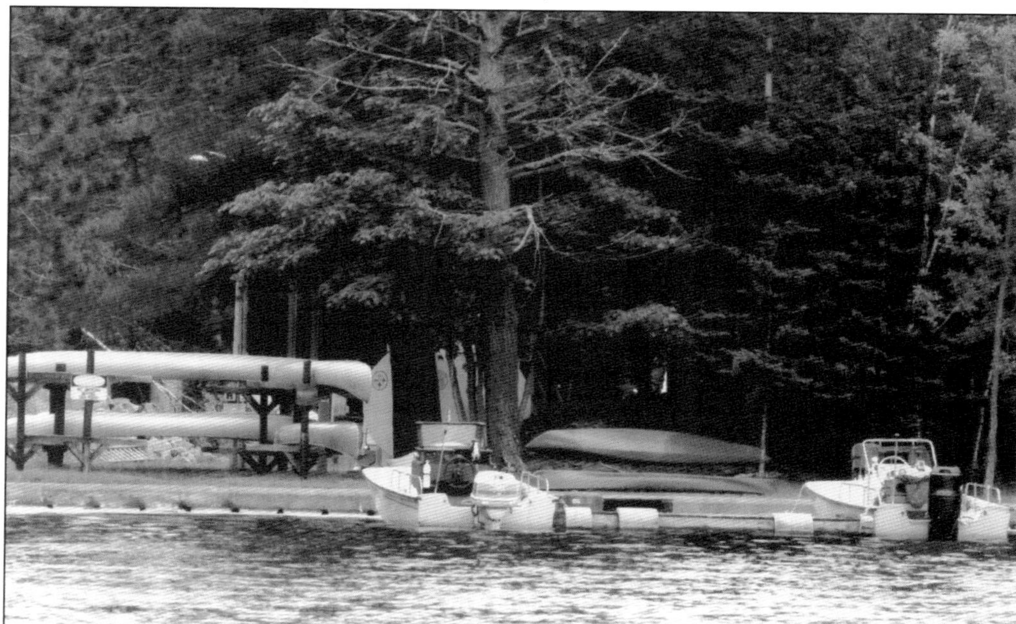

SUNY ESF has an extensive docking facility at Barber Point, where an annual sophomore summer camp associated with the College of Forestry at Syracuse University has a 50-year history. The college also acquired a property on Columbian Road in 1973 for a land base. The *Forester* makes regular round-trips back and forth during the summer season. (Courtesy of Ellen Giraud.)

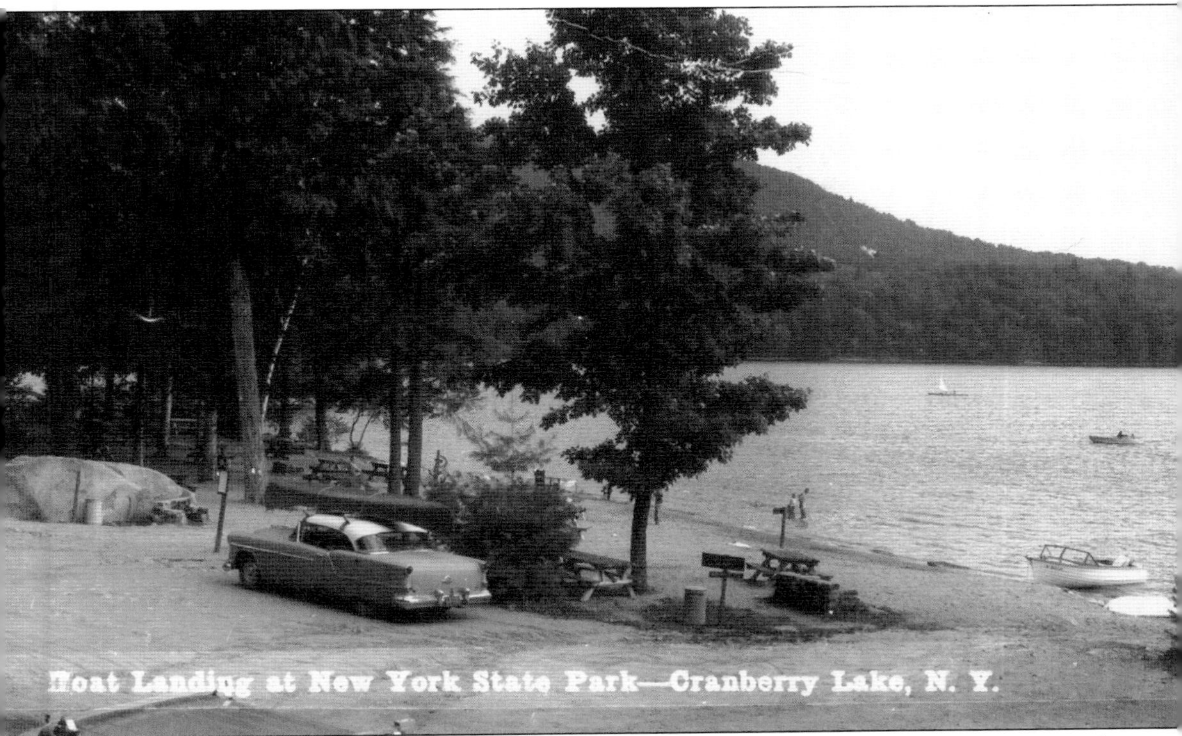

A New York State park at Cranberry Lake opened in 1935. It closed in 1942 for the duration of World War II. By the 1950s, campers from all over were bringing their boats to Cranberry Lake. There was no dock at this picnic area, but a canoe, motorboat, or sailboat could be beached there. (Courtesy of Peter VandeWater.)

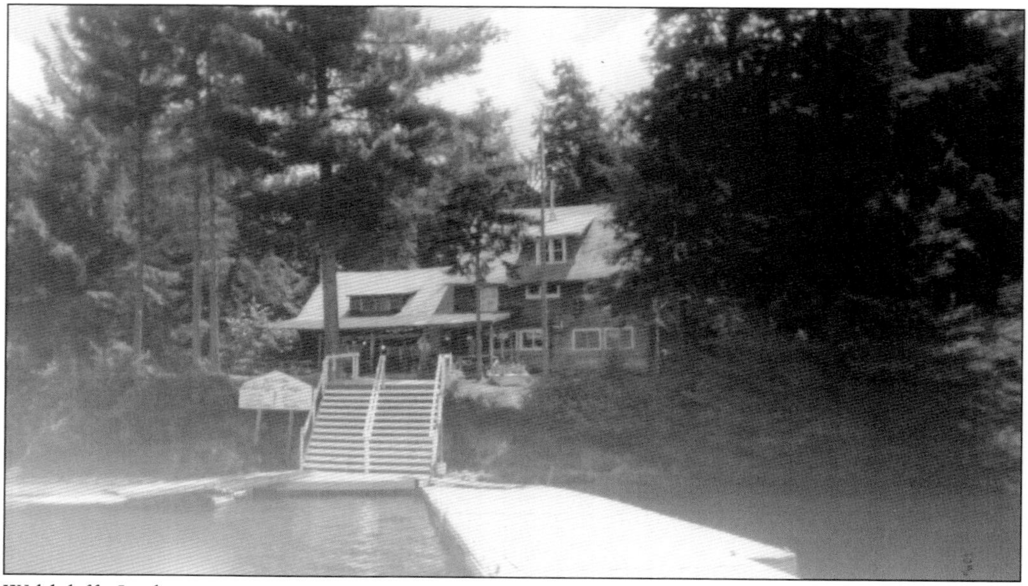

Wildcliffe Lodge was on a water-accessible-only point near South Flow. Al "Hoppy" Hopkins owned the lodge in the 1960s, when it became known as Hoppy's. Guests came to the dock in the summer in their boats and in the winter on their snowmobiles. It closed in 2000, lamented by its many friends. The dock is no longer there, and the boathouse sign reads, "Closed." (Courtesy of Jay Edel.)

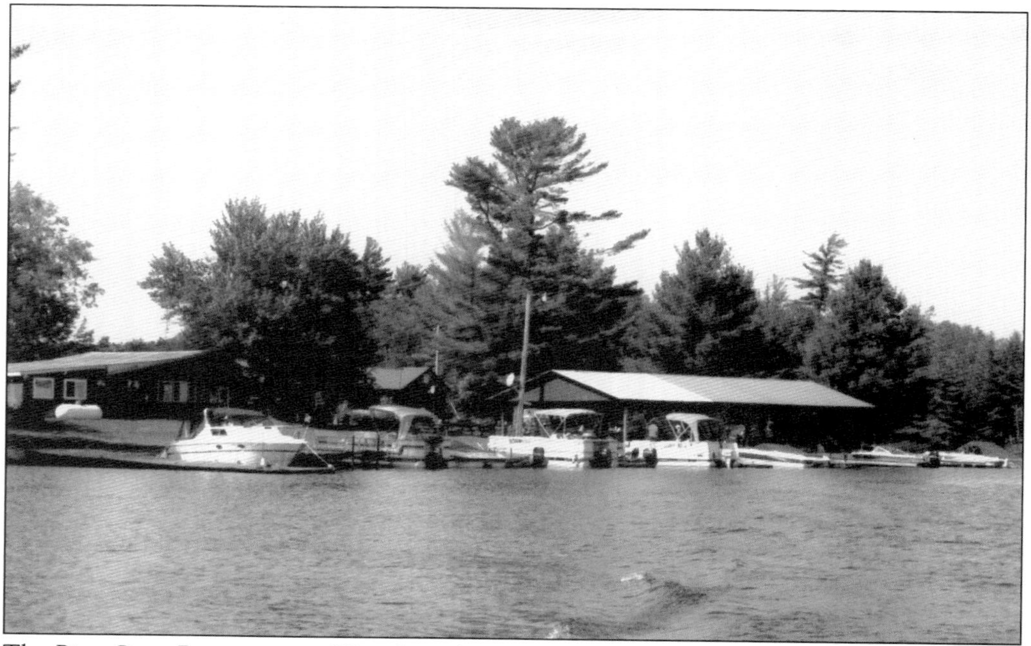

The Pine Cone Restaurant in Wanakena has operated since the 1960s. It is accessible by road or by boat from Cranberry Lake following the winding Oswegatchie River. The ride is popular with pontoon boats and motorboats alike. Local kayakers also make the trip. There are a number of boat slips to accommodate guests. The Cranberry Lake Boat Club holds its annual summer picnic here. (Courtesy of Ellen Giraud.)

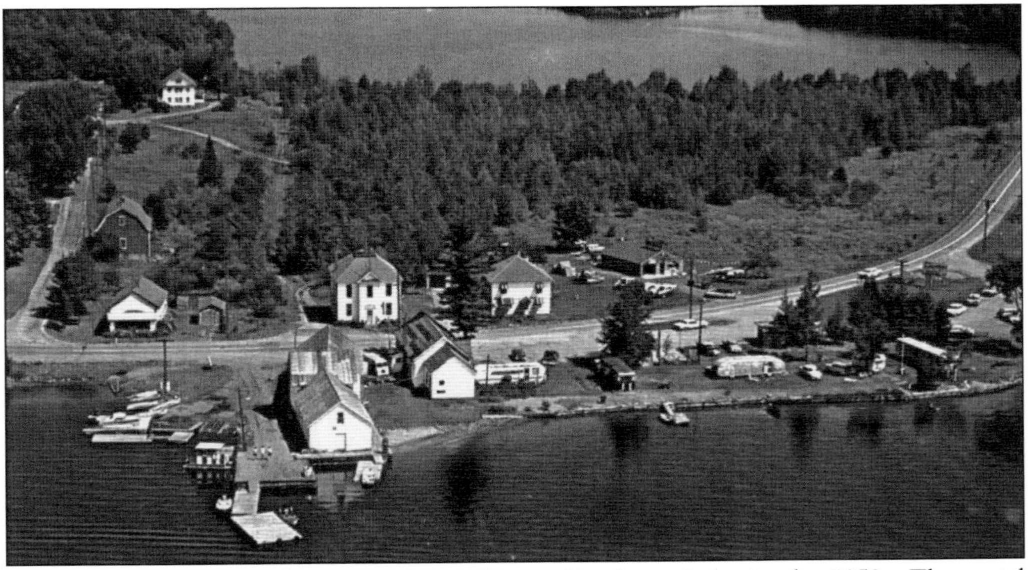

The Emporium Marina dock extended well into Cranberry Lake in the 1950s. The aerial photograph looking north provides a good view of the area at the time. Behind the marina is State Route 3 connecting Cranberry Lake with Star Lake to the west and Tupper Lake to the east. Behind State Route 3 is Silver Lake. William LaFrance operates the marina today. The Cranberry Lake Boat Club leases space for a members dock, just visible near the flagpole. (Courtesy of Peter VandeWater.)

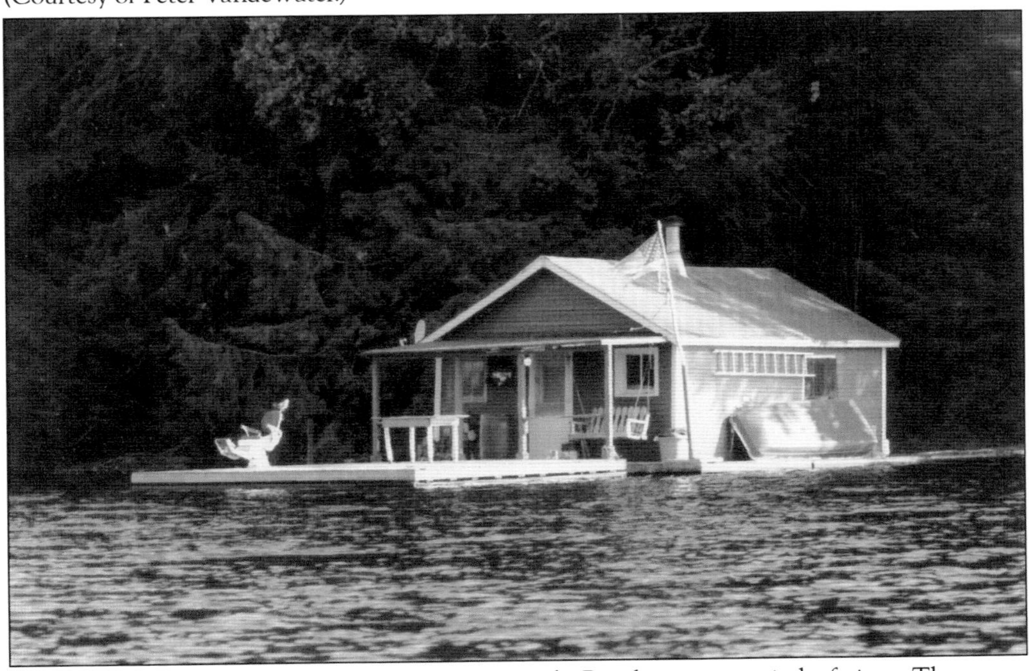

Floating camps spontaneously appeared on Brandy Brook over a period of time. They were really docks with boathouses on them that a person could live in. They were used for years by fishermen and hunters until the State of New York banned them in 2008, and they were removed. (Courtesy of Ellen Giraud.)

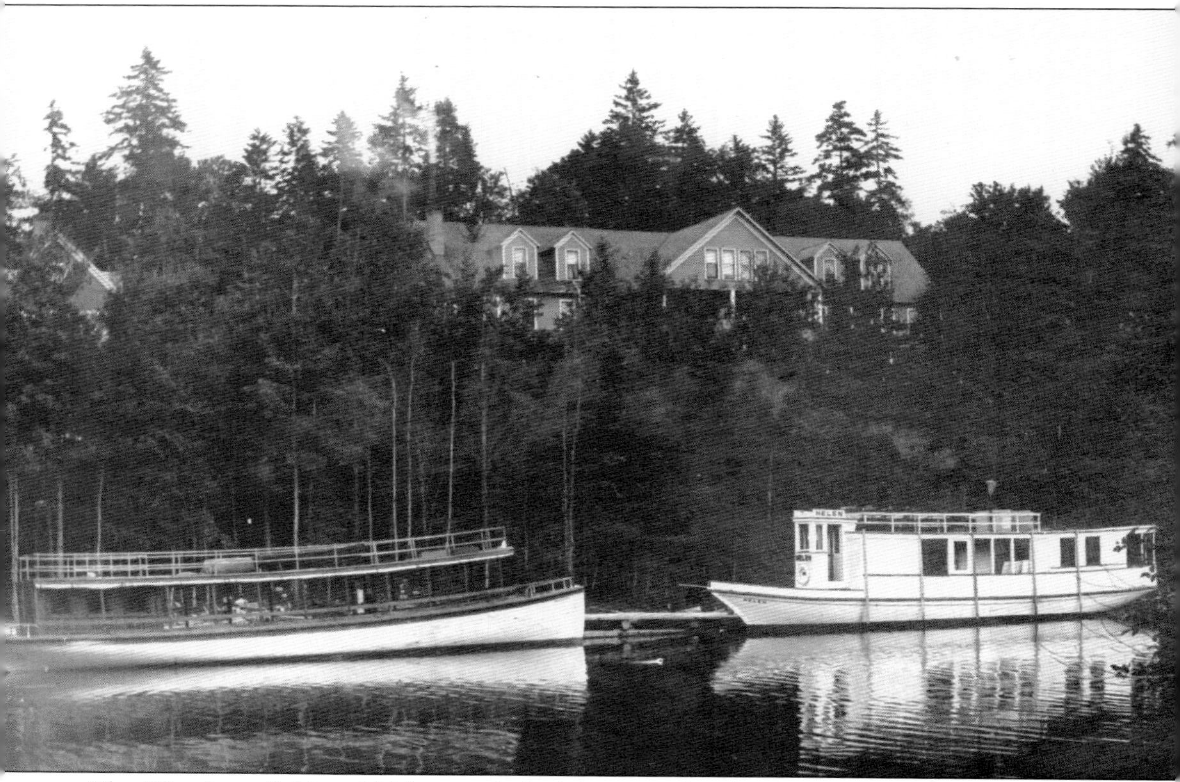

The *Wanakena* (left) and *Helen* are docked facing each other below the Hotel Wanakena in this unusual photograph taken before 1906. These hugely useful and popular workboats were the mainstay of commerce between the villages of Cranberry Lake and Wanakena in this period and symbolize the long history of boats and boating on Cranberry Lake. (Courtesy of Susan Smeby.)

About the Cranberry Lake Boat Club

The Cranberry Lake Motor Boat Club began in 1909. The initial meeting of the group took place in a grove of trees at the head of the lake (near or at Nunn's Inn). The organization wished to promote powerboating, improve boating conditions, and encourage socialization among summer visitors and residents. Boating remains the central interest of members.

The club's original aims were expanded in 1937. Then commodore George Terry said, "The name 'Boat Club' does not limit our usefulness to boat owners. Its aims are far broader. Its purpose is to protect life and property; to promote wholesome sport; through united effort, to improve fishing and do all in its power to stabilize the water level of the lake, especially during the vacation periods; and last but far from least, to promote a healthy community spirit."

The Cranberry Lake Boat Club was formally incorporated in 1956. Since then, the boat club has become more active in the Cranberry Lake community. The boat club provides volunteers for the Cranberry Lake Fire and Rescue Squad, maintains the town beach and a shelter that it built, and plants flowers to enhance the community. Navigation safety, water quality, fishing conditions, camp security, and docking facilities remain on annual agendas. Community interests are considered whenever projects are undertaken by the boat club. The interdependence of the Cranberry Lake Boat Club and the community is evident. The majority of boat club members remain seasonal. A conscious effort is made to include year-round residents as directors and officers. Faculty and staff of the Ranger School, the College of Forestry at Syracuse University, and SUNY ESF have served in that capacity.

The Cranberry Lake Boat Club offers more than annual traditional events. Equally important are the friendships cultivated among members. The Cranberry Lake Boat Club is a community within a community, vigilant in safeguarding the lake, and conscious of its civic responsibility.